T0331843

Interdisciplinary Advances in Adaptive and Intelligent Assistant Systems:
Concepts, Techniques, Applications, and Use

Gunther Kreuzberger, Ilmenau Technical University, Germany

Aran Lunzer, Hokkaido University, Japan

Roland Kaschek, Gymnasium Gerresheim, Germany

INFORMATION SCIENCE REFERENCE

Hershey · New York

Director of Editorial Content:	Kristin Klinger
Director of Book Publications:	Julia Mosemann
Acquisitions Editor:	Lindsay Johnston
Development Editor:	Joel Gamon
Publishing Assistant:	Casey Conapitski
Typesetter:	Casey Conapitski
Production Editor:	Jamie Snavely
Cover Design:	Lisa Tosheff

Published in the United States of America by
Information Science Reference (an imprint of IGI Global)
701 E. Chocolate Avenue,
Hershey PA 17033
Tel: 717-533-8845
Fax: 717-533-8661
E-mail: cust@igi-global.com
Web site: http://www.igi-global.com

Library of Congress Cataloging-in-Publication Data

Interdisciplinary advances in adaptive and intelligent assistant systems : concepts, techniques, applications and use / Gunther Kreuzberger, Aran Lunzer and Roland Kaschek, editors.
    p. cm.
 Includes bibliographical references and index.
 Summary: "This book discusses how collaboration between humans and intelligent systems can potentially improve access to and processing of complex information, contributing to the synthesis, storage and integration of knowledge"--Provided by publisher.

 ISBN 978-1-61520-851-7 (hardcover) -- ISBN 978-1-61520-852-4 (ebook) 1.
Intelligent control systems. 2. Expert systems (Computer science) I.
Kreuzberger, Gunther, 1968- II. Lunzer, Aran, 1965- III. Kaschek, Roland H.,
1955-
 TJ217.5.I5453 2010
 006.3--dc22

British Cataloguing in Publication Data
A Cataloguing in Publication record for this book is available from the British Library.

All work contributed to this book is new, previously-unpublished material. The views expressed in this book are those of the authors, but not necessarily of the publisher.

Table of Contents

Section 1
Enabling Technologies

Chapter 1
Aylin Akaltun, Christian-Albrechts-University Kiel, Germany
Patrick Maisch, Christian-Albrechts-University Kiel, Germany
Bernhard Thalheim, Christian-Albrechts-University Kiel, Germany

Chapter 2
Shin-ichi Minato, Hokkaido University, Japan
Nicolas Spyratos, Université de Paris-Sud, France

Section 2
Applications and Results

Chapter 9

*Alexander Krumpholz, CSIRO ICT Centre & Australian National
University, Australia
David Hawking, Funnelback, Australia
Tom Gedeon, Australian National University, Australia*

Detailed Table of Contents

Section 1
Enabling Technologies

Chapter 1
Towards Next Generation Web: Knowledge Web 1

Aylin Akaltun, Christian-Albrechts-University Kiel, Germany
Patrick Maisch, Christian-Albrechts-University Kiel, Germany
Bernhard Thalheim, Christian-Albrechts-University Kiel, Germany

This chapter discusses how to build a computerized web retrieval aid taking user characteristics into account. The authors provide an approach that matches retrieved content against particular life cases, user models and contexts. For clarification an example application is provided that deals with matching content against information available regarding various kinds of users.

Chapter 2

Shin-ichi Minato, Hokkaido University, Japan
Nicolas Spyratos, Université de Paris-Sud, France

The work introduced in this chapter stands as an enabling technology for letting users express, in simple ways, their information interests as handled in a large digital library organised by a rich, hierarchical taxonomy of terms. The key to the technique is Binary Decision Diagrams. By automatically taking into account the structure of the taxonomy of keywords used to tag the documents in the library, the proposed system allows users to build subscriptions based on a free mix of highly specific and more general terms, depending on the specificity of their interests. With respect to the medical examples cited in the chapter provided by Krumpholz et al., this chapter gives insight into how the expansion of simple queries given by users can be handled without overwhelming the servers on which the repositories are held.

Chapter 3

Jun Fujima, Hokkaido University, Japan
Shohei Yoshihara, Hokkaido University, Japan
Yuzuru Tanaka, Hokkaido University, Japan

This chapter also deals with the challenge of providing users a simplified way to access and make use of potentially rich information resources, in this case by supporting the combination of resources offered by Web applications. For the kind of ad hoc combinations of resources that users call on every day it is still difficult without advanced programming skills to set up even the simple form of assistance involved in automating data transfer, so as to save time and effort in subsequent use of the same resource combination. The authors' proposal is to enable the use of a standard spreadsheet environment – Microsoft Excel – as a platform for such automation, on the basis that a large body of computer users, though not considering themselves programmers, find the simple declarative semantics of spreadsheet calculations to be unintimidating and useful. They demonstrate a basic range of facilities that enable users to set up "orchestrations" of Web applications that not only automate the data transfers between applications but also provide a way to generate sets of related results to assist the user in making comparisons.

Chapter 4
A Component-Based 3D Geographic Simulation Framework and its Integration
with a Legacy GIS

Zhen-Sheng Guo, Hokkaido University, Japan
Yuzuru Tanaka, Hokkaido University, Japan

Similar to the prior chapter, this chapter is reporting work designed to enable users
who are not sophisticated programmers to build or configure their own specialised
information-access applications, in this case in the domain of Geographic Information Systems. The form of assistance being demonstrated is that while the end
user performs only simple operations such as visually repositioning and/or reconnecting knowledge-media components, these components assemble and transfer
rich data structures to drive complex simulation tools and display advanced 3D
simulation results. Building on the framework developed by the authors, two application examples are explained in detail, demonstrating how straightforward it
is to replace the key simulation elements and thereby obtain, on the same three-
dimensional GIS substrate, the modelling of quite different phenomena.

Section 2
Applications and Results

Chapter 5
A Web-Enabled, Mobile Intelligent Information Technology Architecture
for On-Demand and Mass Customized Markets

M. Ghiassi, Santa Clara University, USA
C. Spera, Zipidy, Inc., USA

In this chapter, the authors deal with the challenges of increasing product customization and customer requirements demanding new strategies for "Mass Customisation". The approach proposed here is based on the assumption of a customer-
centric production system involving many businesses each of which focuses on
its core competencies, resulting in products that are outcome of a collaborative
effort. In fact, the authors envision the idea of users assisted by IT applications,
namely distributed and specialized software agents, by proposing and applying a
taxonomy that accounts for some core functionalities of assisting entities and sufficient roles in the value chain. Accordingly, the authors introduce an architecture
for the dynamic instantiation and interaction of the agents, and give examples of
their approach through a number of case studies.

This chapter presents a system for producing customised presentations of videos, in which some parts of the video are emphasised relative to others by appropriate automatic use of the playback controls. The author's view is that this can be seen as an assistant-like functionality whereby the system recognises and reproduces the user's habitual behaviour, so that once the system has been appropriately trained it will automatically show newly arrived videos in the way the user would probably have wanted to watch them anyway. The author shows that because his system represents such "viewing styles" as knowledge objects that can be transported from one user to another, and can be manipulated so as to produce various forms of composition of alternative viewing styles, users are able to benefit from the use of viewing styles defined by others – such as, in the recording of a football match, a style that would be used by a football coach when demonstrating or analysing a team's tactics.

An empirical study regarding the utilisation of a knowledge management system (KMS) in the tertiary education sector is presented. From an evaluative perspective, the authors examine the impact of the KMS, i.e., its utilisation and potential barriers preventing such utilisation, and present results from two studies. In a first, exploratory study they identified typical behaviour patterns and search strategies, looked for difficulties in use and attributed them to a set of personal and non-personal barriers. A second, quasi-experimental study was conducted to determine the impact of utilization barriers on usage patterns. The findings provided by the authors clearly give empirical evidence that even untrained users can benefit from assistance offered by training courses and KMS. These findings do not conflict with but clarify (at least some of) the assumptions made by Akaltun et al., in their chapter on the idea of a knowledge web, regarding limited user capabilities.

In this chapter the authors look into possible improvements of human communication in the web utilising social virtual worlds by means of mobile software agents. They provide interaction schemas applying to communication between humans and machines, between machines, and between humans through machines. Thereby communication is supported by personalised agents acting as intelligent messengers or even as humans' substitutes within the virtual world. Humans can focus on the interaction with friends, regardless of the social network to which they belong.

Chapter 9

This chapter deals with the application domain of literature retrieval. It focuses on literature retrieval for computer scientists, and on medical literature retrieval for clinicians or medical researchers. The authors describe existing search aid systems and identify a number of search purposes that might warrant a specialised approach to literature search. They examine in detail the domain of medical literature search, as a frequently occurring and important task in a problem area with a highly standardised terminology. In addition to developing a context-aware perspective, the authors call for a user-centric approach by using an ad hoc interpretation of Web retrieval processes as a guiding metaphor for understanding search processes. Pointing out that in Web search one is usually provided with a large number of result documents, thus creating a follow-on need to check these results for relevance, the authors point to further potential for assisting search.

Foreword

The PISA endeavour on "Perspectives of Intelligent Systems Assistance" was launched in 2005 by a workshop under this title hosted by Roland H. Kaschek at Massey University, Palmerston North, New Zealand. The PISA brand, so to speak, was introduced and the term PISA coined in preparation for the workshop. A consolidation of the scientific discussion initiated within that workshop led to a first book entitled "Intelligent Assistant Systems: Concepts, Techniques and Technologies" which appeared in December 2006. That may be seen as the first PISA book. The PISA idea and concepts have been around since at least that time.

To keep it short and easy to grasp, PISA is about the trend of transforming tools into assistant systems. We speak in particular about computerized tools and, thus, about computerised assistant systems.

A tool is something that does not do anything by itself unless a user is wielding it appropriately. Tools are valuable for numerous simple tasks and in cases in which a human knows precisely how to operate the tool. Those tools have their limitations as soon as dynamics come into play. There are various sources of dynamics, such as a changing world or human users with different wishes, desires, and needs.

The trend toward ubiquitous and pervasive computing is bringing with it a steadily growing community of naive users of computerized systems. If those users are not able to use properly the systems that are offered as tools, one of the many ways out might be to transform those systems into assistants, releasing the users from decisions they are unable to make properly for themselves. At least in the developed countries, the trend toward an aging society gives similar reasons for such transformations.

When tools are no longer sufficient, we have to think about substitutes. A moderate approach is to transform tools gradually into assistants bringing in only as much flexibility and freedom as necessary. It is advisable to be careful in giving autonomy to human-made artifacts - as we all know, at least, from science fiction: one just has to think of Stanley Kubrick's film "2001: A Space Odyssey", made in 1968, in which the assistant computer HAL 9000 becomes a bit too independent.

However dangerous, the independence of assistant systems is highly desirable. In the case of human assistance, in the very end the most helpful assistants are those who have own ideas, go their own ways, and - from time to time – surprise us with unexpected outcomes. Mankind will surely go to an extreme, because more independent and creative assistants, even if they are only computer programs, will allow for unexpectedly valuable results, at least in a certain number of relevant cases.

Consequently, there is no chance to ban assistant systems, even if they may sometimes turn out to be dangerous. The only way is to learn about the potentials of intelligent assistant systems, about technologies of development and implementation, about strategies and process models of employment. That's what PISA is about.

At the reader's fingertips, the present publication is the second PISA book, hopefully a milestone in a growing series of fruitful publications.

Klaus Peter Jantke,
Fraunhofer IDMT Ilmenau & Erfurt

Klaus Peter Jantke *born in Berlin, Germany, studied Mathematics at Humboldt University Berlin. He graduated with an honours degree in Theoretical Computer Science and received both his doctorate and his habilitation at Humboldt. Jantke won the Weierstrass Award for his diploma thesis and the Humboldt Prize for his PhD. Klaus Jantke started his academic career as a full professor at Kuwait University and simultaneously at Leipzig University of Technology, aged 35. Since then he has been teaching at several German Universities such as Chemnitz, Cottbus, Darmstadt, Ilmenau, Leipzig, and Saarbrücken. He sees himself as a logician in the school of Heinrich Scholz and Karl Schröter. Jantke's scientific interest ranges from universal algebra and algorithmic learning through digital games to qualitative and quantitative research into the impact of media. Fraunhofer Society, Germany's largest research institution with currently 17,000 scientists and 60 institutes in operation, decided to establish its own children's media research center. In January 2008, Klaus Jantke was put in charge of developing this research center in Erfurt, Germany,*

Preface

This book is the second publication of the loosely organized PISA (Perspectives of Intelligent Systems' Assistance) project on assistant systems. In our first book (Kaschek, 2006) we tried to set the stage for a general debate of assistance and tried to push the development and use of assistant systems to the level of what was possible back then. With this book we try to highlight the role of interdisciplinarity and adaptivity. There is good reason for that. First, from our definition as given in the preface of the earlier book, intelligent assistant systems inherently are adaptive; it turns out that this adaptivity is a key issue, that we try to explore in more detail here. Second, and going beyond what we saw back in 2006, interdisciplinarity is very important too. Maybe not for each and every assistant system, but certainly many instances of requiring computer-based assistance will have to take into account a number of different disciplines at the same time. As is customary for a preface we first introduce our subject, discuss some of the related work, and then briefly summarise the chapters of this book.

As we did in 2006, we still feel that the most fundamental concept we have to deal with is that of information. Our related view is one in which we take into account structural aspects of modern life and do not necessarily restrict ourselves to the individual human using a computer. We consider an information society as a society in which information is the overwhelmingly dominant item in production, management, support and consumption. What we did not really understand at the time of the first PISA book is that information is becoming key even in consumption processes. That process is driven by the following causes: (1) many products or services are complex, and using them appropriately is not necessarily a trivial task; (2) providing the product or service meta-information required for a conscious choice about whether and how to buy them (i.e., what business model to use for purchasing or, more generally, for acquiring access or consumption rights), as well as how to consume or use them, is expensive. One way of getting an edge over competitors is to offer that information in computer-readable electronic format only; that way it can be kept up to date much more easily and effectively. Also, that way the information can be made much more meaningful to consumers, as it can be computer processed and turned into a shape useful for the consumer. That processing could even involve the consumption context and boost meta-information usage. Obviously, the act of product or service purchase can also be subject to computerised support. On the horizon we see a stage of society in which, without one's personal digital assistant (PDA), one will not reasonably be able to go shopping in a supermarket, to buy products or services at standardised points of sale, to navigate within the city (including getting timetables for buses or trams) or on the highway. The technology of informational infrastructure is going to change fundamentally. PDAs enable that process, and require it as a precondition of general usage in modern society. The ability to produce powerful PDAs is creating new needs that rely on their availability. Since information technology is a major modern industry it is very likely to find ways of convincing citizens to use these devices on a large scale.

Information is becoming the raw material of modern society. According to a definition that goes back to Bateson (1979), information is the "difference that makes a difference". It is the driving force of modern service industry. It is customary to use the metaphor of information space to characterise the effects of the ongoing change process. Our information spaces have been technologised, and their size as well as their complexity increased. Access to information spaces and the capability to use them effectively and efficiently have become key economical success factors. Kuhlen (1999) diagnosed an information dilemma. The alternatives he identifies are (1) searching the information spaces oneself, spending an increasing amount of time for satisfying one's information needs; and (2) delegating that searching task to an information assistant, whose performance is time-consuming to control and whose effectiveness is hard to assess. Obviously, the only way out of that dilemma is the emergence of information brands, in other words, information quality, as certified by a trusted and trustworthy agency. While many of the contributors to Wikipedia, for example, are not necessarily aware of that issue, it was foreseen in philosophy of science when Popper discussed the fundamental role of authority for truth. Also Fleck (1935) discussed this when he commented on the emergence of scientific fact, the role of this emergence, and the role of the related community that has established a fact and keeps maintaining it.

Currently the first of Kuhlen's choices dominates. However, using such an information assistant must be the ultimate goal, as one cannot reasonably expect that technologisation will stop or even be undone. In fact the technologising of the world has a long history and must be considered as one of the most fundamental driving forces of human civilisation. It is inextricably connected with technologising the word (Ong, 1996, p. 101), as "(s)poken words are always modifications of a total situation which is more than verbal. They never occur alone, in a context simply of words." According to Ong, technologisation has significantly restructured human consciousness. What we are witnessing right now should be understood as the latest step in the process of technologising the word. That process began with the invention of script (about 3200 – 3100 BCE), and was followed by the invention of letters (about 1500 BCE), and print (1540 CE), (Ifrah, 2000, pp. 3 – 25) – although some recent research suggests somewhat different dates. The latest step of technologisation is the automation of uttering and understanding words and text, in which we here include calculation and computation. This sums up the capability of verbally controlling processes of all kinds. Enzensberger (1970) reports the analogy that El Lissitsky drew in 1923 between language use and modes of transportation and, in particular, vehicles. He related articulated language to upright gait; writing to the wheel; and the printing press to animal-powered carts. El Lissitzky did not suggest analogies in language use for automobiles and aeroplanes. One is tempted to suggest that computers correspond to automobiles, and the Web to aeroplanes. Would it be venturing too far to relate intelligent assistants to spacecraft?

The idea of assistant systems is not a new one. Rather, it has been around for 30 years. Recently the interest in assistant systems has been refreshed by various authors because of a need to address a deep-rooted worrying issue. That issue is the role that is played by computers and humans respectively during their interaction. A number of advanced general approaches to computer-based technologisation of words and text were proposed in the past but were not heavily used in application systems, a point made by Sowa (2002). We expect that this will not happen to intelligent assistant systems. They will make their way to mass systems. That they did not do so already is, on the one hand, due to aspects of the genesis and evolution of computers. Computers were only invented in the fifth decade of the 20th century, and as they came into widespread use in the sixth and seventh decades they continued to become ever more powerful, so that solutions of practical problems became feasible that were not feasible only a short time earlier. Miniaturisation of computers along with ongoing increases of computational power and storage capacity has now led to a situation in which the devices required for general usage of assistant systems are starting to emerge. The economic need identified above to completely reorganize the informational infrastructure towards a situation in which the human individual without a PDA is lost in information spaces is going to enforce the mass usage of assistant systems.

It was as early as at the end of the eighth decade of the 20th century that Winograd (1979) (relying on a study of the US Department of Defense) wrote that computers "are not primarily used for solving well-structured mathematical problems or data processing, but instead are components in complex systems. ... Many computer scientists spend the majority of their time dealing with embedded computer systems such as message systems and text editing and formatting systems." By about 1975 the task focus of computers had changed from computation to communication (Hevner & Berndt, 2000). With the dominant use of computing technology today being for business application (p. 13), a significant increase has taken place in the number of individuals who are directly affected by computers and are engaged in using them. They also use computers in an increasing number of domains and tasks. The complexity of problems for whose solutions computers are key components continues to increase. The traditional approaches of using computers turn out to be ineffective for these problems of higher complexity. On the one hand, these approaches require the human problem solver simultaneously to maintain a good understanding of both the overall solution architecture and the solution detail. Many humans experience difficulties meeting this requirement. On the other hand, the approach fails to let computers work out the problems and their solutions, as humans working under their own resource restrictions cannot understand and validate these solutions.

The Oxford English Dictionary Online defines 'complex' as "(c)onsisting of parts or elements not simply co-ordinated, but some of them involved in various degrees of subordination; complicated, involved, intricate; not easily analyzed or disentangled." A related but more operationalised definition was given by Victor Basili, (see Banker et al., 1993). He defined the term 'complexity of a system' as the resources needed to successfully use that system. If we consider a problem as a system the main components of which are a current state C, a future state F, and an actor A who wants to transform C into F given the boundary conditions B, then problem complexity can be understood as a particular instance of system complexity, i.e., as the resources required to transform C into F. That definition can be looked at from a quantitative point of view. Then problem complexity can, for example, be understood in terms of the number of points being used to score a problem. This approach is similar to the one taken in the Function Point methodology (see Garmus & Herron, 1996). Alternatively to this standpoint, problem complexity can be considered qualitatively. Then problem complexity can be understood in terms of the kind of resources needed for solving the problem at hand. New levels of problem complexity then call for new kinds of resources or for new ways of using known ones.

In terms of computer applications, we think that new resources and new ways to use old resources can best be understood as what could be called "the interlocutor metaphor" or "role" that a computer system plays in an interaction with a human. We focus here on the various different ways of understanding the interlocutor role. We identify the roles from a dominance perspective and reuse what already has been suggested in the preface of (Kaschek, 2006), namely the roles tool, collaborator, peer, or master in the 1:1 human-computer-interaction. For a more elaborated list of such interlocutor metaphors we refer the reader to, for example, Buschmann et al. (1999). Our interlocutor metaphors for 1:1 human-computer interaction were taken from human cooperative labour organisation. The generalness of computers enables them to embody many different interlocutor metaphors and thus to appear as qualitatively different resources. Computers can therefore be used for solving problems of quite different complexity.

The mentioned interlocutor metaphors for one-on-one human-computer interaction are discussed in more detail below.

- **master – tool**, i.e., in this relationship the master is superior to the tool and the latter has no or only little latitude in performing the tasks allocated to him / her. The success criterion applied to that relationship is that the tool exactly carries out what it is instructed to. Successful use of a tool depends on the master's capabilities of, first, structuring problem-solving procedures into steps that can be carried out by the tools at hand and, second, handling the tools appropriately. A currently employed version of this relationship is the chain of command in the military all over the world.

- **master – collaborator**, i.e., in this relationship the collaborator has a relatively large latitude regarding what tasks to perform and how to do them. However, the master is superior. The success criterion applied to this relationship is that the master achieves his / her goals. For that, the collaborator appropriately contributes his / her capabilities to the problem the master tries to solve. Successful use of a collaborator depends on his / her capability to learn about and to adapt to the master's way of conceptualizing and solving problems, as well as the master's ability to use the collaborator's capabilities and to delegate tasks to him / her, i.e., let the collaborator do what he / she is good at. A currently employed version of this relationship is the relationship between an enlightened manager and his / her subordinates.

- **peer – peer**, i.e., in this relationship partners interact with each other and neither of them has power over the other or dominates him/her. They cooperate according to their individual goals for tasks and in a way that appears advisable to them. Successfully employing this relationship means perpetuating it and depends on the capability of finding peers who are willing to achieve compatible goals and to engage in communication processes that stimulate the ongoing process of goal achievement. A currently employed version of this relationship is the relationship between collaborating colleagues.

These three relationships between interlocutors cause five different roles in 1:1 relationships to exist in which computerized systems can interact with humans. The role of collaborator has two obvious specialisations, namely agent (one might consider the notorious 007 as an archetype) and assistant (an archetype of which might be Sherlock Holmes' well known companion Dr. Watson). In this book we mainly discuss aspects of the assistant role occupied by a computer in the master – collaborator relationship. While authors of chapters of this book were free to express their own definitions for agent and assistant, the editors believe that this distinction, as introduced in the preface of (Kaschek, 2006), is a reasonable one. If we would want to extend the range of our concepts then, among other domains, we would certainly have to deal with gaming applications. Under certain circumstances they can be considered as assistant systems, insofar as they aid humans in "pleasantly killing time" (recreation). This then gives rise to a different model of assistance. What we have sketched above can be regarded as interlocutor assistance. In addition we see now that an assistant might enhance the reality of the human it is assisting, and that as a consequence that human gains the power to accomplish things they could not accomplish before. A simple example of this is a parking assistant that issues signals to the driver indicating the distance to the next physical obstacle; this clearly simplifies parking cars in overcrowded cities. Hence we feel that assistant systems should not be limited in purpose to avoiding human mistakes; clearly there is another ever-present goal of improving the quality of human life. Therefore user-centric perspectives matter. This is the ultimate reason why Intelligent Assistant Systems as a research topic is necessarily interdisciplinary.

We forecast that the trend will continue towards more (ubiquitous) computing power pervading everyday life and enabling mankind to deal with ever more complex applications. We therefore anticipate that "computers in the role of human-like peers" will continue to attract attention. For example, the ongoing demographic process of an aging population in industrialised countries will create a need to provide companions for elderly people whose loved ones have passed away, but who do not need the constant attention of a human nurse. It is not hard to forecast that for the younger members of society, too – children of all age groups – specific electronic companions will come into existence. In fact with the tamagotchi (see for example the related Wikipedia article) and the various kinds of artificial dogs we have seen a number of such attempts. Obviously, the performance characteristics of such companions may differ considerably from one to another. A few examples of what might be the focus of such devices are (1) performing helpful jobs in the household, including nursing the elderly, babies or toddlers; (2) aiding human users with pleasant ways to pass the time; or (3) serving as a general purpose interlocutor. It might not even be too far-fetched to assume that such an interlocutor device will one day come with a placeholder for a mental and physical fingerprint, in such a way that after adding the related parameter instances in most cases (perhaps in 95 % of all cases) one cannot really tell the device apart from the human being whose prints were taken. That way mankind really and for the first time would defy death. It is, of course, clear that there are immense cultural obstacles to overcome for a vision of this magnitude to become reality. Also, the cultural consequences of systems of that kind becoming used on a large scale would be enormous. And it is certain that for all of this there are not only civilian applications; rather, due to the large amount of resources that will have to be spent it is likely that the first creators and users of such advanced assistant systems will be the military.

The analysis regarding the increasing complexity of problems that have to be solved is not entirely novel. It is actually quite old. Engelbart (1962) writes, for example, that "Man's population and gross product are increasing at a considerable rate, but the complexity of his problems grows still faster, and the urgency with which solutions must be found becomes steadily greater in response to the increased rate of activity and the increasingly global nature of that activity. Augmenting man's intellect ... would warrant full pursuit by an enlightened society if there could be shown a reasonable approach and some plausible benefits." Engelbart even used a particular instance of the interlocutor metaphor. He called the resource that he was asking for a "clerk". There are at least two respects, however, in which we differ in our approach from Engelbart's and others that are comparable. First, we do not aim at creating a particular artifact that would be capable of aiding a human user in all contexts, situations, and conditions. Rather, we aim at domain dependent aids. We furthermore concede that "agent", "assistant", and "clerk" are unlikely to be the only reasonable instantiations of the interlocutor metaphor that can be employed in solving complex problems.

We follow Winograd (1972) in conceiving of assistants as systems that understand what they do and that are capable of answering relevant questions. However, we regard assistants of this kind as intelligent assistants, and distinguish these from reality-enhancing assistants that do not necessarily have to understand anything they do. In Winograd's spirit, Robertson, Newell, and Ramakrishna, cited after (Sondheimer, Relles, 1982, p. 106) write, "One does not wield an intelligent assistant, one tells it what one wants. Intelligent assistants figure out what is necessary and do it themselves, without bothering you about it. They tell you the results and explain to you what you need to know." From an architectural view, that spirit suggests that assistants contain a domain model, a user model, and a situation model that combines the state of affairs of these two models as far as they are relevant for the task at hand. We do not aim at conceiving all sorts of assistant systems as a particular kind of information system, as the latter are understood from a functional view as, according to Hirschheim et al. (1995, p. 11), "technologically implemented [media] for the purpose of recording, storing, and disseminating linguistic expressions as well as for the supporting of inference making.". For several modern assistant systems this would be too narrow a definition, since it presupposes a human as one of the communicators, and the communication as employing a language. To cover these modern systems one must conceive assistant systems as embedded systems, i.e., systems that are embedded in other systems and store, record, exchange, and process signals. If one matches the master-assistant communication against Shannon's communication model (Shannon, 1993) then one finds that certain encoding or decoding steps may be superfluous. Additional to this more technical point one finds that the assumption of a deliberate choice of messages does not necessarily apply to the input that is fed into an assistant system. Rather, such input may result from a master activity that is independent of the assistant. Consider for example a power-steering or braking assistant. The master's activity (steering or braking respectively) occurs as a natural problem-solving behaviour, and sensors derive the assistant system's input from this behaviour. Furthermore, the technical problem of Shannon's communication theory (i.e., the reconstruction of a message that was chosen at a particular point in space at a different point in space at a later time) is not the technical problem of an assistance theory. The technical problems of assistance theory are to identify (1) the master's state of affairs, intent, and activities; (2) those responses to a master's activity that are likely to aid the master in their current course of action; and (3) the most suitable way of telling the master what they need to know.

With respect to those cases in which a human is supposed to communicate verbally with the assistant, we can, however, stick to understanding the assistant as an information system. The kind of linguistic expressions that the assistant system is then supposed to handle successfully depends on the purpose of that system. According to our understanding of assistant systems as highly capable, adaptive, cooperative, domain-specific problem-solving aids, the mentioned linguistic expressions must enable an assistant to autonomously find solutions for problems for which the master needs a solution, but is unwilling or unable to find one alone. The assistant's capabilities must be such that they can be tailored towards as smooth as possible an interaction with the master. A promising approach to this was suggested by Maes (1994), based on a three-valued logic ("yes", "maybe", and "no" being the truth values). The assistant would obtain a confidence value with respect to its current suggestion to the master. The assistant would then match this confidence value with one of the truth values, and would use for that the corresponding master-definable confidence-threshold values. Further action to be taken would then depend in the obvious way on the resulting truth value.

Intelligent assistant systems are knowledge media, which, according to Tanaka (2003, p. 11), are defined as media to "externalize some of our knowledge as intellectual resources and to distribute them among people". Until now the archetype of knowledge media is the book. Tanaka (p. 30–31) provides interesting details regarding the history of books. While books are very effective in disseminating knowledge, they are less effective in terms of operationalising (i.e., putting knowledge to action) and reusing it, as the book is a passive medium. Tanaka points out that each knowledge medium, in addition to the knowledge represented in it, is equipped with an access method. The computer is an active knowledge medium. The access methods that can be used with respect to the knowledge stored in a computer can thus be more effective and efficient than the ones that can be used with respect to a book. Also, parts of the knowledge stored in a computer can be stored in "active form", i.e., as a program that can actually be executed. Consequently the computer has the potential to substitute the book as the number-one knowledge medium. For that to be achieved, however, the computer's powers must be harnessed and end-user interfaces provided. These interfaces would enable modification and reuse of the stored knowledge with high-level end-user-proof operations. This is what Tanaka and his collaborators have aimed at and achieved with their implementation of meme media. These media are highly relevant for assistance theory, as they seem to have the potential for effective reuse of existing knowledge.

Assuming two systems interacting with each other, Liebermann and Selker (2000, p. 618) define the context of an interaction step as any aspect of that system interaction which is not explicit in that step. With this definition, obviously adaptive knowledge media such as assistant systems have to be context sensitive because adaptation means changes carried out without the issue of an explicit command but only an incomplete or syntactically invalid one. As Liebermann and Selker note (p. 623), computer applications always include an application model, a user model, and a task model. Traditionally these models have been only implicit in the application's code. They further argue that better suited for contextual computing are "systems that represent a system model explicitly and try to detect and correct differences between the user's system model and what the system actually can do." Winograd's 1972 request that intelligent assistant systems should understand what they are doing seems to suggest that an intelligent assistant has an explicit and dynamic model of itself.

If one tries to identify computerized systems that implement the interlocutor metaphors mentioned above then one easily identifies tools such as case-tools, text-processors, compilers, etc as implementing the master – slave relationship. Regarding assistant systems the situation appears to be more difficult, however various works (e.g., Winograd, 1972; Marcus, 1982; Kaiser et al., 1988; Boy, 1991; Maes, 1994; Burke et al., 1997, O'Connor, 2000) show assistants that were constructed as examples for programming / software development and software project planning; email processing; meeting scheduling; retrieving bibliographic information, piloting aircraft, and browsing (selecting new cars, choosing a rental video, finding an apartment, selecting a restaurant, and configuring home audio systems). There are several assistant systems in modern cars, for example for steering, braking and accelerating. As an aid in the rather well understood area of software component installation, intelligent assistants have found quite widespread use. In this book we bring some new examples. Of course there are not only success stories. Realising intelligent automated assistance is quite difficult for domains that are not well understood, such as everyday office work. To illustrate this, Liebermann and Selker (2000) use the example of Microsoft Word's capability of forcing the first non-blank character after a full stop to be in upper case. MS Word often, even after a user has for some reason undone that correction, re-"corrects" to the capital letter. It wouldn't be too hard to stop MS Word from doing that. However, the vendor would have to see this as a sensible feature. Microsoft, Inc, for example, has acknowledged difficulties with their office assistant by making it easier to switch on or off. They also have changed the default for this assistant from switched-on to switched-off in the latest versions of MS Word.

According to the Oxford English Dictionary Online, an assistant is "(o)ne who gives help to a person, or aids in the execution of a purpose; a helper, an auxiliary; a promoter; also, a means of help, an aid." This book is supposed to promote the genesis of assistant systems as gear for everyday life. According to our analysis so far, assistant systems are interactive, user-adaptive problem solving aids that understand what they do, accept input in terms of goals rather than instructions, or deduce such goals and, once these goals are identified, aim at solving them independently from their user. Assistant systems that interact with humans will often incorporate a question-answering component as well as an explanation component. We assume that intelligence can improve effectiveness and efficiency of assistants. We thus anticipate assistants to be intelligent. For us that means that available information is exploited as effectively as possible for aiding the master in achieving his / her / its goals. It is a characteristic of assistance (by information systems) that (1) the responsibility remains with the master; (2) the master may ask or cause the assistant to execute a task whenever the master wishes so or it becomes necessary; and (3) the assistant may be pro-active such that it is ready for upcoming tasks, provided the associated preparation does not interfere with the current activities (Boy, 1991).

Agent systems are similar to assistant systems. We distinguish these from each other by noting that agents are systems that have an operational mode in which they are not necessarily interactive, adaptive, or even accessible. Again querying the Oxford English Dictionary Online one finds that "agent" may be applied for referring to persons or things. The most important of the given definitions are (1) "One who (or that which) acts or exerts power, as distinguished from the patient, and also from the instrument"; (2) "He who operates in a particular direction, who produces an effect. ... The efficient cause."; (3) "Any natural force acting upon matter, any substance the presence of which produces phenomena, whether physical as electricity, chemical as actinism, oxygen, medicinal as chloroform, etc."; and (4) "One who does the actual work of anything, as distinguished from the instigator or employer; hence, one who acts for another, a deputy, steward, factor, substitute, representative, or emissary. (In this sense the word has numerous specific applications in Commerce, Politics, Law, etc., flowing directly from the general meaning.)". These explanations seem to be consistent with our belief that agents are different from tools, as agents act on their own in achieving complex user goals while tools require successive instructions to carry out even relatively simple tasks. It also appears to be justified to distinguish agents from assistants. Agents often do their job without much or any interaction with the user. Assistants would typically do their job in close interaction with the user, observe what he or she is doing, and propose aid that he or she is likely to find acceptable.

With this book, we continue our efforts as part of a group of researchers working to popularise assistant systems. Many of the chapters are extended and quality-assured versions of the most relevant papers presented at the PISA workshop held in August 2007 in Sapporo, Japan. These submissions were put through two further reviewing stages before being accepted here.

To widen the book's scope beyond the horizon of the PISA-related group, we advertised on mailing lists and also directly contacted researchers who had previously published or shown an interest in this area. We obtained both new contributions, which went through our full review process, and enhanced versions of existing published work.

We now briefly summarise the book's chapters, in alphabetical order of the first authors' names.

Akaltun et al.

Akaltun et al start out with the observation that "[the] more unspecified content [is] published, the more general usability of the World Wide Web is lost." They then claim that the "(t)he next generation's Web information services will have to be more adaptive to keep the web usable." While it might seem a little questionable whether in fact computer support may enable an uneducated web user to perform highly in their searches, it certainly is worth trying to find out the boundaries of what can be achieved with computerised aid. Akaltun et al "present a new technology that matches content against particular life cases, user models and contexts." They start out with a discussion of the term "knowledge" and then discuss an example application that matches different types of content against information available to it about various kinds of users.

Akaltun et al. address the problem that in the web, due to lack of authoritative knowledge brands, a user is frequently unable to determine the value of a number of accessible documents. From an epistemological point of view the indispensable role of authority for knowledge has been addressed by Popper decades ago. To some extent the problem may be solvable by automated means that evaluate a large part of what is available. Akaltun et al. implicitly use the aphorism, mentioned above, that information is a difference that makes a difference, by employing a five-layer model that they retrieve from the literature, and according to which information is suitably organised and connected data. Akaltun et al. then make a very important point, namely that users are imperfect and that computerised aid to some extent needs to take into account these imperfections.

For computerised web retrieval aid to be able to take into account user imperfections it is necessary to have access to a user model. According to Akaltun et al. the next generation web will be forced to focus on matching these user models and web content. Clearly, the specifics of web content as weakly structured data is going to impact any matching of web content with user models.

As Akaltun et al. do not believe in all-purpose solutions they propose an approach that focuses on ease of use, high-quality content delivery in respect of user life cases that also corrects the defects of adaptability by taking into account the construction of the web story. It is clear that, to some extent, combinatorial difficulties of matching content and user models can be solved by incorporating into that comparison the usage context. It will, however, be a challenge to cope with the complexities of combining three items reasonably rather than only two.

Erfurth & Schau

One of the assumptions of the earlier, traditional systems analysis was that the systems themselves as well as their users were stationary. In modern life that assumption is no longer necessarily true. Accordingly Erfurth and Schau drop that assumption, and consider the task of achieving "a seamless integration of users in on-line communities". Their chapter discusses "the potential of software agents for sophisticated interaction in ubiquitous, mobile applications by utilizing the example of social networks as a practical scenario."

Erfurth and Schau claim that humans "are on the starting blocks to integrate and share our daily life within the context of web communication channels. That is the new understanding of mobile access and modern life. Thereby, mobile communication devices and applications are primarily designed to increase efficiency and productivity, as well as to manage our rapid way of life. For many people, particularly younger users, interaction functions of cell phones, smart phones, and other handhelds are paramount (Eagle & Pentland, 2005)." Obviously this new style of life is at the same time the cause and effect of technological innovation and business opportunity. Consequently informatics cannot refrain from discussing the related phenomena.

According to Erfurth and Schau, "humans are no more able to conceive the possibilities and to utilize available services efficiently." They thus conclude that a kind of intelligent broker is needed that would translate a human's requests into suitable service calls. These would then result in what they call "purified information". Obviously, heavy use of computerised media may make humans accommodate more to virtual reality. This creates the need to provide computerised aid to bridge the gap between realities. Due to their autonomous nature, "mobile software agents are in addition well suited to provide essential support in this matter"

Erfurth and Schau look into possible improvements of human communication in the web utilizing social virtual worlds by means of mobile software agents. They provide interaction schemas applying to communication between machines and humans, between machines, and between humans (through machines). Thereby communication is supported by personalized agents acting as intelligent messengers or even as humans' substitutes within the virtual world. Humans can focus on the interaction with friends, regardless of the social network to which they belong.

Fujima

The chapter by Fujima et al. is one that deals with the challenge of providing users a simplified way to access and make use of potentially rich information resources, in this case by supporting the combination of resources offered by Web applications. Despite the recent emergence of numerous technologies that enable the "mashing up" of Web-accessible data sources (such as use of the Google Maps API to map announcements of house sales, or of crime reports), there is a tendency for the technologies either to require sophisticated programming skills (as is the case with Google Maps) or to be constrained to information delivered in a form explicitly designed for merging with other sources, such as RSS feeds. For the kind of ad hoc combinations of resources that users call on every day – such as taking a price from a shopping site and feeding it to a currency-conversion application – it is still difficult for users without advanced programming skills to set up even the simple form of assistance involved in automating that data transfer, so as to save time and effort in subsequent use of the same resource combination. Fujima et al.'s proposal is to enable the use of a popular spreadsheet environment – Microsoft Excel – as a platform for such automation, on the basis that a large body of computer users, though not considering themselves to be programmers, find the simple declarative semantics of spreadsheet calculations to be unintimidating and useful. The result is a set of custom extensions to Excel, demonstrating a basic range of facilities that enable users to set up "orchestrations" of Web applications that not only automate the data transfers between applications but also provide a way to generate sets of related results (such as overall purchase costs from a range of competing shopping sites) to assist the user in making comparisons.

Although for simplicity of explanation the examples in this chapter address only straightforward lookups on shopping sites and bioinformatics repositories, the potential power of this platform becomes apparent when one considers that it can be applied equally to Web applications that incorporate intelligent, adaptive techniques. It is now common for sites to keep long-term records of the activities of individual users, enabling the sites both to adapt the information displayed according to an individual user's history of use, and to pool these histories in support of techniques such as collaborative filtering, thereby driving suggestions and recommendations as to what each user might like to try or buy next. Users who add such applications into the spreadsheet-driven mix stand to benefit from a dramatic new level of customised access to the Web resources that interest them.

Ghiassi & Spera

In their chapter, Ghiassi and Spera deal with the challenges of increasing product customisation and customer requirements, demanding new strategies for "Mass Customisation". Providing an architecture for a web-enabled, intelligent agent-based information system to support on-demand and mass customised markets such as car manufacturing, their approach is based on the assumption of a customer-centric production system involving many businesses each of which focuses on its core competencies, resulting in products that are outcome of a collaborative effort. In fact, they envision the idea of users assisted by IT applications, namely distributed and specialized software agents. Based on a taxonomy that accounts for the core functionalities (monitoring, analyzing, acting, and coordinating) of assisting entities and sufficient roles in the value chain, these agents systematically "address the needs of end users, manage product demands, and coordinate supply and resource management continuously". Accordingly, the authors introduce an architecture for the dynamic instantiation and interaction of the agents and give examples of their approach through a number of case studies. With an interdisciplinary combination of economic demands and computer scientific solutions, they encourage efforts to consider user-centric issues in production chains. Moreover, the case studies, although relying to some extent on simulation results, clearly show how to assist users such as end-customers in IT supported environments.

Guo

Similar to Fujima et al., Guo and Tanaka are reporting work designed to enable non-sophisticated programmers to build or configure their own specialised information-access applications, in this case in the domain of Geographic Information Systems. The form of assistance being demonstrated here is that while the end user performs only simple operations such as visually repositioning and/or reconnecting knowledge-media components, these components assemble and transfer rich data structures to drive complex simulation tools and display advanced 3D simulation results. The key to enabling this is that the components conform to local standards, established by the framework developer, for accessing a limited but useful subset of the capabilities of the underlying simulation tools. It is the framework developer's careful choice of the capabilities to be made available, and a simplified inter-component communication model based on custom-designed data formats and a flow-graph-style protocol for update propagation, that is crucial in obtaining a good balance between ease of use and breadth of capabilities. Guo and Tanaka explain in detail two application examples that have been built on their framework, demonstrating how it is possible to replace the key simulation elements and thereby obtain, on the same three-dimensional GIS-enabled substrate, the modelling of quite different phenomena. This form of framework can be seen as offering at least two levels for applying intelligence-supported assistance: one is above the level of the components, for example augmenting the user's simple construction operations with automatic sensing and resolution of mismatches in data formats and protocols; another is below the components – in other words, building components that offer simplified access to assistant services. Both can be seen as potentially profitable extensions of the principles demonstrated here.

Krumpholz et al.

Krumpholz et al. point out the crucial role of librarians in days gone by, when "Librarians … fetched the needed materials and passed them out to the reader. … Later, librarians got access to computers and translated readers' needs into queries to retrieve the meta-information about the requested literature. Beyond their retrieval tasks, experienced librarians also helped students to identify popular books or drew their scientists' attention to new publications in their field.", and ask whether, now that most researchers have access to search engines through their own computers, the literature retrieval services available to them match up to the job being done by librarians.

They describe a number of currently existing search aid systems and research efforts to improve literature retrieval, focusing on literature retrieval for computer scientists, and on medical literature retrieval for clinicians or medical researchers.

The authors note that the need for literature retrieval depends on the role and the field of the researcher as well as the task they wish to achieve. In order to better understand search tasks, Krumpholz et al. identify a number of search purposes that might warrant a specialised approach to literature search. These are: (1) Finding a specific publication, (2) Finding related publications, (3) Staying up to date in the field, and (4) Entering a new field. Krumpholz et al. additionally address medical research as a particular domain for study – a focus that makes sense, as medical literature search is a particularly frequently occurring and important task in a problem area with a highly standardized terminology. As a guiding metaphor for understanding search processes, Krumpholz et al. use an ad hoc interpretation of Web retrieval processes. They assume that a query provided by a user contains a number of search terms and that as a response a ranked list of matching documents is returned. A commonly used strategy of dealing with that response is skimming the first few results and, based on the acquired information, altering the query and searching again. This cycle of output creation and limited-scope evaluation of it can then be repeated for as long as the results seem to be improving, or until the strategy clearly fails. The key query change goals are (1) improving output quality; and (2) adapting output size. Employing literature retrieval systems differs from Web search in that it frequently exploits specific metadata for improving output quality. In particular this shows in using links to further publications of a given author.

Krumpholz et al. point out that in Web search one usually gets access to a large number of documents, which creates the need to check them for relevance; that in itself implies further potential for aiding search.

Minato

The work introduced in the chapter by Minato and Spyratos stands as an enabling technology for letting users express, in simple ways, their information interests as handled in a large digital library organised by a rich, hierarchical taxonomy of terms. The key to the technique is Binary Decision Diagrams, a way of encoding complex logic formulas into a compact representation by taking advantage both of the sparseness of the formulas relative to the total number of possible terms, and of the terms shared between formulas that are being calculated in parallel. By automatically taking into account the structure of the taxonomy of keywords used to tag the documents in the library, the system proposed by Minato and Spyratos allows users to build subscriptions based on a free mix of highly specific and more general terms, depending on the specificity of their interests. In one of the examples that they give, a user who is interested in documents dealing with a specific sorting algorithm could subscribe using that specific term, whereas a user who is interested in sorting algorithms in general could subscribe at that higher level without needing to worry about the sub-categories that this encompasses; not only will the subscription ensure that the latter user receives notification of every document dealing with any such sub-category, but if the taxonomy is later changed all subscriptions can be automatically recompiled so that they continue to deliver all documents that the users were expecting.

The need to be able to expand simple queries given by users into the complex combinations of keywords that will deliver what the users had in mind is clearly demonstrated in the medical examples cited in the chapter by Krumpholz et al.; this chapter gives insight into how such expansions can be handled without overwhelming the servers on which the repositories are held.

Sturm & Igel

The chapter provided by Sturm and Igel presents an empirical study regarding the utilisation of a knowledge management system in the tertiary education sector. The KMS was designed to meet the perspectives of both learners and teachers. It therefore provides so called teaching-learning modules to be experienced by the learners, as well as a multimedia database storing the digital material to support lecturers during their apprenticeship. By means of the KMS, "digital information and knowledge objects can be retrieved and selected, collected in a separate download domain and, where required, archived and downloaded. Alternatively, users can make digital information and knowledge objects ...created [by] themselves available to the (scientific) community". Thus the two functionalities "search" and "submit" essentially characterize the use of the KMS. From an evaluative perspective, the authors examine the impact of the KMS, i.e., its utilisation and potential barriers preventing such utilisation, and present result from two studies. In a first, exploratory study they identified typical behaviour patterns and search strategies, looked for difficulties in use and attributed them to a set of personal and non-personal barriers. A second, quasi-experimental study was conducted to determine the impact of utilisation barriers on usage patterns. Sturm and Igel were able to confirm their assumption that a variety of aspects prevent existing as well as potential users from using all capabilities offered by the KMS. According to this finding the authors also show that having complete technical equipment, network-connected computers or Internet access does not automatically guarantee a new level of quality in teaching and learning. Interestingly, their studies show that system training, i.e. retrieval training, "helps system novices with a low level of task-solving knowledge when completing specific, detailed set tasks more than it does system novices with a high system competence". Going into more detail they found that "course participants with a low system expertise tend to be more motivated and focused, and therefore probably handle tasks more conscientiously. They ask more questions in the scope of the system training and assure themselves of the fact that their user identification is still active at the end of the test phase". Hence, their studies clearly give empirical evidence that even untrained users can benefit from assistance offered by training courses and KMS. However, these findings do not conflict with but clarify (at least some of) the assumptions made by Akaltun et al., in their chapter on the idea of a knowledge web, regarding limited user capabilities.

Takashima

Takashima's chapter presents a system for producing customised presentations of videos, in which some parts of the video are emphasised relative to others. The form of emphasis supported by the current version is the automatic use of the playback controls (including slow-motion and fast forward) to slow down for sections that are deemed to be especially interesting, and to skip through the sections of least interest. Takashima's view is that this can be seen as an assistant-like functionality whereby the system recognises and reproduces the user's habitual behavior, so that once the system has been appropriately trained it will automatically show newly arrived videos in the way the user would probably have wanted to watch them anyway. The main example used for his experiments is segments of football games, which form a convenient object of study because the play tends to be divided relatively cleanly into scenes of different types (goal shots, game pauses, etc), and camerawork conventions ensure that these differences are quite straightforward to detect. Takashima shows that because his system represents viewing styles as knowledge objects that can be communicated from one user to another, and can be manipulated so as to produce various forms of composition of alternative viewing styles, users are able to benefit from the use of viewing styles defined by others – such as, in the football example, a style that would be used by a football coach when demonstrating or analysing a team's tactics.

Gunther Kreuzberger, Ilmenau Technical University, Germany
Aran Lunzer, Hokkaido University, Japan
Roland Kaschek, Gymnasium Gerresheim, Germany

REFERENCES

Ahituv, N., Neumann, S. (1990). *Principles of information systems fore management*. Dubuque: Wm. C. Brown Publishers, third printing.

Banker, R., Datar, S., Kemerer, C., & Zweig, D. (1993). Software complexity and maintenance costs. *Communications of the ACM, 36(11), 81 – 94.*

Barstow, D., Shrobe, H. & Sandewall, E. (Eds.) (1984). *Interactive programming environments*. New York et al.: McGraw – Hill.

Bateson, G. (1979). *Mind and nature: a necessary unity*. New York: Dutton.

Boy, G. (1991). *Intelligent assistant systems*. Academic Press.

Burke, D., Hammond, K. & Young, B. (1997). The FindMe approach to assisted browsing. *IEEE Expert, 12(4), 32 – 40.*

Buschmann, F., Meunier, R., Rohnert, H., Sommerlad, P. & Stal, M. (1999). *Pattern – oriented software architecture: a system of patterns*. Chichester et al.: John Wiley & Sons, 4th printing.

O'Connor, R. (2000). *An architecture for an intelligent assistant system for use in software project planning*. PhD thesis, Department of Computing, City University of London.

Engelbart, D. (1962). *Augmenting human intellect: a conceptual framework*. Excerpt from Summary report AF0SR-3223 under contract AF 49(638)-1024, SRI Project 3578 for Air Force Office of Scientific Research, Menlo Park, California. Reprinted as (Wardrip-Fruin, N., Montfort, N., 2003, pp. 95 – 108).

Engelbart, D., English, W. (1968). A research centre for augmenting human intellect. AFIPS conference proceedings 33, part 1, 395 – 410. Fall Joint Computer Conference. Reprinted as (Wardrip-Fruin, N., Montfort, N., 2003, pp. 233 – 246).

Enzensberger, H.(1970). Constituents of a theory of the media. *New Left Review, 64(Nov / Dec), 13 – 36.* Reprinted as (Wardrip-Fruin, N. and Montfort N., 2003, pp. 261 - 275).

Fleck, L. (1935) *Entstehung und Entwicklung einer wissenschaftlichen Tatsache. Einführung in die Lehre vom Denkstil und Denkkollektiv*. Schwabe und Co., Verlagsbuchhandlung, Basel.
Garmus, D. & Herron, D. (1996). *Measuring the software process: a practical guide to functional measurements*. Upper Saddle River: Prentice Hall.

Haase, K. (1997). Do agents need understanding? *IEEE Expert, 12(4), 4 – 6.*

Häuble, G., Trifts, V. (2000). Consumer decision making in online shopping environments: the effects of interactive decision aids. *Marketing Science, 19(1), 4 – 21.*

Hevner, A., Berndt, D. (2000). *Eras of business computing*. Advances in Computers, 52, chapter 1. Academic Press.
Hirschheim, R., Klein, H., & Lyytinen, K. (1995). *Information systems and data modeling: conceptual and philosophical foundations*. Cambridge, UK: Cambridge University Press.

Ifrah, G. (2000). *The universal history of numbers III: the computer and the information revolution*. London: The Harvill Press.

Kaiser, G., Feller, P., & Popovich, S. (1988). Intelligent assistance for software development and maintenance. *IEEE Software, 5(3), 40 – 49.*

Kaschek, R. (2006). *Intelligent assistant systems: concepts, techniques and technologies*; IDEA Group Publishing, Inc.: Hershey, PA. 2006.

Kuhlen, R. (1999) (In German). *The consequences of information assistants.* Frankfurt: Suhrkamp Verlag.

Liebermann, H., Selker, T. (2000). Out of context: computer systems that adapt to, and learn from context. *IBM Systems Journal, 39(3/4), 617 – 632.*

Maes, P. (1994). Agents that reduce work and information overload. *Communications of the ACM, 37(7), 31 – 40, 146.*

Marcus, R. (1982). User assistance in bibliographic retrieval networks through a computer intermediary. *IEEE Transactions on Systems, Man, and Cybernetics, March/April, 116 – 133.*

Ong, W. (1996). *Orality and literacy: the technologizing of the word.* London and New York: Routledge, 7th. printing.

Sandheimer, N., Relles, N. (1982). Human factors and user – assistance in interactive computing systems: an introduction. *IEEE Transactions on Systems, Man, and Cybernetics, 12(2), 102 – 107.*
Satzinger, J., Jackson, R., & Burd S. (2004). *Systems analysis and design in a changing world.* Thomson Course Technology, 3rd edition.

Shannon, C. E., (1993). *A Mathematical Theory of Communication.* In Sloane, N. J. A., Wyner, A. D. (Eds.), Claude Elwood Shannon, Collected Papers, (pp. 5–83). New York: IEEE Press.

Sowa, J. (2002). Architectures for intelligent systems. *IBM Systems Journal, 41(3), 331 – 349.*

Tanaka, Y. (2003). *Meme media and meme media market architectures: knowledge media for editing, distributing, and managing intellectual resources.* IEEE Press and John Wiley & Sons, Inc.

Wardrip-Fruin, N., Montfort N. (2003). *The new media reader.* Cambridge, London: The MIT Press.

Winograd, T. (1973). Breaking the complexity barrier (again). *Proceedings of the ACM SIGPLAN – SIGIR interface meeting on programming languages – information retrieval,* November 1973, 13 – 30. Reprinted as chapter 1 of (Barstow, Shrobe & Sandewall, 1984).

Winograd, T. (1979). Beyond programming languages. *Communications of the ACM, 22(7), 391 – 401.* Reprinted as chapter 25 of Barstow et al. (1984).

Acknowledgment

The editors would first like to thank all the researchers who took part in the PISA 2007 workshop in Sapporo, and in particular Yuzuru Tanaka for hosting the event and for his continued support of our project.

We also express our thanks to all the reviewers and Editorial Advisory Board members who have helped in producing this book, and to Joel A. Gamon, our Development Editor at IGI Global, for patiently guiding us through the publication process and answering our many questions.

Gunther Kreuzberger, Ilmenau Technical University, Germany
Aran Lunzer. Hokkaido University, Japan
Roland Kaschek, Gymnasium Gerresheim, Germany

Section 1
Enabling Technologies

Chapter 1
Towards Next Generation Web:
Knowledge Web

Aylin Akaltun
Christian-Albrechts-University Kiel, Germany

Patrick Maisch
Christian-Albrechts-University Kiel, Germany

Bernhard Thalheim
Christian-Albrechts-University Kiel, Germany

ABSTRACT

The rapid growth of information demands that new technologies make the right information available to the right user. The more unspecified content published, the more general usability of the World Wide Web is lost. The next generation's Web information services will have to be more adaptive to keep the web usable. User demands for knowledge reflecting his or her life case, specific intentions, and therefore a particular quality of content must be served in an understandable way. As a possible solution, the authors present a new technology that matches content against particular life cases, user models and contexts. In a first approach the authors give a quick overview of knowledge, the way it is perceived and an example application dealing with content matching and different views of information required for different kinds of audiences.

DOI: 10.4018/978-1-61520-851-7.ch001

INTRODUCTION

The Right Needle from the Right Haystack

Among the technological generations of World Wide Web, content of any kind and for any audience grew and grew. Meanwhile the user is overwhelmed by a flood of information offered to him indiscriminately by the World Wide Web, which leads to a significantly decreasing usability. Search engines have not (yet) improved this picture. They introduce their own policies and biases. They filter out useful information and direct the searcher in a specific way. Search is moreover still bound to addresses which may be known or unknown to the searcher.

The user is typically not able to determine the quality of data obtained. He or she can

- neither judge accuracy, currency, appropriateness, completeness, correctness, independence, learnability, maturity, reliability, stability, suitability, or understandability,
- nor decide whether data obtained are at the right moment of time, of the right kind, in the right dose, of the right form, in the complete extent, and within the restrictions agreed upon in advance.

There is no authority for quality. The business model for the World Wide Web is based on freedom of content to a certain extent. This freedom may be nicely used or may be misused. Wikipedia is a typical example of partially very useful and partially completely confusing information.[1]

Missing Adaptivity and User Orientation

Information as processed by humans is perceived in a very subjective way. For a web information system, the determining factor as to whether the user can derive advantage from the content delivered is the user's individual situation (Kobsa, 2005), i.e., the life case, user model and context. The same category of information can cause various needs in different life cases. For instance, a divorcee has a completely different need for information in fatherhood than a prospective father, although both of them reside in the same category. It is not the case that any user can deal with any kind of content. For the casual user or the novice other content has to be delivered than for experts. The common web information system doesn't reflect the user's situation and neglects the user's specific needs. As a result, the user is spammed with information which is predominantly out of focus. The abundance of information also makes it impossible for the user to separate useful from useless content. By the absence of metadata, any unspecified information reduces the usability of the World Wide Web as a whole. Whether the content obtained from the web may be classified as information depends on the user. There is no commonly agreed definition of information. We may define information as follows within the five layer model of (Mortiz, Schewe, Thalheim, 2005)(Murphy, 2001)(Schewe and Thalheim, 2007):

Information, as processed by human users of web sites, is

* *data*
* *perceived* or noticed, *selected* and organized by its receiver,
* because of his subjective human *interests*, originating from his instincts, feelings, experience, intuition, common sense, values, beliefs, personal knowledge, or wisdom,
* simultaneously *processed* by his cognitive and mental processes and
* seamlessly *integrated* in his recallable knowledge.

Therefore, web site modeling must include a description of the *information need* of actors. The information need can be specified as

* conceptual incongruity in which a person's cognitive structure is not adequate to a task,
* when a person recognizes that something is wrong in their state of knowledge and desires to resolve the anomaly,
* when the current state of possessed knowledge is less than is needed,
* when internal sense runs out and
* when there is insufficient knowledge to cope with voids, uncertainty or conflict in a knowledge area.

Moreover, users are limited

* in their abilities for verbalization,
* in their abilities for digestion of data and
* by their habits, practices and cultural environment.

These limitations may cause intellectual overburdening of users. Most systems that require sophisticated learning courses for their exploration and utilization did not consider these limitations and did not cope with real life situations. The approach we use for avoiding overload is based on observation of real applications before developing the web information system.

Content Matching as the Challenge of the Next Generation Web

Content in its current definition is any kind of information that is shared within a community or organization. In difference to data in classical database systems content usually refers to aggregated macro data which has complex structure. Structuring of content can be distinguished as follows:

- The structure of the aggregated micro data is preserved but micro data was combined to build larger chunks of information. Examples are scientific datasets such as time series of certain measurements. There is a common (or even individual) structuring and meaning for each sampling vector, but the compound of all sampling vectors adds additional semantics.
- The structure of content is only partially known. A typical example is the content of web pages: structuring is known up to a certain level of detail which may also be varying within one instance.
- Content may be sub-symbolic, such as pictures, videos, music or other multimedia content.

Users typically request or need various content depending on their situation, on material available, on the actual information demand, on data already currently available and on technical equipment and channels ready to hand. Therefore, we need a facility for content adaptation depending on the context of the user (Schewe and Thalheim, 2008). Content matching and adaptation may be thus considered as one of the 'grand challenges' of the modern internet.

To meet this challenge, the information has to be matched against the particular needs of the user (Paech, 2000). Since the imaginable combinations of user life cases, user models and context (Kaschek, Schewe, Thalheim and Zhang, 2003) are unlimited, the definition of life cases(Schewe, Thalheim,2008) has to be determined for the content and matched against the users' situations. For a web information system, there should not only be concrete definitions of which content is applicable for which life case; to avoid making useful content useless by presenting it in an inappropriate way to the user, web information systems also have to consider the user's specific profile and context. By processing this data, the web information system should provide different views of information and the appropriate media types for presenting their knowledge to various audiences. The implicit goals of content management and content delivery are:

- to meet all the information (contextual) requirements of the entire spectrum of users in a given application area;

- to provide a natural and easy-to-understand structuring of the information content;
- to preserve the designers' entire semantic information for a later redesign;
- to achieve all the processing requirements and also a high degree of efficiency in processing;
- to achieve logical independence of query and transaction formulation on this level;
- to provide a simple and easy to comprehend user interface family.

Our Approach

Since there cannot be an all-purpose solution, we give an approach for ease of use, high-quality content delivery in respect of user life cases to correct also the defects of adaptability by also taking into account the story of the construction of the web, as follows.

WEB X.0 EVOLUTION AND THE KNOWLEDGE WEB

Web 1.0

For almost two decades the Internet was a linkage of networked Servers, which was entirely used as a worldwide source for research. It resulted in an aggregate of billions of static web sites, which were accessed via hyperlinks. Websites were mainly author-driven, aiming to support users depending on their information need and demand, so the focus was chiefly on the mutual trust between user and provider. The utilization of these sites can be modeled by story spaces. The story space specification results in storyboards that are schemes for utilization by a large variety of users. Web 1.0 is author driven and uses as stories

- at the provider side: publish/provide_story/support or advertise/wait/attract/react/retain and
- at the user side: inform/subscribe/obtain/answer/come_back.

Web 1.0 has mainly been oriented towards content provision, which basically meant to deliver content together with a rudimentary functionality. These main functionalities can be:

- navigation facilities for intra-site or page navigation;

- acquisition possibilities of information for users from simple content that is based on text, media data such as pictures, audio and video data;
- linking facilities;
- search and browse facilities provided to users

Websites are mainly oriented towards content delivery, provide some functionality and use a large variety of presentation facilities. This orientation results in requirements for website development illustrated in Figure 1.

We notice however that early website development methodologies (Dusterhoft & Thalheim,2001) have already paid attention to the specification of the story space. Most website specification languages have however been mainly concentrated on the three dimensions in Figure 1. The acceptance for explicit story modelling came with the evolution of Web 1.0 to Web 2.0.

The Web 2.0 Generation

The Web has rapidly developed over two decades. In its early days, Web 1.0 made author-driven static content available to numerous users. Users could access exclusively the web pages for research and personal investigations. The control and management from the 'top' didn't provide any scope or client-side opportunities for development. This has changed with the evolution of Web 2.0, the so-called social web, as a development process powered by collaborative brainstorming, in which collective cooperation is to the fore. Meanwhile there are no bounds set to the today's web. With the establishment of user communities, users obtain an abundance of information by high-tech sophisticated services, interchange experiences, and benefit from the mass collaboration every single day, because data acquisition and data diffusion are basically accomplished by user interactions inside the whole web

Figure 1. Web 1.0 is oriented towards content, provides some functionality and a variety of presentation

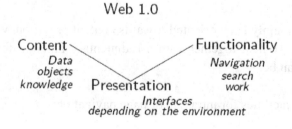

story space. But as time draws on, the advantages of this evolution fade ever more into the background. More and more deficiencies of Web 2.0 are brought to light. The error-proneness of data and distribution of information increases exponentially; incorrect information gives no warranty against falsified, faked or even stolen content. Also privacy is despite collective identity a quite back number. The challenging question is which knowledge in the web we can rely on. The call for quality-based content is rising and cannot be neglected. Figures 1 and 2 illustrate the differences between Web 1.0 and Web 2.0. Web 1.0 has already made progress in adaptation to the user. The story spaces have however been hardwired into the website. Context has been mainly neglected. The sudden and very dynamic development of Web 2.0 is mainly due to the activation of users, of support for the intensive participation and to the demand of collaborating societies. But the advantages over Web 1.0 entail also indefensible disadvantages: it is just a question of time before misuse of data happens in a grand style.

The context and user dimensions are still not treated very well. The context dimension can be specified through the explicit presentation of the user's context, the story context, the system context and the content context (Schewe and Thalheim, 2008). The functionality context plays a minor role since most websites are content-driven. Users must be specified through a *user model*. The most important information about the user is the intention of the user or of groups of users and the situation which is typical for the user while interacting in the internet.

Figure 2. Web 2.0 allows context injection and is user-centered and story-centered

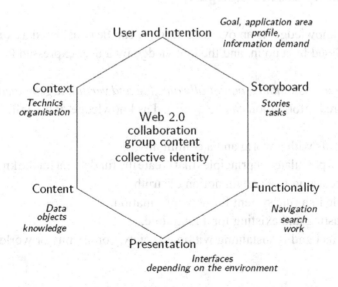

Knowledge Dimensions in the Next Generation Web

While Web 2.0 integrates collaboration, Web 3.0 provides annotation techniques. But what is missed in the future of web is quality. We want to reach this level of quality with the aid of semantics and pragmatics in respect of the user profile and life cases. We are convinced that lexical semantics composes the base frame of the Next Generation Knowledge Web. That is the reason why we conduct intensive research in the field of linguistics and the development of high-quality web information systems. Therefore it is absolutely essential to consider linguistic branches. With syntactics, semantics and pragmatics, which constitute the semiotics, it is necessary to concentrate on conceptualisation of content for a given context considering annotations with respect to user intentions, motivations, profiles and tasks. Description of scenarios inside a certain story space and preliminary considerations of general user behaviour guarantee with reliable data acquisition quality based content coordinated to user groups (Schewe & Thalheim, 2006). So the knowledge space is composed of the content space, the concept space, the topic space and the information space (Kiyoki & Thalheim, 2008).

For this reason we imagine using knowledge chunks as a suite of knowledge pieces consisting of content, concepts, topics and information. These dimensions are interdependent from each other. Figure 3 displays the knowledge space.

KNOWLEDGE FOR THE USER

The Dichotomy of Knowledge

The notion of knowledge[2] is an overused term. It can be considered as knowledge in general, defined by a noun, and the knowledge by a user expressed by the verb 'to know'.

Knowledge as sustainable, potentially durable and verifiable grounded consensus. The required information can be qualified as knowledge, if the information:

1. is consensus with a world and a community,
2. is based on postulates or principles that create the fundament for the knowledge,
3. is true according to a certain notion of 'truth',
4. is reusable in a rule system for new information,
5. is long-lasting and existing for a long time,
6. has an effect and is sustaining within a society, community or world, and

7. is not equivalent to other information that can be generated with the aid of facts or preliminary information in the particular inventory of knowledge by a rule system.

Knowledge as the state of information of a user. Different kinds of knowledge are:

1. The state or fact of knowing.
2. Familiarity, awareness, or understanding gained through experience or study.
3. The sum or range of what has been perceived, discovered, or learned.
4. Learning; erudition: teachers of great knowledge.
5. Specific information about something.
6. Carnal knowledge.

We conclude therefore that within the scope of the Next Generation Knowledge Web, it is necessary to deliver knowledge as enduring, justified and true belief to users depending on context, users' demands, desiderata and intention, whereby these aspects are supported by social facets, the environment, the profile, tasks and life cases of the users. Life cases, portfolios and tasks constitute the information demand of every user. The information demand of users requires a special content quality. It results in the requested knowledge, which also depends on the understanding and motivation of users. So, the requested knowledge of users is a composition of understanding, and information demand, whereby the information demand is an aggregated component of life cases, motivation, intention and quality.

Figure 3. The four dimensions of the knowledge space: data dimension through content, foundation dimension through concepts, language dimension through topics, and user dimension through user information

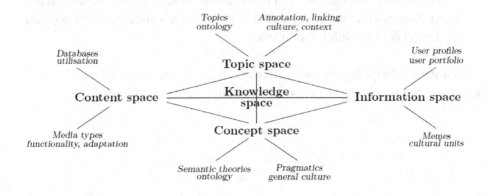

The Quality Characteristics of Knowledge

It is surprising that the literature treats knowledge as a 100% quality criterion. We can however distinguish between:

- *validated knowledge* that is satisfiable within a scope of axioms and derivation rules (application domain), within a certain generality, and that has validity and timeliness,
- *verified and correct knowledge* based on axioms and rules within a proof system that can be verified within a finite time, obeys correctness criteria (depending on profiles), and has some known interaction with other knowledge, and finally
- *quality knowledge* defined by the quality of use (understandability, learnability, operability, attractiveness, appropriateness), by the external quality (privacy, ubiquity, pervasiveness, analysability, changeability, stability, testability), and by the internal quality (accuracy, suitability, interoperability, robustness, self-contained/independence).

These quality characteristics result in differences of the value of knowledge for the user.

Quality is thus characterised by certain main characteristics. These characteristics can be ordered within the tree shown in Figure 4.

We may also observe that these quality characteristics are of different *value* and *importance* depending on the needs of the user. We may differentiate knowledge depending on

- the role of the user such as learner, teacher, scientist, writer, etc.,
- the application area such as sciences, engineering, daily life,
- the timeliness of the information depending on the needs,
- the background necessary for transferring the data to the user's information space, the user's recognition and perception abilities, the user's attention and interest, the user's processing abilities, and the user's abilities to integrate the data into his or her information space.

For instance, the quality characteristics are of very different importance. Compare for instance the following two opposite evaluations shown in Figure 5.

Figure 4.

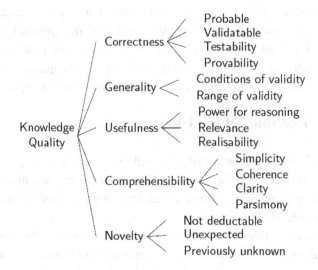

The Content Space, Topic Space and the Concept Space for Knowledge Management

We apply the separation of the knowledge space for the user into the content space, the concept space and the topic space. We furthermore assume that the information space can be defined on top of the three spaces. In this case we can use the content management system approach that has already been used in our research group

Figure 5.

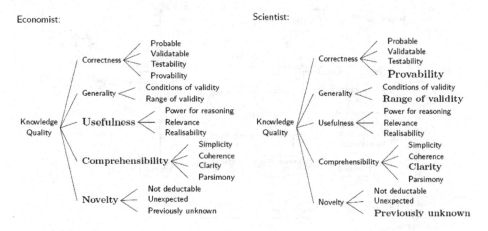

for a number of applications. Using this separation we define a *knowledge chunk* as data that represent content, topics, and concepts. This triptych has already been used for advanced content management. We generalize the approach of (Fiedler& Thalheim, 2009) and may now describe the knowledge chunk database through its rough database schema. The schema in Figure 6 displays the general structure. The main part of the schema is the triptych of concepts, content and topics.

Profiles and Portfolio of the User

User modelling is based on the specification of *user profiles* that address the char- acterisation of the users, and the specification of *user portfolios* that describe the users' tasks and their involvement and collaboration on the basis of the mission of the WIS (Schewe & Thalheim, 2006).

To characterize the users of a WIS we distinguish between *education*, *work* and *personality* profiles. The education profile contains properties users can obtain by education or training. Capabilities and application knowledge as a result of educa- tional activities are also suitable for this profile. Properties will be assigned to the

Figure 6. Main Schema for Content, Concept and Topic Databases representing Knowledge Chunks

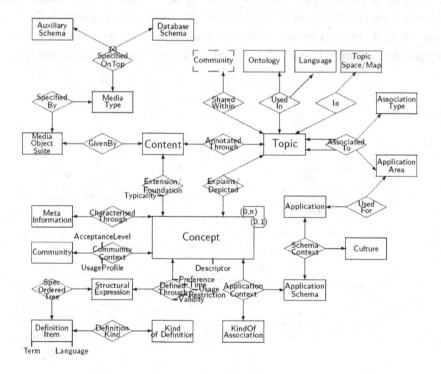

work profile if they can be associated with task-solving knowledge and skills in the application area, i.e. task expertise and experience as well as system experience. Another part of a work profile is the interaction profile of a user, which is determined by his frequency, intensity and style of utilization of the WIS. The personality profile characterises the general properties and preferences of a user. General properties are the status in the enterprise, community, etc., and the psychological and sensory properties like hearing, motoric control, information processing and anxiety.

A *portfolio* is determined by responsibilities and is based on a number of targets. Therefore, the actor portfolio (referring to *actors* as groups of users with similar behaviour) within an application is based on a set of tasks assigned to or intended by an actor and for which s/he has the authority and control, and a description of involvement within the task solution (Schewe & Thalheim, 2007). A *task* as a piece of work is characterized by a problem statement, initial and target states, collaboration and presupposed profiles, auxiliary conditions and means for task completion. Tasks may consist of subtasks. Moreover, the task execution model defines what, when, how, by whom and with which data a task can be accomplished. The result of executing a task should present the final state as well as the satisfaction of target conditions.

Users' Life Cases

For task completion, users need the right kind of data, at the right time, in the right granularity and format, unabridged and within the frame agreed upon in advance. Moreover, users are bound by their ability to verbalise and digest data, and their habits, practices and cultural environment. To avoid intellectual overburdening of users we observe real applications before the system development leading to *life cases* (Schewe & Thalheim, 2008). Life cases help in closing the pragmatic gap between intentions and storyboarding. They are used to specify the concrete life situation of the user and characterise thus a bundle of tasks that the user should solve. Syntax and semantics of life cases have already been well explored in (Schewe & Thalheim, 2006).

In addition, each user has an *information portfolio*, which specifies the information needs as well as the information entered into the system. We do not model the information portfolio as part of a user, but instead of this we will model the information consumed and produced with each more detailed specification of a user request.

Requirements Issued by the User to Knowledge Web

We may now summarise the knowledge delivery task of the Knowledge Web based on user-oriented and life-case-based content, concepts and topics as follows:

Deliver the knowledge the user really needs through (1) concepts *at the educational level of the user that are illustrated and extended by (2)* content *which is quality content depending on the external and internal quality of the aggregated data (media object suite) and that are depicted by (3)* topics *in the language, in the culture and in the application portfolio of the user.*

The question is therefore whether such system is achievable and whether there is a chance to build it. We are going to sketch now a system proposal of (Akaltun, 2009) in the next section, refer for a proof of achievability based on generic generators to (Kowski, 2009) and finally illustrate usefulness by a prototypical example in the last section.

KNOWLEDGE WEB ARCHITECTURES

We concentrate on a *Three Tier Knowledge Management Architecture.*

Service-Oriented Architecture

System components of a Service-Oriented Architecture (*SOA*) constitute a group of services that communicate with each other via interoperable services and interfaces. In Global Risk Management Systems (Jaakkola, et al., 2008), for example, these components are partitioned in three levels.

First level: The kernel system provides centralized Knowledge Base (KB) and Knowledge Management (KM) services and gets processed data from next tier nodes, provides also local KB and KM services and provides services to the next tier nodes (SSS, LS)

Second level: The sensing and legacy service(sub-)systems produce (and process) data to the upper-level systems, get data from upper-level nodes and process data or provide specialised services, and also provide special data and use upper-level services via standardized interfaces

Third level: The client system uses services from different levels of nodes based on fixed or service oriented connection

Web-Oriented Architecture

The Web-Oriented Architecture (WOA) is an extended version of SOA with web based applications. The service agreement of WOA resources is included; it is the representation that is received. WOA embodies Thomas Erl's essential Principles of SOA (Ma & Thalheim, 2008). Furthermore, it is radically distributed, granular, web-oriented, open and highly consumable.

Figure 7. SOA and WOA

Knowledge-Oriented Architecture

We take a step forward and define a new architecture which is the extension of WOA integrating enterprise scale and integration focus of the SOA with Knowledge features. We consider the new Knowledge Oriented Architecture (KOA), which is grounded on rule systems, metadata structures and which is knowledge driven.

1. Data Repository: Amount of data to which structure is given by the HERM/ER scheme;
2. User Group Specification: Users are classified into types or user groups by the analysis of the click behaviour, the profile, and the topics the user is interested in;

Figure 8. The Knowledge- Oriented Architecture

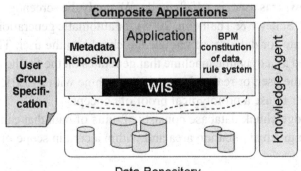

Data Repository

3. Metadata Repository is the repository for the metadata modelling schemes. These schemes can be defined for every user in respect of the web story space and the possible scenarios;
4. BPM, constitution of data, Rule System: Rule System defines the navigation structure, constitution of data and the functionality.
5. The Web Information System constitutes the interface between the metadata repository and the BPM/ Rule System. It represents the Business Logic.
6. Composite Applications give services to the clients.

Database Technology Applied for Knowledge Delivery

Database technology has brought a large number of facilities for advanced knowledge management. We shall combine this approach with the technology developed for web information systems and e-learning systems. Classical database systems provide a facility for view generation. It is well known that views can also be parameterised. This facility has been used for the development of the technology of media types (Schewe & Thalheim, 2007) that enhance views by playout facilities and functionality that support the work of the user such as import/export, marking, specialisation, generalisation, survey, reordering, browsing, sequentialisation, linking, searching and join functions. Media objects are defined over media types and can be combined into containers that deliver or stream them to the user within a web playout system.

We also use the approach of (Binemann-Zdanowicz, Thalheim & Tschiedel, 2003) for the delivery of knowledge chunks. This approach has generalised learning objects to learning units and open learning objects. Knowledge chunks consist of elementary content, concept and topic units. These units are stored in the database. They are going to be combined with other chunks based on the media type technology. Media types are the basis for the knowledge chunk stream that can be delivered to the user. This stream can now be filtered against the user portfolio and the system context of the user. The system context also provides information regarding what kind of web browser is used, in which mode. We apply the screenography approach (Moritz, Noack, Schewe & Thalheim, 2005) for automatic generation of the layout that is appropriate for delivery of knowledge chunks to the user. The system can either be realised as a dynamic machine that generates on the fly the corresponding knowledge for the user, or realised as a static machine with a restricted scope. We decided however to use a prototypical proof of concept.

The knowledge chunk database consists of units of data that can be of interest for the user in a given application area and within a certain scope of the user.

- These chunks are combinable and can be delivered to the user. The combination is given by views over the database. The result of applying the view to the database is enhanced by functions that ease the work of the user. A typical function of this kind is marking or extracting of content, concepts and topics from the chunk.
- The result can now be filtered against the context of the user request, against the user portfolio and against the layout facilities the system provides. We envisage that in the future this extract-transform-load approach can be partially automated by term rewriting. In this case, a user request from a user with a known portfolio is automatically transformed to an enhanced user query.

The knowledge web machine thus uses *database extraction* for extraction of content, concepts, and topics from the database consisting of knowledge chunks and generation of media objects, *transformations* of the media objects to knowledge chunk streams thus providing a playout stream, and a *loading facility* that allows to deliver knowledge adapted to the user.

A CHALLENGING APPLICATION

German Law using the example of Final Withholding Tax

As we've seen above, it is by far not enough to present to the user some minimally categorized content or content only specified by common keywords. The delivered information has to satisfy the specific needs of the user and has to be refined in a specific view of the information that is intelligible for the user and suitable for the user's particular situation. A Web information system has to be adaptive (Binemann-Zdanowicz, Thalheim & Tschiedel, 2003), which means it has to reflect the life cases, user model and context. Any collaborative way of providing information has to comply with the information structures claimed for web communities. Our team has built a database to map laws and deliver the aggregated data to different kinds of audience. Besides the techniques to picture law in a relational database, we specially focused on the transport of knowledge to the user. The information within laws is described in a very abstract way. The delivered information can be in a wide range between an abstract, rather scientific level, down to an individually recommended action. The topic is therefore predestined to give an example of how information has to be brought to the user in a way that is understandable for him. To produce the desired quality of information, we recognize the user and discriminate requests by the user's role, application area, timeliness and background. Those parameters have to be made available with the request and lead to different responses from the web information system. To render the rules, in our case the tax law, we use in essence the database scheme in Figure 9.

To make our example more detailed, we mapped the Final Withholding Tax into our system as an important part of German tax law. In 2007 the German Business Tax Reform Act was passed, introducing the Final Withholding Tax. From 1 January 2009, the taxation of income from capital investment became subject to totally new rules in order to simplify taxation. As a result, there are various informational needs among the affected actors. Simplified, we picture the core of the new tax-law as the facts and the legal consequences using the scheme shown in Figure 10. Facts thereby mean the conditions that have to apply. The legal consequence is the result for the underlying conditions. The facts are herein defined in *kind of investment* and *time of investment*. The particular conditions and desired quality will be derived from the user's role-assigned view of data. Let's take three simple examples to picture the different life cases, user profiles and contexts:

1. Arthur Simple is a retired salesman. He bought some shares on the recommendation of his financial advisor when he retired in 2006. He doesn't know much about securities, laws and taxation, but wants to know if he is affected

Figure 9. DB Schema of the Application

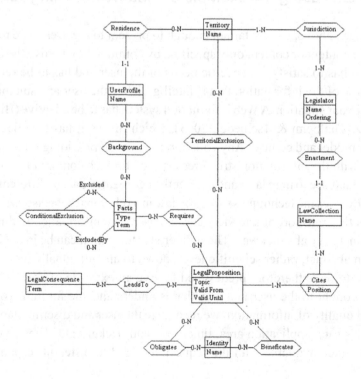

by the reform and whether he has to do something to avoid taxes. Since his eyesight isn't as good as it used to be, he doesn't like reading articles.

2. Britney Average is a broker. She has already heard about taxation, but can't deal with content that is too specific. She needs to explain the new situation to her customers, so she wants detailed information, but needs additional explanations and examples to understand terminologically interspersed content.

3. Tax advisor Colin Expert knows a lot about the matter and just wants to have a quick overview about the changes in his accustomed terminology.

If our actors would search for the term "Final Withholding Tax" they would probably find something like this:

(...) The final withholding tax is applicable on interest and dividends received after 31 December 2008. The taxation of capital gains upon private disposal, which in the future will be effected in any case and without the consideration of a holding period only applies to securities acquired after 31 December 2008. For securities acquired prior to 1 January 2009 the current rules remain applicable. According to the transitory provision in Sec. 52a para. 10 sent. 7 ITA final withholding tax

Figure 10. Flowchart of the Application

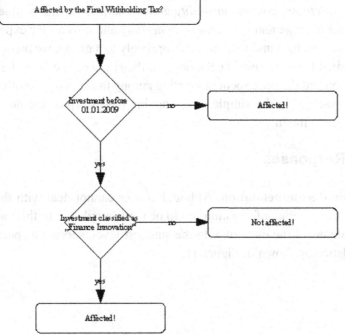

becomes due on sales of capital investments, which already under the current law qualify as Financial Innovations, effected after the year 2008, even if the capital investment was acquired prior to 1 January 2009 (at least this applies to all Financial Innovations acquired after 15 March 2007)." (...) (taken from The Tax Newsletter, http://www.dlapiper.com)

Except Colin Expert, none of actors can use this delivered content, as they demand individual views of the information. So we have to define the user roles for knowledge levels simple, average and expert. Each level has to be served a different view, containing different types of information. Besides the various levels of detail of information delivered for individual views, the available information can be scaled from a scientific-informative level down to a simple recommendation. In our example we therefore define the three mentioned qualities of information with different biases, for every condition of the user's request.

Adaption

In order to become adaptive, the audience has to be categorized in user groups, demanding individual views. Content has to be prepared for each individual group. Furthermore it has to be customized by media type, vocabulary and level of detail. In our example, we use the groups simple, average and expert with the corresponding database views. The content delivered is filtered against the group. The focus is set on *correctness, comprehensibility* and *usefulness* for the simple group, on *generality* for average and *correctness, generality* and *novelty* for experts. To recognize the current user and map him appropriately to a group, we process the click profile, created from the user's behaviour on the site, i.e., the items he chooses in his navigation and the time spent navigating among those items. Another approach is possible, such as in the simplest case having the user pick the desired quality explicitly from a menu.

Sample Responses

1. **Simple Recommendation**. Although a user cannot deal with the matter at all, some suitable information has to be made available. In this case we have to scale down the data view to the smallest level, serving a specific recommendation as shown in Figure 11.

Figure 11. Simple View of Content

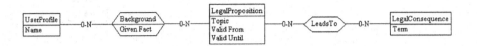

The quality of the information has to be adapted to the user's ability, in this case being focused on correctness, comprehensibility and usefulness. For the legal consequence, a simple statement must be defined. In our example:

"You are not affected by the new tax." or "Your investment is affected by the Final Withholding Tax. Please consult your tax advisor."

For Arthur Simple the conditions from the request would be:

mapped user profile: simple
topic: Final Withholding Tax given facts: kind of investment: shares; time of investment: 01.12.2006
The response from the system is: *"You are not affected by the new tax."*

2. **Average-level information.** For the more advanced user, we prepare an advanced view of data. Going beyond the simple view, the focus is on generality as shown in Figure 12.

In contrast to the simple recommendation, no particular facts have to be processed, since an abstract over all common conditions has to be served.

mapped user profile: average
legal proposition: topic: Final Withholding Tax

The response from the system is a detailed, commonly understandable summary, that makes the user able to explain her customers the new situation like this:

"Capital gains upon private disposal bought after 31.12.2008 are affected by the Final Withholding Tax, regardless how long the securities are held by the owner and kind of investment. The Gains are also affected if bought before 01.01.2009 but coming from securities classified as Finance Innovations."

Figure 12. View Schema for Average-Level Recommendation

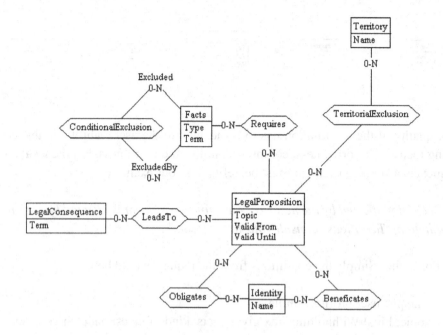

3.   **Expert information.** The expert's view meets the complete scheme in Figure 9 with all available data for a predefined topic. The quality focus is on correctness, generality and novelty.

mapped user profile: expert
legal proposition: topic: Final Withholding Tax
The response is the complete information at scientific quality.

CONCLUSION

In order to save the user from drowning in useless information, next generation web services will have to match the content served to each user against his or her particular needs. Knowledge on demand must, literally, respect the user's demand. For that reason, future web services will have to produce real knowledge for the user by means of particular user profiles condensed to an individual view of information. Since there is a unlimited number of imaginable users and situations, any matching criteria have to be defined from the content site and have to be matched against a user's life case, profile and context. Web 3.0 web information systems will also have more to deal with humans' ways of perceiving knowledge and will have to improve the way that knowledge is presented to the individual user. They will need to make different views of information available for different kinds of users and different intentions of representing their knowledge in an understandable way.

REFERENCES

Aksac, A. (Alkatun). *Knowledge engineering and semantics for the quality based next generation knowledge web.* Master's thesis, Christian-Albrechts University Kiel, Dept. of Computer Science, May 2009.

Binemann-Zdanowicz, A., Thalheim, B., & Tschiedel, B. (2003). *Logistics for learning objects. In eTrain'2003.* Kluwer.

Düsterhöft, A., & Thalheim, B. (2001). Conceptual modeling of internet sites. In Proc. ER'01, (LNCS 2224, pp. 179-192). New York: Springer, 2001.

Fiedler, G., & Thalheim, B. (2009). Towards semantic wikis: Modeling intensions, topics and origin in content management systems. *Information Modelling and Knowledge Bases, XX,* 1–21.

Jaakkola, H., Thalheim, B., Kidawara, Y., Zettsu, K., Chen, Y., & Heimburger, A. (2008). Information modeling and global risk management systems . In Jaakkola, H., & Kiyoki, Y. (Eds.), *EJC'2008, Information Modeling and Knowledge Bases XVI.* Amsterdam: IOS Press.

R. Kaschek, K.-D. Schewe, B. Thalheim, & Lei Zhang.(2003). Integrating context in conceptual modelling for web information systems, web services, e-business, and the semantic web. In *WES 2003,* (LNCS 3095, pp. 77-88). New York: Springer.

Kobsa, A. (2005). User modeling and user-adapted interaction. *User Modeling and User-Adapted Interaction, 15*(1-2), 185–190. doi:10.1007/s11257-005-6468-9

Kowski, S. (July 2009). *Verwaltung von Generatoren auf der Basis des Concept-Driven Engineerings.* Master's thesis, Christian-Albrechts University Kiel, Dept. of Computer Science.

H. Ma & B. Thalheim.(September 2008). *Web information systems co-design and web 2.0.* WISE 2008 Tutorial, Auckland.

Moritz, T., Noack, R., Schewe, K.-D., & Thalheim, B. (2007). Intention-driven screenography. In *Proceedings ISTA 2007,*(Vol. LNI 107, pp. 128-139).

Moritz, T., Schewe, K.-D., & Thalheim, B. (2005). Strategic modeling of web information systems and its impact on visual design patterns . In Frasincar, F., Houben, G.-J., & Vdovjak, R. (Eds.), *WISM'05* (pp. 5–13). Sydney.

Murphy, G. L. (2001). *The big book of concepts*. Cambridge, MA: MIT Press.

Paech, B. (2000). *Aufgabenorientierte Softwareentwicklung*. Berlin: Springer.

Safra, J. E., & Yeshua, I. (2003). *Encyclopedia Britannica*. Merriam-Webster.

Schewe, K.-D., & Thalheim, B. (2004). Reasoning about web information systems using story algebra. In *ADBIS'2004*, (LNCS 3255, pages 54-66,)

Schewe, K.-D., & Thalheim, B. (2006). *Usage-based storyboarding for web information systems*. Technical Report 2006-13. Christian Albrechts University Kiel, Institute of Computer Science and Applied Mathematics, Kiel.

Schewe, K.-D., & Thalheim, B. (2007). Development of collaboration frameworks for web information systems. *In 20th Int. Joint Conf. on Arti̅cal Intelligence, Section EMC07 (Evolutionary models of collaboration)*, (pp. 27-32), Hyderabad.

Schewe, K.-D., & Thalheim, B. (2007). Personalisation of web information systems. *Data & Knowledge Engineering, 62*(1), 101–117. doi:10.1016/j.datak.2006.07.007

Schewe, K.-D., & Thalheim, B. (2008). Context analysis: Towards pragmatics of information system design. In A. Hinze & M. Kirchberg,(eds.) *Fifth Asia-Pacific Conference on Conceptual Modelling (APCCM2008),* (volume 79 of CRPIT, pp.69-78) Hobart, Australia.

Schewe, K.-D., & Thalheim, B. (2008). Life cases: A kernel element for web information systems engineering. In *Web Information Systems and Technologies, Volume 8*. (Lecture Notes in Business Information Processing,).Berlin: Springer.

B. Thalheim.(2007). The conceptual framework to user-oriented content management. *Information Modeling and Knowledge Bases, XVII*, 30-49.

Y. Kiyoki & B. Thalheim.(2008). Knowledge technology for next generation web. *PPP Application to DAAD: Partnership Program with Japan.* September

ENDNOTES

[1]   See, for instance, the English entry "Dresden" for the German city Dresden. Everybody knows something about Dresden and may add also wrong information. We found more than 40 errors for this entry in May 2008.

APPENDIX

(I) as the fact of knowing something:
    (Ia1) the fact or condition of knowing something with familiarity gained through experience or association;
    (Ia2) acquaintance with or understanding of a science, art, or technique;
    (Ib1) the fact or condition of being aware of something;
    (Ib2) the range of one's information or understanding;
    (Ic) the circumstance or condition of apprehending truth or fact through reasoning or cognition;
    (Id) the fact or condition of having information or of being learned;

(II) the body of things known about or in science:
    (IIa) the sum of what is known: the body of truth, information, and principles acquired by mankind;
    (IIb) a branch of learning (synonyms of knowledge: learning, erudition, scholarship) meaning what is or can be known by an individual or by mankind.

We prefer this approach over the approach taken by the Wikipedia community, who distinguish between communicating knowledge, situated knowledge, partial knowledge, scientific knowledge and know-how or know-what or know-why or know-who knowledge.

Chapter 2

BDD–Based Combinatorial Keyword Query Processing under a Taxonomy Model

Shin-ichi Minato
Hokkaido University, Japan

Nicolas Spyratos
Université de Paris-Sud, France

ABSTRACT

Digital libraries are one of the key systems for an IT society, and supporting easy access to them is an important technical issue between a human and an intelligent system. Here we consider a publish/subscribe system for digital libraries which continuously evaluates queries over a large repository containing document descriptions. The subscriptions, the query expressions and the document descriptions, all rely on a taxonomy that is a hierarchically organized set of keywords, or terms. The digital library supports insertion, update and removal of a document. Each of these operations is seen as an event that must be notified only to those users whose subscriptions match the document's description. In this chapter, the authors present a novel method of processing such keyword queries. Our method is based on Binary Decision Diagram (BDD), an efficient data structure for manipulating large-scale Boolean functions. The authors compile the given keyword queries i

DOI: 10.4018/978-1-61520-851-7.ch002

nto a BDD under a taxonomy model. The number of possible keyword sets can be exponentially large, but the compiled BDD gives a compact representation, and enabling a highly efficient matching process. In addition, our method can deal with any Boolean combination of keywords from the taxonomy, while the previous result considered only a conjunctive keyword set. In this chapter, they describe the basic idea of their new method, and then the authors show their preliminary experimental result applying to a document set with large-scale keyword domain under a real-life taxonomy structure.

INTRODUCTION

Digital libraries are one of the key systems toward an IT society, and supporting easy access to them is an important technical issue between a human and an intelligent system. The publish/subscribe interaction paradigm provides subscribers with the ability to express their interest in classes of events generated by publishers. A system that supports this paradigm must be able to find, for each incoming event e, the subscriptions that match e, in order to determine which subscribers should be notified. Many typical web applications can be seen as variants of this general framework, including auction sites, on-line rental offices, virtual bookshops, etc. They act as brokers which store only descriptions of the published items.

We now consider a publish/subscribe system for digital libraries which continuously evaluates queries over a large repository containing document descriptions (Frej, 2006). The subscriptions, the query expressions and the document descriptions, all rely on a taxonomy that is a hierarchically organized set of keywords, or terms. The digital library supports insertion, update and removal of a document. Each of these operations is seen as an event that must be notified only to those users whose subscriptions match the document's description.

In this chapter, we present a novel method of processing such keyword queries. Our method is based on Binary Decision Diagram (BDD) (Bryant, 1986), an efficient data structure for manipulating large-scale Boolean functions. We compile the given keyword queries into a BDD under a taxonomy model. The number of possible keyword sets can be exponentially large, but the compiled BDD gives a compact representation, and enabling a highly efficient matching process than using a naïve representation. In addition, our method can deal with any Boolean combination of keywords from the taxonomy, while the previous result (Frej, 2006) considered only a conjunctive keyword set. In this chapter, we will show the results of an experiment in which we applied our method to document-tagging keywords from the ACM Computing Classification, a taxonomy list with over 1,000 entries. We will also mention our future work to consider more advanced keyword expansion.

PRELIMINARIES

Here we describe the basic framework of subscription-notification service which we consider in this paper.

Subscription-Notification Service in Digital Library

Figure 1 shows the basic processing flow of our system. A document is represented in the digital library repository by a *description* of its content together with an identifier (say, the document's URI) allowing to access the document's content. A number of documents are incoming to the digital library every day, and the identifier list of recent new documents is notified to each user periodically (daily, weekly, or monthly). Each user can specify a *subscription* to show the composed keywords that are of interest to that user. Every document has a description with a set of keywords, and if one of the keywords matches to some users' subscriptions, the identifier of the document is added to the notification list. Here, we assume that a user's subscription is not so frequently updated as the notification periods.

If we consider a nation-wide digital library system, the number of documents and the number of users become quite huge, and it is an important problem to reduce the computation cost for matching (or filtering) of the documents to each user.

Keyword Query and Taxonomy Graph

A subscription represents the topics of interest to the user with some keywords. There are many pieces of previous work (gough, 1995), (aguilera, 1999), (yan, 1999), (demers, 2006), (frej, 2006), however, most of them consider just a keyword match or dealing with relatively simple combinations of multiple keywords, due to the limitation of computation cost for processing large-scale keyword space.

Figure 1. Basic processing flow of subscription-notification service

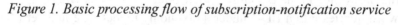
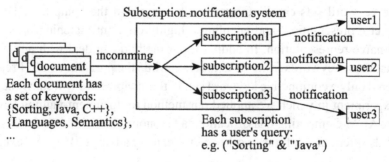

So far we are not aware of a publish/subscribe technique that considers a flexible keyword-based query language and a subsumption relation over the terms. In this chapter, we consider any keyword query that allows all propositional logic operations, conjunction, disjunction and complement. For example,(("languages" & "sorting") | "java") & (! "c++") represents that the user likes to see the documents including the keyword *languages* and *sorting* together, or having the keyword *java*, provided that the document is not related to *c++*.

In addition, we consider the hierarchical taxonomy of the keywords. Figure 2 shows an example of taxonomy graph. In this graph, upper keywords represent more general concept of its descendants. For example, if a user subscribes to the keyword *algorithms*, the incoming documents having any one of the keywords *algorithms, sorting, merge, quick* and *bubble* will be notified to the user. In this example, the taxonomy graph has a tree structure, but in general, some sub-trees can be shared with each other, and the taxonomy graph can be a directed acyclic graph. Employing such a hierarchical taxonomy graph will greatly improve the usability of the system, but the computation cost may grow larger.

Binary Decision Diagrams (BDDs)

In this paper, we discuss a new method of keyword query processing based on Binary Decision Diagrams (BDDs). Here we briefly describe our data structure.

BDD (Binary Decision Diagram) is a directed graph representation of the Boolean function, as illustrated in Figure 3(a). It is derived by reducing a binary tree graph representing recursive *Shannon's expansion*, indicated in Figure 3(b). The following reduction rules yield a *Reduced Ordered BDD (ROBDD)*, which can efficiently represent the Boolean function. (see (Bryant, 1986) for details.)

Figure 2. An example of taxonomy graph

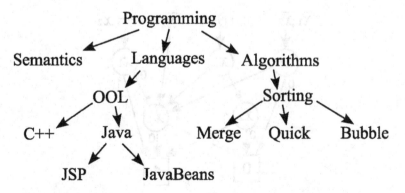

Figure 3. BDD and binary tree: F = a b + c

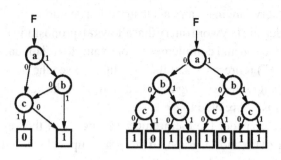

- Delete all redundant nodes whose two edges point to the same node. (Figure 5(a))
- Share all equivalent sub-graphs. (Figure 5(b))

ROBDDs provide canonical forms for Boolean functions when the variable order is fixed. Most researches on BDDs are based on the above reduction rules. In the following sections, ROBDDs will be referred to as BDDs for the sake of simplification.

As shown in Figure 4, a set of multiple BDDs can be merged into one graph under the same fixed variable ordering. In this way, we can handle a number of Boolean functions simultaneously in a monolithic memory space.

Using BDDs, we can uniquely and compactly represent many practical Boolean functions including AND, OR, parity, and arithmetic adder functions. Using Bryant's algorithm (Bryant, 1986), we can efficiently construct a BDD for the result of a binary logic operation (i.e. AND, OR, XOR), for a given pair of operand BDDs. This algorithm is based on hash table techniques, and the computation time is almost

Figure 4. Shared multiple BDDs

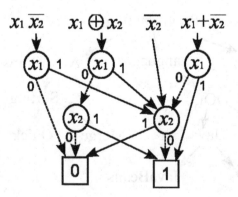

linear to the data size unless the data overflows the main memory. To generate BDDs for a Boolean expression, we first define the input variable order and create a simple single node BDD for each input variable. We then construct complicated BDDs by applying logic operations to the initial BDDs according to the structure of the Boolean expression. Based on these techniques, a number of BDD packages have been developed in 1990's and widely used for large-scale Boolean function manipulation, especially popular in VLSI CAD area.

The computation time for generating BDDs depends on the length of the Boolean expressions and the size of the BDDs to be generated. It is difficult to estimate the time exactly. We know that the time for one logic operation is approximately proportional to the size of the BDDs. In many cases, the BDDs grow larger by repeating logic operations unless the Boolean expression is redundant. Thus, the final few logic operations take the dominant time, and roughly speaking, the total computation time is almost proportional to the size of final BDDs.

BDD size greatly depends on the order of input variables. It is difficult to find the best variable order, as it is an NP-complete problem (Tani, 1996). However, there are some heuristic methods of variable ordering to find pretty good orders in many practical cases. See (Bryant, 1986), (Minato, 1996), or (Knuth, 2009) for detailed techniques of BDD manipulation.

BDD-BASED DOCUMENT FILTERING

In the subscription-notification system, each document is determined whether it matches or not to respective user subscriptions. If we employ the keywords based on the hierarchical taxonomy, the matching procedure becomes complicated. In order to accelerate the matching procedure, we propose a BDD-based method to generate a complete document filter for each user under a structural taxonomy.

Figure 5. BDD node reduction rules

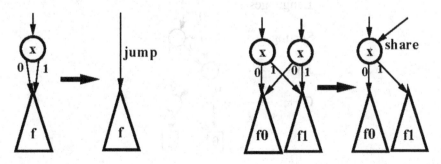

BDD Generation for a Keyword Query

Under fixed variable ordering, a BDD can be generated from the Boolean expression of the user's query. The algorithm is completely the same as the one for generating BDDs from given logic circuits, which has been developed in the area of VLSI CAD. For example, the query: (("Languages" & "Sorting") | "Java") & (! "C++") produces a BDD as shown in Figure 6. In this BDD, each path from the root node to 1-terminal node corresponds to a possible keyword pattern to be notified to the user. When we check a new document to be notified, we may traverse the BDD downward from the root node to the terminal nodes, by choosing one of subgraph so as not to conflict with the keyword set of the document. Eventually we will arrive at either 0- or 1-terminal node and it tells us the result, indicating that the document is irrelevant or relevant, respectively. The computation time is linearly bounded by the height of the BDD, rather than depending directly on the number of BDD nodes. In other words, the Boolean expression of the user's query is compiled into a logic circuit with an efficient BDD-based structure.

Expansion of BDDs based on Taxonomy Graph

Employing the hierarchical taxonomy, we expand the BDD for the user query to take into account all implications of multiple keywords. The method is illustrated in Figure 7. First we look at the top keyword *Programming* in the taxonomy graph. *Programming* has three children *Semantics, Languages*, and *Algorithms*, so we may accept a document with any of three child keywords instead of *Programming*. This can be performed by logic operations as follows. We divide the query function F into the two subfunctions F_{off} and F_{on}, which represent the sub-queries for the documents without the keyword *Programming* and for the documents with

Figure 6. A BDD representing user's query

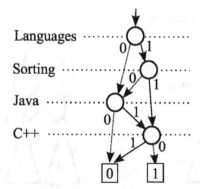

Programming, respectively. In other words, the original query Q can be represented as the following expression.

Q = (! "Programming" & F_off) | ("Programming" & F_on).

Notice that F_{off} and F_{on} do not depend on the logic variable for *Programming*. Extracting these two sub-functions from F can be implemented by primitive BDD operations. This operation requires a constant time if the variable for *Programming* is at the root node of the BDD (just look up the two child nodes), otherwise the operation consumes linear time for the number of BDD nodes located at a higher position than the variable for *Programming*.

We then replace *Programming* with the set of four keywords as

Q = ((! "Programming" & ! "Semantics" & ! "Languages" & ! "Algorithms") & F_off) | (("Programming" | "Semantics" | "Languages" | "Algorithms") & F_on).

By executing the BDD operations for this logic expression, we can obtain a new query BDD where the keyword patterns related to *Programming* are expanded.

Next, we extract different F_{off} and F_{on} based on another variable for *Languages,* and then expand the keyword patterns with its sub-keyword *OOL*. In this way, we expand the BDD for all the other keywords from the top to the bottom in the taxonomy graph. Finally we can obtain the BDD to determine the documents considering all implications of keywords under the taxonomy graph. If we can generate such a BDD in a feasible memory size, the information embodied in the

Figure 7. BDD expansion based on a taxonomy graph

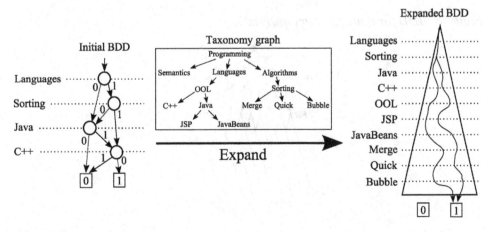

taxonomy structure is already compiled into the BDD-style logic circuit. It will be a very powerful data structure.

COMBINING MULTIPLE USERS' QUERIES

As shown in Figure 1, our subscription-notification system assumes multiple users. Our system aims to reduce the communication cost to deliver unnecessary documents for each user. We may combine a number of users' queries into a single BDD as follows. To handle a total of m users, we prepare the special variables as many as [$log_2 m$], to distinguish respective users by using a binary code. For example, we prepare the three variables u_1, u_2, and u_3 for $m=8$, and here a binary vector (u_1, u_2, u_3) represents a user ID of F. We then combine the logic expression for the queries F_0, F_1, ... F_7 as:

Q = (!u1 & !u2 & !u3 & F0)
| (!u1 & !u2 & u3 & F1)
| (!u1 & u2 & !u3 & F2)
...
| (u1 & u2 & u3 & F7) .

The BDD for this logic expression is shown in Figure 8. We can obtain various information by manipulating this BDD. For example, when we assign 0 or 1 for all keyword variables using the description of a document, then the variable u_1, u_2, and u_3 remain in the BDD. Such a BDD represents the set of users who accept the document with the keyword pattern assigned now. For example, if the binary vec-

Figure 8. BDD for multiple users queries

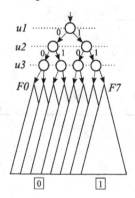

tor $(u_1, u_2, u_3) = (0, 0, 1)$ satisfies the function of the BDD, then we can see that the keyword pattern is accepted by the user with the ID $(0, 0, 1)$.

On the other hand, if we compute a union (logical OR) of the two subgraph of the top node with the variable u_1, the result of BDD represents a filtering circuit to know the keyword patterns which are accepted no matter how is the value of u_1. By applying the same operation to all the user variables we can eliminate all user variables. This BDD shows the set of keyword patterns such that the document is accepted by at least one user.

EXPERIMENTAL RESULT

To evaluate our new method, we conducted an experiment to generate BDDs for given user queries under a real-life taxonomy structure, ACM Computing Classification System (ACM, 1999), which is used for ACM/IEEE documents in EE & CS area. This taxonomy list has 11 top level categories ("A" to "K") and each of which has a tree structure of up to 4-level depth. 1,765 keywords are described in this list. Here we show a part of the keyword list. We assign a unique ID for each keyword.

A General Literature
A_0 General
A_0_0 Biographies/Autobiographies
A_0_1 Conference Proceedings
A_0_2 General Literary Works
A_1 Introductory and Survey
A_2 Reference
A_3 Miscellaneous
B Hardware
B_0 General
B_1 Control Structures and Microprogramming
B_1_0 General
B_1_1 Control Design Styles
B_1_1_a Hardwired control
B_1_1_b Microprogrammed logic arrays
B_1_1_c Writable control store
B_1_2 Control Structure Performance Analysis and Design Aids
B_1_2_a Automatic synthesis
B_1_2_b Formal models
B_1_2_c Simulation
....

H_2 Database Management
H_2_0 General
H_2_0_a Security, integrity, and protection
H_2_0_b Database design, modeling and management
H_2_0_c Query design and implementation languages
H_2_1 Logical Design
H_2_1_a Data models
H_2_1_b Database architectures
H_2_1_c Database integration
H_2_1_d Database models
H_2_1_e Normal forms
H_2_1_f Schema and subschema
H_2_2 Physical Design
H_2_2_a Access methods
H_2_2_b Deadlock avoidance
H_2_2_c Indexing methods
H_2_2_d Physical database design prototypes
H_2_2_e Recovery and restart
H_2_3 Languages
H_2_3_a Data description languages
H_2_3_b Data manipulation languages
H_2_3_c Database (persistent) programming languages
H_2_3_d Database semantics
H_2_3_e Query languages
H_2_3_f Report writers
H_2_4 Systems

We then consider a simple example of user query as:

$Q = (H\_2\_1 \& H\_2\_3\_e) | (! H\_2\_2 \& H\_2\_3)$

Namely, this query represents ("Logical Design" and "Query language") or (not "Physical Design" and "Language"). We can easily generate a BDD of just a 6 nodes for Q, as shown in the left side of Figure 9. We then expand this BDD under the taxonomy structure by applying logic operations. We obtained the following Boolean functions.

$Q' = H\_2\_1 \& H\_2\_3\_e$
$| H\_2\_1\_a \& H\_2\_3\_e$
$| H\_2\_1\_b \& H\_2\_3\_e$
$| H\_2\_1\_c \& H\_2\_3\_e$
$| H\_2\_1\_d \& H\_2\_3\_e$

| H_2_1_e & H_2_3_e
| H_2_1_f & H_2_3_e
| !H_2_2 & !H_2_2_a & !H_2_2_b & !H_2_2_c & !H_2_2_d & !H_2_2_e & H_2_3
| !H_2_2 & !H_2_2_a & !H_2_2_b & !H_2_2_c & !H_2_2_d & !H_2_2_e & H_2_3_a
| !H_2_2 & !H_2_2_a & !H_2_2_b & !H_2_2_c & !H_2_2_d & !H_2_2_e & H_2_3_b
| !H_2_2 & !H_2_2_a & !H_2_2_b & !H_2_2_c & !H_2_2_d & !H_2_2_e & H_2_3_c
| !H_2_2 & !H_2_2_a & !H_2_2_b & !H_2_2_c & !H_2_2_d & !H_2_2_e & H_2_3_d
| !H_2_2 & !H_2_2_a & !H_2_2_b & !H_2_2_c & !H_2_2_d & !H_2_2_e & H_2_3_e
| !H_2_2 & !H_2_2_a & !H_2_2_b & !H_2_2_c & !H_2_2_d & !H_2_2_e & H_2_3_f

The BDD for Q' is shown in the right side of Figure 9. This BDD includes only 27 nodes, so document filtering using this BDD will be easily done. The total number of logic operations (i.e. the length of the script) is linearly bounded by the size of taxonomy graph (1,765 keywords, in this case). Actual computation time for the BDD expansion is only 0.10 second. In this experiments, we used BEM-II (Minato, 1992), a Boolean expression manipulator based on our own BDD package. This program can manipulate up to 30,000,000 nodes of BDDs on a Linux PC with 2GB memory.

Next we applied our method for more complicated example of query. The following Boolean expression represents a set of queries of multiple users.

Q = !u3 & !u2 & !u1 & !u0 & (A_0_1 & B_2 | C_1_1 & !D_4_1)
| !u3 & !u2 & !u1 & u0 & (E_2_1 & F_0 | G_2_2 & !H_3_1)
| !u3 & !u2 & u1 & !u0 & (I_1_1 & J_1 | K_5_1 & !A_0_0)
| !u3 & !u2 & u1 & u0 & (C_4_1 & E_2 | G_3_2 & !I_2_2)
| !u3 & u2 & !u1 & !u0 & (K_3_1 & B_3 | D_2_1 & !F_1_2)
| !u3 & u2 & !u1 & u0 & (H_2_1 & K_4 | A_0_2 & !D_1_5)
| !u3 & u2 & u1 & !u0 & (G_1_1 & J_5 | b_4_1 & !E_1_4)
| !u3 & u2 & u1 & u0 & (H_3_1 & K_1 | C_1_2 & !F_2_3)
| u3 & !u2 & !u1 & !u0 & (A_0_2 & B_1 | C_2_1 & !D_4_3)
| u3 & !u2 & !u1 & u0 & (E_2_2 & F_1 | G_3_2 & !H_3_2)
| u3 & !u2 & u1 & !u0 & (I_1_2 & J_2 | K_4_1 & !A_0_1)
| u3 & !u2 & u1 & u0 & (C_4_2 & E_3 | G_5_0 & !i_2_1)
| u3 & u2 & !u1 & !u0 & (K_3_2 & B_4 | D_3_1 & !F_1_0)
| u3 & u2 & !u1 & u0 & (H_2_2 & K_5 | A_0_2 & !D_1_4)
| u3 & u2 & u1 & !u0 & (G_1_2 & J_3 | B_2_1 & !E_1_3)
| u3 & u2 & u1 & u0 & (H_3_2 & K_3 | C_3_2 & !F_2_2)

This example includes 16 users' different queries. Each query has the same form $(a \ \& \ b) \ | \ (c \ \& \ d)$ but the keywords are randomly selected from the taxonomy

Figure 9. BDD structures before and after expansion

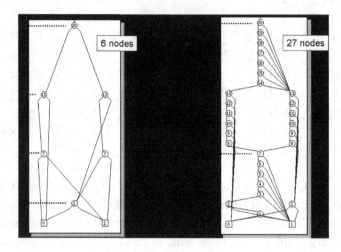

list. In this case, the original BDD for Q has 87 nodes, and expanded one includes 533 nodes. Computation time for the BDD expansion requires 0.13 second. In this experiment, we use the variable order such that user variables u0, u1, u2, u3 are located at the top as shown in Figure 8. However, when we located the user variables at the bottom, the BDD for Q exploded as more than 30,000,000 nodes and memory overflow occurred. Thus, we can see that the BDD variable ordering is important in this method.

CONCLUSION

In this chapter, we presented a new method of processing keyword queries using BDDs. The number of possible keyword sets can be exponentially large, but the compiled BDD gives a compact representation, and enabling a highly efficient matching process. In addition, our method can deal with any Boolean combination of keywords, while the previous result (Frej,2006) considered only a conjunctive keyword set. We presented preliminary experimental results that thousands of possible keyword patterns can be represented compactly by a BDD-based filtering circuit. We applied our method to a document set with large-scale keyword domain under a real-life taxonomy structure such as ACM Computing Classification System. We observed that the BDD variable ordering would be important in this method. Our future work also includes to consider more advanced keyword expansion, for example, to define *distance* of keywords in taxonomy graph and provide a limited keyword expansion. It will be also interesting work to provide *sorted* output of documents under some preference of users to avoid "spam" notifications, which are too frequent or too many notifications for users.

REFERENCES

Aguilera, M. K., Strom, R. E., Sturman, D. C., Astley, M., & Chandra, T. D. (1999). Matching events in a content-based subscription system. *Proc. ACM Intl. Symp. On Principles of Distributed Computing (PODC)*, (pp. 53–61).

Bryant, R. E. (1986). Graph-based algorithms for Boolean function manipulation. *IEEE Transactions on Computers, C-35*(8), 677–691. doi:10.1109/TC.1986.1676819

Demers, A. J., Gehrke, J., Hong, M., Riedewald, M., & White, W. M. (2006). Towards expressive publish/subscribe systems. In *Intl Conf. on Extending Database Technology (EDBT)*, pp. 627–644.

Frej, H. B., Rigaux, P., & Spyratos, N. (2006). User notification in taxonomy based digital libraries (invited paper). *Proc. of ACM SIG-DOC Conference on the Design of Communication,*(pp. 18-20).

Gough, J., & Smith, G. (1995). Efficient recognition of events in a distributed system. *Proc. Australasian Computer Science Conference*.

Knuth, D. E. (2009). *The Art of Computer Programming: Bitwise Tricks & Techniques; Binary Decision Diagrams*, volume 4, fascicle 1. Reading, MA: Addison-Wesley.

Minato, S. (1992). BEM-II: An arithmetic Boolean expression manipulator using BDDs. *IEICE Transactions on Fundamentals . E (Norwalk, Conn.)*, *76-A*(10), 1721–1729.

Minato, S. (1996). *Binary Decision Diagrams and Applications for VLSI CAD*. Amsterdam: Kluwer Academic Publishers.

Tani, S., Hamaguchi, K., & Yajima, S. (1996). The Complexity of the Optimal Variable Ordering Problems of a Shared Binary Decision Diagram, *IEICE transactions on information and systems . E (Norwalk, Conn.)*, *79-D*(4), 271–281.

The ACM computing classification system. (1999). Retrieved August 4, 2009, from http://www.acm.org/class

Yan, T. W., & Garcia-Molina, H. (1999). The SIFT information dissemination system. [TODS]. *ACM Transactions on Database Systems*, *24*(4), 529–565. doi:10.1145/331983.331992

Chapter 3

Spreadsheet–Based Orchestration for Describing and Automating Web Information Access Processes

Jun Fujima
Hokkaido University, Japan

Shohei Yoshihara
Hokkaido University, Japan

Yuzuru Tanaka
Hokkaido University, Japan

ABSTRACT

A spreadsheet is one of the most widely used applications by office workers. It provides an end user, with a programming environment. In this chapter, the authors propose a spreadsheet-based environment in which end users can orchestrate multiple Web applications. First, the authors provide a method for embedding various Web resources in spreadsheet cells as visual components that can be reused on the spreadsheet. Second, they propose a method by which these embedded components can be accessed by using special functions via the formula language. Third, they present these special functions to describe loop structures. Their approach enables users to define the complex coordination of multiple Web applications on

DOI: 10.4018/978-1-61520-851-7.ch003

the spreadsheet using its formula language. Further, they describe their prototype implementation, which uses Microsoft Excel and its user interface support to utilize the embedded Web applications.

INTRODUCTION

Resources on the World Wide Web are now rapidly increasing in terms of their variety and storage volume. Such resources may contain not only static documents in Hypertext Markup Language (HTML) but also dynamic content created by server-side technologies such as Common Gateway Interface (CGI), client-side script languages, and Asynchronous JavaScript + XML (Ajax). Through the Internet, users can access various data and application tools such as search engines and database forms, as well as more advanced systems such as recommendation systems and data-mining applications.

People now commonly perform everyday tasks such as shopping and travel planning in this new environment. For instance, a Japanese person wanting to buy some CDs can access a number of CD shopping sites and retrieve the desired CDs' cost including shipping cost. If, however, a particular person accesses a shopping site that is not a Japanese site, he/she may then have to calculate the total cost of the desired product in Japanese yen by accessing a currency exchange rate software on a currency conversion Web site. After doing such research the shopper may then choose the least expensive shopping sites for that purchase. In this way, even a small but complicated task can be achieved through access to the Web.

Such common, everyday tasks can be better achieved by combining a series of atomic tasks. In the previous example, the following can be considered as such a series of atomic tasks: accessing a number of CD shopping sites, retrieving the price of a specific CD, calculating the total price including shipping cost, and converting the total price to Japanese yen. Although people can perform such tasks in combination by manually transferring data from one to another, it becomes burdensome when such tasks must be done repetitively, and current computer systems offer little support for the automation of such repetitive combined tasks.

Therefore, in order to facilitate people's daily access of information on the Web, it is necessary to provide a framework for describing, reusing, reediting, and sharing combined tasks. In the domain of Web service architecture, the creation of such a combined task is called *orchestration*. Only after externalizing the orchestration in information systems can the combined task be shared among people for reuse and automatic processing by computer systems. The externalization of this orchestration also allows people to edit one or more parts of a combined task in order to create a new combined task.

In this chapter, the authors propose a framework for the construction of an orchestration environment that uses a spreadsheet application. Our framework allows users to describe a combined task and to automate the recorded tasks on a spreadsheet. It comprises a unified method for accessing Web resources, a mechanism for coordinating Web resources on the spreadsheet, and a set of functions for the definition of loop structures. It allows users to embed various Web resources in spreadsheet cells as visual components and to then reuse them in the spreadsheet. Further, it enables users to access these embedded components using a special function in the formula language. Users can then define the complex coordination of multiple Web applications on the spreadsheet by using combinations of the special function, as well as specific predefined functions, such as that which currently exists for conditional statements. We describe our prototype, implemented using Microsoft Excel, and then show how the proposed framework can be applied to practical cases of information access.

This chapter extends the work of an earlier paper by Fujima et al. (2002) by providing some mechanisms for describing loop structures and includes further details and discussions.

BACKGROUND AND RELATED WORK

Nowadays, Web users can access many types of Web resources. Such resources may be not only static HTML documents but also RDF Site Summary (RSS), Web applications, and Web services. RSS is a general term for certain document formats that deliver updates on various Web sites, such as those concerning news or blogs. Web applications and Web services provide various types of processing or services such as database access, search engines, shopping, currency conversion, and so on. Users can utilize these resources when performing their daily tasks.

Under these circumstances, some programmers create new Web resources by combining existing resources to automate the repetitive processing of combined tasks. *Mashup* has come to be used as a paradigm that combines data from multiple existing Web resources to create new applications. Housing Maps (Google + craigslist: http://www.housingmaps.com/) is one of the pioneering examples of a mashup. In order to create mashups, however, programming skills are typically needed.

For this reason, *mashup tools* are emerging to enable non-programmers to create mashups for different purposes by combining multiple existing Web resources. Yahoo pipes (http://pipes.yahoo.com/pipes/) provides a Web-based visual editor for creating new RSS feeds by reordering, filtering, and merging multiple data sources represented as RSS, XML, and JavaScript Object Notation (JSON) through the direct mouse operation of connecting "pipes." Google Mashup Editor (http://code.google.

com/intl/en/gme/) is a more flexible environment for creating mashups. It offers a library and template engine for the construction and deployment of mashups using XML-based templates and JavaScript programming. These technologies support the creation of new XML data sources or Web applications using server-side APIs published by third parties and script programming. Mashup tools act as a technology for enabling end users to assembling multiple Web resources to achieve combined tasks required by them, e.g., new data sources or new Web applications not anticipated by the Web resource providers.

In the domain of Web service composition, the term *orchestration* refers to the creation of business processes from composite Web services (Peltz, 2003). Web services are software components deployed on the Web. Each component provides an Application Programming Interface (API), which is accessible through protocols such as Simple Object Access Protocol (SOAP) or Hypertext Transfer Protocol (HTTP). Since a Web service can be accessed by any client software connected to the Web, it is extremely effective as a method for constructing a reusable service. Certain standard formats, such as Business Process Execution Language (BPEL), are used to describe orchestration as a workflow; some vendors have also implemented BPEL-based workflow editors and workflow engines (Oracle, 2006). The use of these tools does not require programming expertise. Users can create their own new composite services by using procedure descriptions to obtain the desired results.

However, though the functionality of mashup tools and workflow editors may be easy for end users to utilize, the data that they will use in these applications can be difficult for them to apply practically. The reason for this is that they must also possess knowledge regarding the various data sources: schema, data formats, and their meanings. Although Web services may be available in the form of workflow editors, users also need further knowledge of different Web services, such as which parameter should be passed to a specific Web service. Furthermore, there is the question of how users can find data sources or Web services which provide the necessary data or functions that they need.

Form-based Web applications, on the other hand, can be easily used by end users. Such Web applications have Web-based frontends that are described in HTML. They typically submit a form to the corresponding program deployed on a Web server, and the server returns the result to the client Web browser in the form of an HTML document. Users can find the required applications using conventional search engines and can easily use them by supplying appropriate values to the input fields that are presented to them. Form-based Web applications are widely used to provide services on the Web because they are easy to deploy, since users will need no additional software apart from their Web browsers.

Typically, it is difficult to combine multiple form-based Web applications. Web applications are not interoperable because they do not provide APIs available from programming languages, and their data is not well structured for reuse in other software. It is only written in HTML for human understanding. The above-mentioned Web mashup tools only support a combination of RSS, XML, and Web services. To enable end users to define a series of tasks by combining multiple Web applications, it is necessary to extract data in reusable forms from Web applications, and to do so without programming. There are many systems known as Wrappers (Laender, 2002) that support people in the extraction of information in the form of structured data from existing Web applications. Moreover, there are now many mashup tools that enable one to create mashups without programming, by integrating such wrappers into various frameworks of data integration (Dntcheva, 2007; Lin 2009). Here again, however, users need additional knowledge about each particular mashup tool and its data-integration frameworks.

By considering the above observations, we have developed a framework for the orchestration of Web applications. Our target users are office workers who can create a spreadsheet using its formula language but who do not have strong expertise in programming. To this end, we propose an orchestration environment that is based on a spreadsheet application. The spreadsheet is a very popular application, and it allows end users to create a document for statistical data analysis or end-user programming through formula language. We have, therefore, sought to integrate the functionalities that access Web applications via a spreadsheet, since the global pool of spreadsheet users far outnumbers the pool of workflow editors or people with knowledge of other mashup tools.

The spreadsheet paradigm is used in many other domains. For example, Chi et al. utilized a spreadsheet to show multiple visualization results using various parameter values (Chi, 1997; 1998). Query by Excel (QBX) (Witkowski, 2005) offers a user interface for accessing RDBMS on an Excel spreadsheet. The function instance sheet (Jones, 2003) provides an end-user programming environment based on spreadsheets. In this system, users can reuse a series of calculations described in other sheets and define it on a different sheet as a new function. The analytical spreadsheet package in Smalltalk-80 (Piersol, 1986) is a pioneering environment that can embed various types of objects in its cells. A1 (Kandogan, 2005) is a spreadsheet-based programming environment for system administrators that allows cells to contain arbitrary Java objects and allows users to call methods using the formula language. Although these systems are very powerful, they remain difficult to manipulate for non-programmers who have no knowledge of the programming paradigm and the class libraries of each programming language. Another spreadsheet-based framework for coordinating multiple visualizations of Web resources has been proposed (Itoh, 2007). It provides a component-based mechanism for association between a visual component and a cell. The accessing method provided in this chapter uses a formula function that is more suitable for current Excel users because it does not require them to have any specific knowledge in order to use the special components.

There are a number of mashup tools that employ the spreadsheet paradigm. Mash Maker (Ennals, 2007) is a mashup tool that supports the extraction, aggregation, and visualization of Web contents. This allows users to combine components, called widgets, with existing Web pages through common browsing operations such as the clicking, copying, and the pasting of widgets. Although its basic data structure is a tree, not a table, it borrows many features from spreadsheets, such as the mixing of data and operations, and the ability to apply an operation to multiple nodes simultaneously. Mashroom (Wang, 2009) is another mashup tool that borrows spreadsheet features such as a visual menu, direct manipulation of data, and loop execution through the selection of a range of cells. It introduces a nested table structure and a set of operations for the data structure into the traditional spreadsheet paradigm.

REQUIREMENTS AND FRAMEWORK OVERVIEW

In order to construct an orchestration environment for Web applications, it is necessary to provide the following two functions: a unified method of access for Web applications and a framework for the coordination of multiple Web applications.

Unified Method of Access for Web Applications

Unlike Web services, Web applications are not interoperable. Since different Web sites have different styles of Web pages and different interfaces for Web applications, it is difficult to programmatically combine different Web applications. Moreover, Web applications often have their own user interfaces for the display of data or calculated results. It is necessary to provide a method for wrapping both the functions and the visual representations of Web applications as reusable components, and to do so without programming.

In this chapter, we uniformly manage various types of Web resources as visual components. We provide a method by which arbitrary Web applications can be wrapped as visual components through the mouse operation of users. Since wrapped components have a standard access interface, they can be operated from within the coordination framework through a unified mechanism. This method also makes it possible for their visual representations to be reused in the coordination framework.

Coordination of Multiple Web Applications

In order to facilitate the orchestration of Web applications by end users, we require a coordination framework that enables us to represent flexible control structures such as a conditional statement or a loop structure that are described by general programming languages. Such a representation should be described in a way that can be readily understood by users who do not have expert programming skills.

We use spreadsheets as a base environment for the coordination of Web applications. A spreadsheet is one of the most popular applications used by office workers since it provides an attractive environment for statistical data analysis and end-user programming. Users can construct a table on a spreadsheet for the comparison of multiple data. A spreadsheet has multiple fields that are deployed in a grid-like configuration of individual units called cells. Users can input a string or numerical values into these cells, and can also apply formulae that define data relationships and perform computational linkages among the cells. Since these cells are labeled using letters and numbers, users can refer to their values using cell references such as A1 or B5:C8 in order to reuse them as reference values for other cells.

We provide a function called *padeval* that provides access to embedded visual components that are created by the wrapping of Web applications. In addition, to enable end users to represent more complex control structures, we provide three loop functions: *fornext*, *while*, and *foreach*. A conventional spreadsheet provides a simple conditional *if* function in order to change a calculation according to a specified condition. Therefore, users can construct an orchestration by combining *padeval*, three types of loop functions, *if*, and other predefined functions.

Framework and Architecture

Figure 1 shows an overview of the proposed framework. To realize a spreadsheet-based orchestration environment for end users, we provide the following functions:

- a method for embedding different Web applications in a spreadsheet,
- a method for accessing embedded resources from spreadsheet formulae, and
- a method for describing loop structures on a spreadsheet.

To enable end users to reuse Web applications in an Excel spreadsheet, it is necessary to provide a unified method for accessing Web applications. Our framework utilizes the 2D meme media system called IntelligentPad (Tanaka, 1989; Tanaka, 2003) for the wrapping of such resources. In IntelligentPad, information and processing components are represented as 2D visual objects called pads. Each pad stores its state data in named slots, which also form an interface for the functional connection

Figure 1. Overview of proposed framework

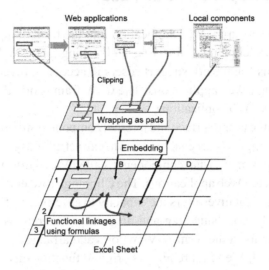

with other pads. By pasting one pad onto another pad and specifying a connection between their slots (in this chapter we denote a slot name as *#slotname*), users can easily define both the compound document layout and the functional linkage among these pads. In the IntelligentPad environment, each compound object is internally represented as a tree structure because each pad has only one parent. Wrapping different resources as pads and embedding them in a spreadsheet enables end users to operate different types of resources in a uniform manner.

In addition, we provide a utility formula function that permits the accessing of embedded pads. By using this function, users can call upon embedded Web applications and extract their results into cells in a spreadsheet. Users can also define complex control structures using this function in combination with predefined formula functions.

Moreover, we provide three types of loop functions from the formula language that end users can utilize. In many cases, users can perform loop processing by repeating "copy" operations over multiple cells. However, in order to increase the options available to users, we provide functions to define loop processing in a spreadsheet. By using one of these functions, users can define loop structures in a spreadsheet.

We utilize Microsoft Excel as our spreadsheet platform. This is because Excel is a popular spreadsheet environment, and thus, there are many Excel users who have the necessary sufficient expertise to write formulae and create Excel documents. By using Excel as a spreadsheet environment, users can define complex task processes to create Excel documents that include multiple Web applications and can share such documents with other Excel users.

Wrapping Web Applications as Pads

In order to wrap an arbitrary Web application into the form of a pad, we proposed the C3W framework (clipping, connecting, and cloning for the Web) (Fujima, 2004; Tanaka, 2006). This framework supports users in accessing diverse resources that are available through Web applications. The C3W framework allows users to clip portions of multiple Web applications.

Figure 2 shows the user interface and internal component structure of the clipping function. The ClippingBrowser enables users to extract arbitrary elements from Web applications in the form of visual components, called ViewPorts, which function as portals to the extracted Web applications. The ClippingBrowser is an extended form of Internet Explorer that gives users the capacity to specify a particular element using XPath (Clark, 1999). Using drag-and-drop mouse operations, the user extracts the specified elements in the form of ViewPorts and arranges them on a C3Sheet. On the C3Sheet, each ViewPort retains its original functionality as a region that is used for either parameter input or result display. The ViewPort created by the user's drop operation is automatically correlated with the corresponding slot that stores its data. These slots are also automatically created and named using alphabetic characters (e.g., *#A*) according to the order in which the clips are dropped onto the C3Sheet. The user may assign meaningful names to these slots after all clipping operations are done. In Figure 2, the user names the slot receiving input value *#in* and the slot outputting the process result *#out*. ViewPorts are typically extracted from a particular navigation that spans multiple Web pages. When a user navigates using the Clipping Browser, the user's operation history (called the navigation path) is recorded by the browser. The navigation path is transferred to the C3Sheet when the user drags an HTML element and drops it on the C3Sheet. The C3Sheet coordinates each clip according to its input-output relationship, as calculated from the corresponding navigation path. When a user provides a new value for the input slot, the appropriate navigation steps are replayed to deliver the results to any associated result slots.

Figure 2 presents the case in which a user clips an input field that corresponds to the currency amount from the *Yahoo! currency conversion* page (http://finance. yahoo.com/currency-converter), enters a sample amount, presses the "convert" button, and then clips the conversion result. When the user supplies a new value to the input slot of the C3Sheet, it automatically accesses the original Web application and updates the value of the output slot with the corresponding converted result.

Figure 2. Clipping mechanism of C3W framework

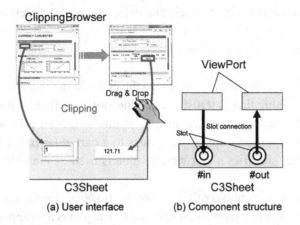

(a) User interface   (b) Component structure

Embedding Pads into Cells

In this framework, we use PlexWare (http://www.k-plex.com), a commercial version of IntelligentPad. Since PlexWare is provided as an ActiveX control, users can easily embed it into ActiveX container applications such as MS Excel or MS Word. We use this mechanism to embed pads into Excel sheets.

In our framework, users can embed only one composite pad in a cell. This allows users to identify one of the multiple composite pads embedded in a spreadsheet by using cell reference descriptions such as "A1" or "C2." An embedded pad is arranged to have the same size as the corresponding cell. When a user changes the cell size, the size of the corresponding pad is changed accordingly.

A user may first create a base pad on a cell. The base pad also works as an IntelligentPad environment. Then, the user can create or load new composite pads on the base pad. The user can also paste a pad from another IntelligentPad environment via drag-and-drop operations.

Accessing Pads via Spreadsheet Formulae

In order to utilize the functions of pads on Excel sheets, the following two mechanisms are required:

- transfer of a cell value to a pad slot, and
- transfer of a pad slot value to a cell.

For these purposes, we provide the utility function *padeval*, which uses the user-defined function mechanism of Excel. The definition of this function is as follows:

$$\text{padeval}(pc, v_1, s_1, v_2, s_2, ..., v_n, s_n, os)$$

Here, *pc* is a cell reference that refers to the cell where the target pad is located. Further, v_n is the value that is transferred to the slot specified by a slot name s_n of the target pad. Since the pair of arguments v_n and s_n can be used any number of times, users can supply multiple input values to a particular pad. Furthermore, *os* is a slot name that specifies a slot whose value is used as the output value of the *padeval* function.

Figure 3 shows an example of the use of the *padeval* function. In this figure, it can be seen that the user places a pad in cell B1. The pad is a wrapper of the *Yahoo! currency conversion* application and has two slots: *#in* and *#out*. These slots correspond to the currency amount input field and the converted result, respectively. The formula inputted into cell B3 transfers the value of cell B2 (Figure 3 (1)) to slot *#in* of the pad embedded in cell B1 (Figure 3 (2)) and returns the value of slot *#out* as the output (Figure 3 (3)). Therefore, cell B3 displays the converted result. If the user inputs a new value into cell B2, the formula in cell B3 is automatically recalculated and returns the corresponding converted result.

Users can omit the pair of arguments v_n and s_n. When a user omits these arguments, the *padeval* function does not transfer any input value to the corresponding pad, and only the value of the specified pad slot is obtained as the return value.

Users can use two types of cell references: absolute references and relative references. An absolute cell reference is fixed to a particular cell. If a formula includes an absolute cell reference and if a user copies and pastes that formula to another cell, the cell reference is fixed to the original cell. On the other hand, a relative cell reference changes its reference according to the position of the formula. In Figure

Figure 3. Example of using padeval function

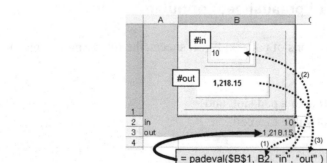

3, it can be seen that the user sets up the absolute cell reference B1 to specify the target pad. Then, the user uses a relative reference B2 as the input parameter for currency conversion. When the user copies and pastes the formula into another cell, its calculation is performed using the same pad with the value of the upper cell as its input.

Representing Loop Structures

In order to represent loop structures, we provide three functions: *fornext*, *while*, and *foreach*. We have designed these functions with reference to the loop statements in the Visual Basic language, such as the "For...Next" or "For Each...Next" statements.

fornext Function

The *fornext* function has a functionality similar to that of the "For...Next" statement in Visual Basic. Users can use this function when they would like to repeat a formula a particular number of times. The definition of the *fornext* function is as follows:

fornext(counter, start, end, step, formula)

Here, *counter* is a string value that represents the name of the control variable for the loop; *start* is the initial value of the *counter*; *end* is the final value of the *counter*; *step* is the amount by which the *counter* is incremented for each loop; and the formula specified in *formula* is executed the specified number of times. In the description of the *formula*, users can use the value of the *counter* as the parameter value of a formula in *formula*. The result values for each *formula* in each step are collected as a one-dimensional array and exported to a column of cells starting with the one below the cell holding the *fornext* function call.

while Function

Users can use the *while* function when they want to repeat a formula an indefinite number of times as long as a given condition is satisfied. The definition of the *while* function is as follows:

while(condition, formula)

The *while* function repeats the specified *formula* as long as the given *condition* returns "TRUE." When the *condition* returns "FALSE," the repetition is stopped. Users can use a formula which returns a Boolean value from the *condition*. The output of this function is exported as a range containing the values returned from the formula in each step.

foreach Function

When users want to repeat a set of formulae for each element in a cell range, they can use the *foreach* function. The definition of the *foreach* function is as follows:

foreach(element, range, formula)

Here, *element* is a string value that specifies the name of the variable used to iterate through the elements of the range. Further, *range* refers to the range of cells over which the *formula* is evaluated. As in the *fornext* function, users can use the value of the *element* in the *formula*. This function also returns multiple evaluated results in the form of an array. In the section "Applications," we present an example of the use of this function.

Describing Control Structure using Formula Language

Users can define a complex control structure involving multiple Web applications using the *padeval* function in combination with predefined functions in Excel.

In a spreadsheet, users can use cell references in a formula to define dependency relationships among cells. Our framework allows users to use cell references to define data linkages among embedded Web applications. Figure 4 shows the simple composition of two applications. In this figure, a user defines a data flow sequence: (1) the value of cell B2 is transferred to the pad in cell B1 as its input, (2) the processing result is exported to cell B3, (3) the value of cell B3 is transferred to cell D2 by the substitution expression inputted into cell D2, (4) the value of D2 is transferred

Figure 4. Sequential data linkage between two applications using padeval function

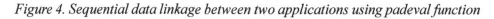
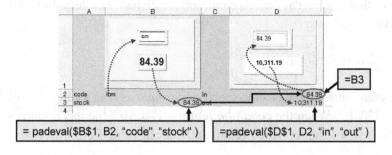

to the pad in cell D1 as its input, and (5) finally, the result of the processing of the pad is exported to cell D3.

Users can also set up conditional branches using the *if* function. The *if* function checks the logical condition of a statement and returns one value if it is true and a different value if it is false. The syntax is *if(condition, value if true, value if false)*.

By using the *padeval* function in combination with the *if* function, for example, users can change the target pad according to a specified condition. Figure 5 shows an example of changing the target pad according to a given condition. In this figure, a user embeds two Web applications: a currency conversion application for convert-ing from Japanese yen to US dollar in cell B1, and another conversion application that converts from US dollar to Japanese yen in cell D1. The user sets a formula for cell B4 by which can change the target Web application on the basis of the symbol specified in cell A3. If the user inputs "JPY" into cell A3, the calculation of the currency conversion is executed using the pad in cell B1.

User Interface Support

In order to assist users in the use of our framework, we have provided several user interface supports. We have provided a toolbar comprising a set of buttons that can: (a) create a base pad, (b) show the slot list in cells, and (c) input the *padeval* function (Figure 6).

When users click button (a) to create a base pad, the system creates a new base pad in the currently selected cell. Users can then paste an arbitrarily selected pad onto the base pad.

It is difficult for Excel users to view the slot information of the target pad. There-fore, it is necessary to provide a method for displaying it. When users click button (b) to display the slot list, the system lists the names and the current values of all

Figure 5. Changing target pad using if function

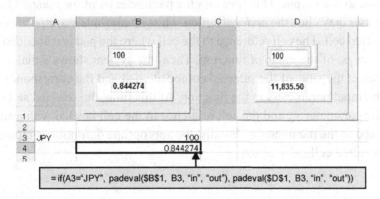

Figure 6. Toolbar for supporting users with pad operations in Excel and its usage

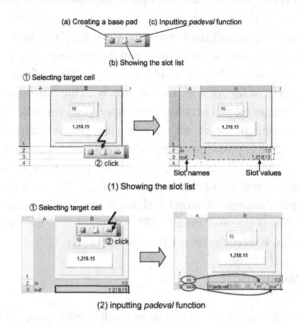

the slots defined in the pad pasted on the selected cell, and changes the background color of the corresponding cells that display the slot names and slot values (Figure 6(1)). The slot values are arranged in the cells below the cell in which the target pad is placed, and each slot name is displayed in the cell to the left of the cell that displays the corresponding slot value. This function supports users in recognizing slot names and values in the target pad.

Button (c) is used for inputting the *padeval* function in the selected cell, and by means of a dialog, it provides support for setting up the parameters of the *padeval* function. Clicking this button allows users to define the input–output relationships among cells and pads. A user may select a cell that displays a value that the user wants to use as the output. This specifies the parameter *os* of the *padeval* function. Then, the user may click the *padeval* button. The system finds a composite pad near to the selected cell. The cell reference to the cell where the pad is embedded is used as parameter *pc* of the *padeval* function. Then, the system shows a dialog so that one can select the slots of the selected composite pad and the corresponding cells used as the input parameters in the function. At this time, the selected slot name is used as the parameter s_n, and the cell reference to the cell labeled with a specified name is used as the parameter v_n. Finally, the appropriate definition is inputted into the first selected cell.

Figure 6 (2) shows an example of the use of the *padeval* button. In this figure, a user first selects cell B3 to specify both the target pad and the output slot, clicks the *padeval* button, and selects slot "in" as the input parameter. As a result, the formula "=padeval(B1, B2, "in", "out")" is inputted into cell B3.

APPLICATIONS

We have constructed some orchestrations to evaluate the capabilities of the discussed framework. In this section, we present three examples of the application of our framework.

CD Price Iteration

A user who wants to buy several CDs may want to know their total price. The user may open *Amazon.com* using a conventional Web browser, enter the name of a CD in the input field of the CD search application, and obtain the price of that one CD. The user must then repeat this process, however, for each CD that is desired. By using our framework, the user can automate this process.

Figure 7 shows an Excel sheet that represents the orchestration for automating this process. First, a user may have a list of the names of the desired CDs somewhere in a spreadsheet. In this figure, the user lists nine CDs in the range A2:A10. The user opens the *Amazon CD search* Web application using the Clipping Browser and clips the input field for a CD title onto the C3Sheet placed in cell B1. Then, the user performs a CD search in order to obtain the price of the target CD on the Clipping Browser. The user clips the portion that displays the price. The user inputs a formula "=foreach("e", A2:A10, padeval(B1, "e", "title", "price"))" to cell B2. This formula iterates the retrieval of the price of the corresponding CDs and outputs the prices in the range B2:B10. The user can then calculate the total price using the SUM function of Excel. When the user changes the given CD titles or adds a CD title to the inputted list, the total price is automatically updated.

An Example in Bioinformatics

In bioinformatics, there are many types of services for databases, analyses, and related reference information. Most of them are available as Web applications. Figure 8 shows the simple composition of three bioinformatics applications: *NCBI BLAST* (http://blast.ncbi.nlm.nih.gov/Blast.cgi) for homology searches, *CLUSTALW* (http://align.genome.jp/) for multiple alignments, and *ATV* (http://sourceforge.net/projects/

Figure 7. Automating multiple CD price search using foreach function

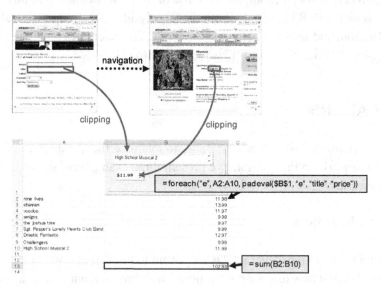

forester-atv/) for the visualization of a phylogenetic tree. *BLAST* and *CLUSTALW* are provided as Web applications and *ATV* is implemented as a local component.

In Figure 8, it can be seen that a user opens the *BLAST* Web application using the Clipping Browser and clips the input field of a protein sequence onto the C3Sheet placed in cell B1 (Figure 8 (1)). Then, the user performs a homology search to obtain a list of sequences on the Clipping Browser. The user selects the top five sequences and navigates to obtain their FASTA format (Figure 8 (2)). The user clips the entire Web page as an output to the C3Sheet in cell B1 (Figure 8 (3)). In the same manner, the user clips the input and output of *CLUSTALW* to the C3Sheet in cell C1 (Figure 8 (4)). Then, the user may set up formulae "=padeval(B1, A3, "sequence", "result")" in cell B3 and "=padeval(C1, B3, "sequences", "tree")}" in cell C3. The user pastes the wrapper pad of *ATV* in cell E3 to visualize a phylogenetic tree and sets up the formula "=padeval(E3, C3, "tree", "result")" in cell D3. If the user inputs another sequence into cell A3, the sequence is transferred to *BLAST* and the top five result sequences are transferred to the *CLUSTALW* application. As a result, the user can obtain a new phylogenetic tree visualization that corresponds to the input sequence.

Moreover, using the standard copy-paste operation, the user can duplicate a set of cells by using their dependency relationships with other cells in the spreadsheet. The user can thus easily perform a side-by-side comparison of different visualization results for different input sequences.

Figure 8. Phylogenetic tree visualization using multiple Web applications

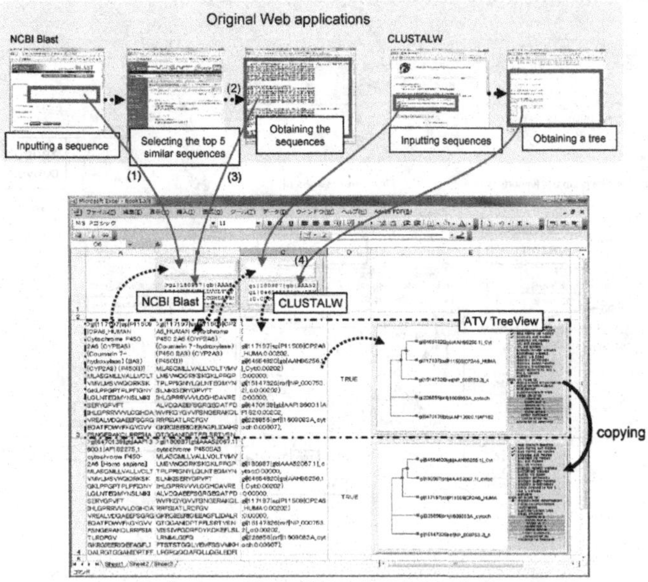

The Excel spreadsheet which coordinate three applications

Comparison of CD Prices among Different Sites

Let us consider a Japanese customer who wants to buy some CDs by foreign artists. Although he/she can buy them at *Amazon.co.jp*, it might be cheaper to buy them at some foreign shopping site that is not in Japanese. How does the customer compare the prices in such a shopping process?

Figure 9 shows a spreadsheet that includes three Web applications and that automates this comparison. The user clips CD search functions from both *Amazon. co.jp* and *Amazon.com* onto cells B1 and E1. In addition, the user clips the input and output portions to convert the dollar amount to yen from the *Yahoo! currency conversion* Web application. Then, the user defines the relevant input–output relationships among the cells and pads using the *padeval* function to obtain the search results. In this example, the user also has to convert string values to numerical values to reuse them as input parameters for other Excel functions. In the case of *Amazon.com*, the shipping charge can be calculated from the number of shipping items. The user adds the shipping charge to the original price and converts the total price obtained from *Amazon.com* to Japanese yen using the *Yahoo! currency conversion* application. The user makes two extra copies of the input and output cells for the CD search service in order to buy three different CDs. The user may click cell H15 to open a

Figure 9. CD price comparison using three different Web applications Amazon. co.jp, Amazon.com, and Yahoo! currency conversion

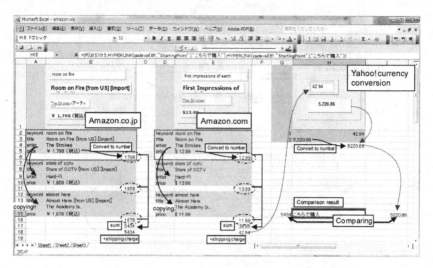

Web page on which the total price is cheaper. When the user supplies a new search keyword, these comparison processes are automatically updated.

FUTURE RESEARCH DIRECTIONS AND DISCUSSION

In this chapter we have presented a spreadsheet-based environment that enables end users to orchestrate multiple Web applications. This framework allows end users to extract certain functionalities from multiple Web applications and create an orchestration that reuses these functionalities. Users can create an orchestration spreadsheet using proposed mechanisms such as *padeval* functions. The proposed mechanisms give typical Excel users the ability to streamline daily tasks by assembling multiple atomic functions derived from Web applications into a spreadsheet. Although this chapter only describes examples that combine simple form-based Web applications, users can also make use of sophisticated intelligent applications such as recommendation systems and knowledge-mining systems. These applications could interact with each other to pool their intelligence with the support of the spreadsheet-based orchestration approach. This approach need not be limited to functioning only with Excel. The authors are considering a future extension of this work in which this framework is modified for use in a Web-based spreadsheet environment such as Google Spreadsheet.

In this chapter, the authors have presented a method for handing Web applications as visual components on a spreadsheet. This method makes the functions and displays of Web applications reusable. Users can reuse functions through the *padeval* function and displays by embedding visual components into cells. Because there are many Web applications which show calculated or processed results in specific formats such as images, having the wrapped visual components in cells becomes useful when users want to reuse the original display interface on the Web applications.

Our framework is especially suitable for simple data-lookup applications that receive certain input parameters, execute certain types of processing, and return the result as an HTML document. The proposed framework offers a way of using those Web applications as tools to perform calculations on a spreadsheet.

Users can use not only simple data-lookup applications, but also perform some real actions on a spreadsheet. Such active applications include Web-based email systems and other types of communication services such as Internet messengers or Twitter. The proposed framework, however, is not suited to these types of Web applications. This framework automatically recalculates the *padeval* function when the referred cells are updated, which may cause unnecessary access to the corresponding Web applications. Moreover, in the current implementation, each time a *padeval* function is recalculated, it causes the corresponding Web application to be executed one time. When a user uses multiple *padeval* functions to obtain multiple result values from a common Web application, there is no guarantee that all the result values will be correctly related to each other, since the Web application might change the program's behavior between executions.

In order to resolve these issues, we need to provide a method for controlling the timing of Web application access. For example, in Excel, there is a functionality to control the automatic recalculation of formulae in a spreadsheet. By turning off this functionality, users can specify the timing of the recalculation. We may also consider improving the *padeval* implementation so that the timing of recalculations is presented to users as a more fundamental activity.

Since we use structure-based information extraction mechanisms using XPath, changes in the structure of Web pages may break a wrapper pad. In the case that advertisements are irregularly embedded in a Web page or the structure of the result page changes depending on the input value, there will be a failure of the reevaluation process of the wrapped Web application functionality such that the XPath recorded during the clipping process becomes invalid. We can resolve this by incorporating other methods such as those used for enhancing the robustness of element identification to accommodate changes in the underlying pages and for capturing a broad range of user actions across applications of different types.

The proposed framework provides a function for the display of slots that are defined by users. However, in a more complex orchestration, it would be helpful for the user to be able to view the relationships among slots or cells in a graphical representation such as a workflow diagram. Excel provides a functionality with which the dependency relationships among cells can be displayed. Users can utilize this functionality to display the dependency relationships among multiple Web applications.

Although the proposed mechanisms require users to have less additional knowledge than that needed for other mashup tools or workflow systems, users do need to learn some specific mechanisms beyond conventionally used spreadsheet functionalities. Such mechanisms include the management of IntelligentPad components, the function of a slot, and the use of the *padeval* function. As a more elegant approach, for example, it would be possible for a spreadsheet itself to function as a C3Sheet. This would make it possible for users to directly clip parts of Web applications onto a spreadsheet, associating a cell with the Web clip. In this case, one ViewPort would be directly associated with one cell, and the value of the ViewPort would be automatically synchronized with the value of the associated cell. Hence, users would not have to use the *padeval* function to pass parameters from the spreadsheet. By using only the ordinary functions in the formula language, users would gain access to Web application functionality on a spreadsheet. Such an implementation would be feasible for programmers who have full access to the source code of the spreadsheet, which was not the case for us.

CONCLUSION

In this chapter, we have proposed a spreadsheet-based environment that enables end users to orchestrate multiple Web applications. We have provided a method for embedding various Web resources as visual components in cells in a spreadsheet that can be reused in the spreadsheet. We have also provided a method by which embedded components can be accessed by using a special function in the formula language. Our framework enables users to define the complex coordination of multiple Web applications on a spreadsheet using combinations of this special function along with predefined functions.

REFERENCES

Chi, E. H.-H., Konstan, J., Barry, P., & Riedl, J. (1997). A spreadsheet approach to information visualization. In *Proceedings of the 10th annual ACM symposium on User interface software and technology*, (pp. 79-80). New York: ACM Press.

Chi, E. H.-H., Riedl, J., Barry, P., & Konstan, J. (1998). Principles for information visualization spreadsheets. *IEEE Computer Graphics and Applications, 18*(4), 30–38. doi:10.1109/38.689659

Clark, J., & DeRose, S. J. (1999). *XML Path Language (XPath) Version 1.0. W3C Recommendation.* Retrieved December 21, 2009, from http://www.w3.org/TR/xpath

Ennals, R., & Gay, D. (2007). User-friendly functional programming for web mash-ups. *SIGPLAN Notices, 42*(9), 223–234. doi:10.1145/1291220.1291187

Fujima, J., Lunzer, A., Hornbæk, K., & Tanaka, Y. (2004). Clip, connect, clone: combining application elements to build custom interfaces for information access. In *Proceedings of the 17th Annual ACM Symposium on User Interface Software and Technology*, (pp. 175-184). New York: ACM Press.

Fujima, J., Yoshihara, S., & Tanaka, Y. (2007). Web application orchestration using Excel. In *Proceedings of the 2007 IEEE/WIC/ACM International Conference on Web Intelligence* (pp. 743-749). Washington, DC: IEEE Computer Society.

Itoh, M., Fujima, J., Ohigashi, M., & Tanaka, Y. (2007). Spreadsheet-based framework for interactive 3D visualization of Web resources. In *Proceedings of the 11th International Conference on Information Visualisation*, (pp. 65-73). Washington, DC: IEEE Computer Society.

Jones, S. P., Blackwell, A., & Burnett, M. (2003). A user-centered approach to functions in Excel. In *Proceedings of the Eighth ACM SIGPLAN International Conference on Functional Programming*, (pp. 165-176). New York: ACM Press.

Kandogan, E., Haber, E., Barrett, R., Cypher, A., Maglio, P., & Zhao, H. (2005). A1: enduser programming for web-based system administration. In *Proceedings of the 18th Annual ACM Symposium on User Interface Software and Technology*, (pp. 211-220). New York: ACM Press.

Laender, A. H. F., Ribeiro-Neto, B. A., da Silva, A. S., & Teixeira, J. S. (2002). A brief survey of web data extraction tools. *SIGMOD Record, 31*(2), 84–93. doi:10.1145/565117.565137

Lin, J., Wong, J., Nichols, J., Cypher, A., & Lau, T. A. (2009). End-user programming of mashups with vegemite. In *Proceedings of the 13th international conference on Intelligent user interfaces* (pp. 97-106). New York: ACM Press.

Oracle: Oracle BPEL Process Manager Quick Start Guide (2006). Retrieved December 21, 2009, from http://download.oracle.com/docs/cd/B31017_01/integrate.1013/b28983.pdf

Peltz, C. (2003). Web services orchestration and choreography. *IEEE Computer*, *36*(10), 46–52.

Piersol, K. W. (1986). Object-oriented spreadsheets: The analytic spreadsheet package. In *Proceedings on Object-Oriented Programming Systems, Languages and Applications* (pp. 385–390). New York: ACM Press.

Tanaka, Y. (2003). *Meme media and meme market architectures: Knowledge media for editing, distributing, and managing intellectual resources*. New York: IEEE Press & Wiley-Interscience. doi:10.1002/047172307X

Tanaka, Y., & Imataki, T. (1989). IntelligentPad: A hypermedia system allowing functional compositions of active media objects through direct manipulations. In *Proceedings of the IFIP 11th World Computer Congress* (pp. 541-546). North-Holland/IFIP.

Tanaka, Y., Ito, K., & Fujima, J. (2006). Meme media for clipping and combining web resources. *World Wide Web (Bussum)*, *9*(2), 117–142. doi:10.1007/s11280-005-3043-6

Wang, G., Yang, S., & Han, Y. (2009). Mashroom: end-user mashup programming using nested tables. In *Proceedings of the 18th international conference on World Wide Web*. (pp. 861-870). New York: ACM Press.

Witkowski, A., Bellamkonda, S., Bozkaya, T., Naimat, A., Sheng, L., Subramanian, S., & Waingold, A. (2005). Query by Excel. In *Proceedings of the 31st International Conference on Very Large Data Bases*, (pp. 1204-1215). VLDB Endowment.

Chapter 4
A Component–Based 3D Geographic Simulation Framework and its Integration with a Legacy GIS

Zhen-Sheng Guo
Hokkaido University, Japan

Yuzuru Tanaka
Hokkaido University, Japan

ABSTRACT

There is an increasing demand for 3D geographic simulation systems. Most systems currently available are closed and based on fixed architectures. Some systems allow us to develop and customize a 3D geographic simulation system, but this usually requires the writing of extensive program code. Especially in 3D geo-disaster simulations, for example, we need to dynamically integrate 2D legacy GIS with 3D geographic simulation systems in order to investigate the details about the damaged areas and the consequences of the disasters. The authors propose a component-based application framework for 3D geographic simulation that can integrate a legacy 2D GIS with geographic simulation systems in a 3D visual environment. Their framework provides a set of 3D visual components required for the development of a new interactive 3D visual geographic simulation. In their framework, component integrators can construct 3D geographic simulation systems by composing the 3D visual components. Moreover, the authors' integration framework provides

DOI: 10.4018/978-1-61520-851-7.ch004

two fundamental integration mechanisms, view integration and query integration mechanisms, to integrate it with legacy 2D systems. The view integration function maps the 2D rendering of a legacy 2D GIS onto the surface of the 3D geography used in a 3D visual geographical simulator, and then dispatches every event on the in a 3D visual environment. geographic surface to the original 2D GIS. The query integration automatically converts each 3D simulation result that is shown as a set of highlighted regions on the surface of the geography to the corresponding regional query to the 2D GIS. mechanisms, to integrate it with legacy 2D systems. The view integration function maps the 2D rendering of a legacy 2D GIS onto the surface of the 3D geography used in a 3D visual geographical simulator, and then dispatches every event on the geographic surface to the original 2D GIS. The query integration automatically converts each 3D simulation result that is shown as a set of highlighted regions on the surface of the geography to the corresponding regional query to the 2D GIS. The proposed framework is based on their 3D meme media architecture in which components are represented as meme media objects, and their interoperation is defined by slot connections between them. As a result, their framework enables users to compose 3D geographic simulation systems and to integrate a legacy 2D GIS with a 3D geographic simulation system simply by composing display objects.

INTRODUCTION

Various geographic simulation systems have been developed to meet the growing need for 3D geographic simulation of disasters, such as avalanches, floods, and landslides. In general, the development of each has been primarily independent with closed and fixed architectures, it is therefore difficult to introduce existing functions of one existing geographic simulation system to others. Moreover, although the geographic simulation systems generally have strong disaster simulation capability, they often lack the information necessary for analysis and evaluation of the disaster, whereas many legacy geographic information systems (GIS) can provide visual map and region query functions for disaster analysis and evaluation. For this reason, GIS and geographic simulation systems often need to be integrated. However, in general, the development of the 3D geographic simulation systems and legacy GIS have been primarily independent and integrative uses are still at an early stage.

There are many conventional GIS, and simulators have become more advanced. Because these types of software are usually independent, closed systems, they are difficult to customize and to integrate with others. Although some systems, such as GRASS (GRASS) and ArcGIS (ArcGIS), can be customized with library packages, they still require users to write lengthy programs. Other systems, such as GeoVista

(Takatsuka, 2002) and AVS (Upson, 1989), provide a visual programming environment for the development or customization of the 3D simulation systems. These systems allow users to interact only with their visual programs; users cannot interact with their visual output to develop a new 3D system or modify their input parameter values. Component object model (COM) is a model for linking software modules. When such a link is established, the modules can communicate with each other through standard communication interfaces. These links require users to be skilled in programming. Open Geospatial Consortium (OGC) standards (OpenGIS) can be used to integrate different Web services through an OGC-standard Web service interface. This integration demands OGC-compliant Web services. However, most of the currently available Web services are not OGC-compliant (Alves, 2006).

This chapter proposes a component-based 3D geographic simulation framework. Our framework provides basic composite components for 3D geographic simulation, and two fundamental legacy GIS integration mechanisms for component integrators. Our framework enables component integrators to easily build 3D geographic simulation systems by visually combining the required components and by defining data flows among the components. The component integrators need to have knowledge about the legacy systems, for example, knowledge about the display and query APIs and their parameters for the legacy GIS, the input and output data formats of the legacy simulators, and the data flows among components. The component integrators also need to know how to combine the required components together. The end users of this framework only need to replace some component with another of the same functionality, by mouse manipulation, to carry out 3D geographic simulations integrated with a legacy GIS.

The component-based 3D geographic simulation framework presented here incorporates the basic components of 3D geographic simulation systems and two legacy GIS integration mechanisms into an integrated environment. This framework provides a set of 3D visual basic components required for the development of a new interactive system that can integrate legacy 2D GIS and legacy geographical simulators to make 3D geographic simulation systems. In the integration framework, construction of a new 3D geographic simulation system only requires combining the necessary 3D visual components. To support this framework of integrating a legacy GIS, we also propose two fundamental integration mechanisms: view integration and query integration. The view integration maps the 2D rendering of a legacy 2D GIS onto the surface of the 3D geography used in a 3D visual geographical simulator, and then dispatches every event on the geography surface to the original 2D GIS. The query integration automatically converts each 3D simulation result that is shown as a set of highlighted regions on the surface of the geography to a corresponding regional query on the 2D GIS. We used the 3D meme media system called IntelligentBox (Tanaka, 2003; Okada, 1995) as the basic platform of our framework.

IntelligentBox is a component-based 3D visual software development system. In IntelligentBox, each primitive component called a box has a special function and some state holders called slots, as well as a special 3D shape. End users can define a functional and visual composition using primitive boxes and slot connections among them. Users can construct 3D applications just through direct manipulation of visual components. Moreover, each component, once created, provides a simple API for its reuse with other components in different applications.

The remainder of this chapter is structured as follows: section 2 shows an overview of the component-based framework, the detail of the framework, and its integration mechanism with a legacy GIS. In section 3, we describe an application of our framework. Finally, we make some concluding remarks.

COMPONENT-BASED FRAMEWORK

This section describes the proposed component-based 3D geographic simulation framework. Figure 1 shows the framework, which consists of three types of 3D visual components used to develop a 3D geographic simulation system. Our framework allows component integrators to use a mouse to combine these visual 3D components together to construct geographic simulation systems. Moreover, in our framework, the display and query functions of a legacy 2D GIS are integrated with the 3D geographic simulation systems. Our framework involves three basic technologies: 3D visual components, component composition, and integration of a legacy 2D GIS with 3D geographic simulation systems technology.

Details of the 3D Visual Components

This subsection describes the three basic components. The 3D terrain component visualizes terrain data stored in the elevation database as a 3D terrain model. It also works as a provider of the terrain data to other components in the simulation environment. The geographic simulation component is used for integrating legacy simulators into our simulation framework. It also calculates the necessary parameters for the geography simulator and for visualizing the results of simulation. The query component integrates the query function of the legacy 2D GIS into the 3D simulation environment. In this research, we used a type of 3D meme media called IntelligentBox as a basic system. IntelligentBox offers a series of interactive 3D components. Each 3D component has its own function and a standardized data access interface called slots. Component integrators can interactively define the parent-child relationships between the 3D components to transfer data between them by connecting slots. We will explain the slots and the data that are kept in each component.

Figure 1. The component-based framework

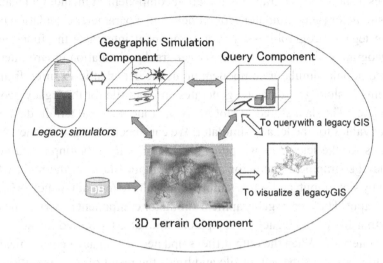

Figure 2 shows the 3D terrain component. It has slot #terrain_data and slot #displayAPI, which hold the terrain data and the map range parameters. The terrain data include the list of the elevation data and the coordinate location of the mesh point. The 3D terrain component can display a 3D terrain model in the 3D environment using the terrain data that are saved in slot #terrain_data. This component obtains a map image from a legacy 2D GIS and maps the map onto the 3D terrain surface using the necessary data (position, size, scale) saved in slot #displayAPI. We call the integration of the display function of the legacy GIS with the 3D terrain component view integration. It is explained below in detail.

Figure 2. 3D terrain component

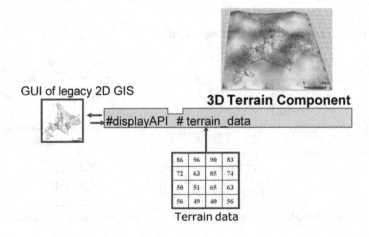

Figures 3 show the geographic simulation component. It includes a legacy geographic simulator (geo-simulator) component and a parameter calculation component. The legacy geographic simulator component integrates the functions of a legacy geography simulator into the 3D geography simulation environment. The legacy geographic simulator component holds the data that is acquired from other components in slot #geo_data and generates an input file for the legacy geographical simulator. The data stored in slot #geo_data includes the terrain data and the parameter values for the legacy simulator. We can specify the path of the input and output files for the legacy geographical simulator with slots #input and #output. The legacy geographical simulator obtains the input file from the path, which is specified by slot #input, and sends simulation results to the path, which is specified by slot #output. The legacy geographical simulator component observes the update of the output file of the legacy geographical simulator (specified by slot #output) at regular intervals. When the output file is updated, the legacy geographical simulator component reads the output file and holds the result of the simulation in slot #result. The simulation result is generally an array, each element of which corresponds to a grid cell, and takes as its value either 0 or 1. Finally, this component visualizes the result in the same 3D environment. The parameter calculation component calculates the necessary parameters for the geographical simulator and visualizes the calculation result. The parameter calculation component holds the data needed to calculate the parameter in slot #geo_data and saves this calculation result in slot #result. Moreover, if it is necessary, this component can visualize the result data in a 3D environment.

Figure 4 shows the query component. It has slot #geo_data, slot #queryAPI, and slot #result, which hold the simulation results, query parameters, and query results respectively. The query component receives the simulation result and keeps it in slot #geo_data. The simulation result includes the terrain data and the simulation

Figure 3. Geographic simulation component

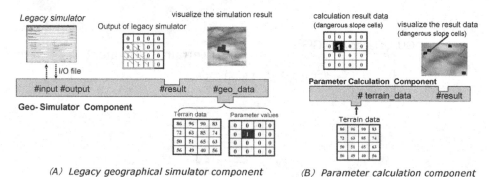

(A) *Legacy geographical simulator component*   (B) *Parameter calculation component*

result values (for example, the damage zone data). Next, the query component uses the data in slot #geo_data to generate a range parameter and calls the query function of the legacy 2D GIS with this parameter through slot #queryAPI. For example, the range parameter of a grid cell in the damaged area takes the value 1. Then, the query component obtains a query result from the legacy 2D GIS and holds it in slot #result. Finally, the query component displays the query result (i.e., the damaged road IDs) in the 3D environment. We call the integration of the query functions of the legacy GIS with the 3D geographic simulations query integration, described in detail below.

Our framework allows component integrators to combine these components to construct geographic simulation systems. The interoperation of visual components is defined by slot connections among them. As a result, they can be combined with other components by connecting their slots. They interoperate by exchanging messages through slot connections. Our framework also enables end users to integrate a legacy 2D GIS with a 3D geographic simulation system simply through the composition of their display objects.

Component Composition

In our framework, component integrators can combine the 3D components arbitrarily as desired. To combine more than one component, the processed data and parameters must be exchanged among the components. In our approach, the data and parameters can be exchanged through the slots. In addition, we use the view integration and query integration mechanisms to integrate the display and query functions of the 2D legacy GIS with the 3D simulation environment.

Figure 4. Query component

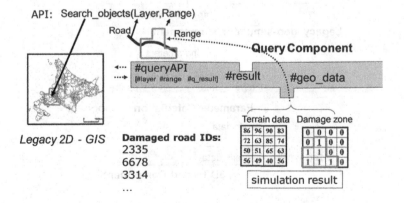

Figure 5 shows an example of a composition. In this example, we combine four components: a 3D terrain component, a parameter calculation component, a legacy geo-simulator component, and a query component. The processed data and parameters are exchanged among these components through the slots. First, the parameter calculation component obtains the terrain data from the 3D terrain component through slot #terrain_data. The parameter calculation component calculates the parameters using the terrain data and holds the parameter values in its slot #result. Next, the legacy geographical simulator component obtains the parameter data from the slot #result of the parameter calculation component and holds the parameter values in its slot #geo_data. The legacy geo-simulator component uses the parameter data to create simulation and holds the simulation result in its slot #result. Finally, the query component obtains the simulation result from the slot #result of the legacy geo-simulator component and holds the simulation result in its slot #geo_data. The query component uses the simulation result to generate a query for integrating the simulation result with a legacy GIS and holds the query in its slot #queyAPI. The query component integrates the simulation result with the legacy GIS through the slot #queyAPI and holds the query result in slot #result.

Figure 5 shows the basic composition structure of our framework. In addition, our framework allows vertical and horizontal extension. Vertical extension means that we can combine other different legacy geo-simulation components or legacy GIS components with the topmost query component in Figure 5 to simulate a sec-

Figure 5. An example composition

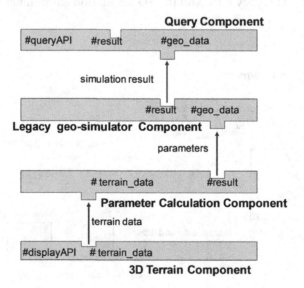

ondary or tertiary disaster caused by the preceding damage. Horizontal extension means that we can combine two or more different legacy simulation components and legacy GIS components with the same 3D terrain component to comparatively study different disaster simulations for the same area. Moreover, we can simply change the input data of the 3D terrain component to immediately apply the same simulation system to another area. Such flexibility and extensibility characterizes our framework.

Integrating a Legacy 2D GIS with 3D Geographic Simulation Systems

We integrated the display and query functions of a legacy 2D GIS with a 3D simulation system. We call the two integrations view integration and query integration.

The view integration function maps the 2D rendering of a legacy 2D GIS onto the surface of the 3D terrain model used in a 3D visual geographical simulation, and it dispatches every event on the terrain surface to the original 2D GIS. We use the 3D shadow-copy mechanism (Ohigashi, 2005; Ohigashi, 2006) to map the 2D graphical user interface (GUI) of a legacy GIS onto the surface of the 3D terrain model. Moreover, the 3D shadow-copy mechanism dispatches every mouse event that occurs on the mapped surfaces of the 3D terrain component to the original 2D legacy GIS with an inverse transformation of the texture mapping process. Therefore, we can easily extend the GUI of a 2D legacy GIS to a 3D geographic information system. We use the 3D shadow-copy mechanism to map the 2D GUI of a legacy GIS onto the surface of the 3D terrain model.

Figure 6 shows a view integration of a legacy 2D GIS with 3D terrain model. We call this the 3D map component. First, the 3D map component calculates the position, size, and scale information from the original terrain data that is kept in slot #terrain_data, which is used for generating terrain polygons, as shown in Figure 6 (i). Next, this component displays the appropriate part of the 2D map from the whole map by calling the display API of the legacy 2D GIS as shown in Figure 6 (ii). Then, this component maps the clipped map onto a 3D terrain using a 3D shadow-copy mechanism as shown in Figure 6 (iii). Finally, we obtain a 3D map as shown in Figure 6 (iv).

The query integration function integrates query functions of a legacy 2D GIS with 3D geographic simulation systems. We propose a query integration function that uses the query API of the legacy 2D GIS. For example, query integration automatically converts each 3D simulation result that is shown as a set of highlighted regions on the surface of the geography to a corresponding regional query to 2D GIS. In general, to search for objects in a given area, we usually integrate a database and use SQL to retrieve the objects from the database. For instance, for a query

Figure 6. Integrating the GUI of a legacy 2D GIS with a 3D terrain model

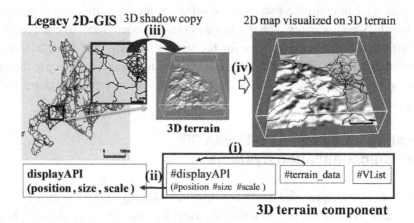

searching for a damaged cell to obtain its population saved in GisDataList (GD), the GD schema would be

GisDataList (Population: integer, CellID:integer)

Moreover, the damaged cell can be referred to by its ID. Therefore, this query can be expressed in SQL as

SELECT GD.Population
FROM GisDataList GD
WHERE GD.CellID=ID

Alternatively, if the query is searching for railways across damaged cells, we have to query an object-oriented database with an object-oriented query. The schema of railway (RAILWAY) and damaged cell object (DCELL) is shown as

RAILWAY (RouteID: integer, Line: line)
DCELL (CellID:integer, Cell:area)
Therefore, the query can be expressed in an object-oriented query as
SELECT x.Line inside (y.Cell)
FROM x in RAILWAY
y in DCELL
WHERE y.Cell=DamagedCell and
x.Line inter (y.Cell),

where x.Line is a line object that belongs to RAILWAY and y.Cell is a cell object that belongs to DCELL.

However, these query expressions are long and complex. Furthermore, it is possible that the database we want may not exist. On the other hand, in many cases, the legacy GIS provide APIs to develop new systems. We can call only one query API function for retrieving the information we want. A query integration mechanism for integrating the 2D GIS query function with 3D geographic simulation results by calling its query API is proposed.

Figure 7 shows the integration of a legacy 2D GIS query with a geographic simulation. The right is a query component, and the left is a legacy 2D GIS (a road map). The legacy 2D GIS offers a query API of searching for objects within a specified range from some layer. For instance, the query function could be *SearchForObjects(Within(range), From(layer))*.

If we want to find damaged roads in damaged zones, which can be obtained from a simulation result, we can call the query function *SearchForObjects (Within(damaged zones), From(road layer)*. The query component receives the simulation result and keeps it in slot #geo_data as shown in Figure 7 (i). Next, the query component uses the data in slot #geo_data to generate a range parameter and calls the query function of the legacy 2D GIS with this parameter through slot #queryAPI as shown in Figure 7 (ii). Then, the query component obtains a query result from the legacy 2D GIS and holds it in the parameter slot #q_result of slot #queryAPI as shown in Figure 7 (iii). Figure 7 (iv) shows that slot #result holds the query result and the terrain data. Finally, the query component displays the query

Figure 7. Integrating the query function of a legacy 2D GIS with 3D geographic simulations

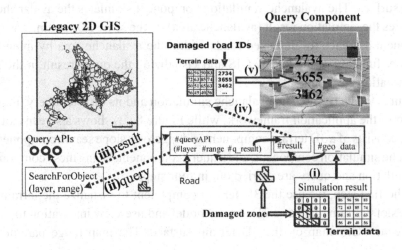

result (i.e., the damaged road IDs) in the 3D environment as shown in Figure 7 (v). The query result and terrain data are stored in slot #result to be used by the next simulation or query.

APPLICATIONS

We present two applications of our framework to demonstrate its effectiveness. The two application systems were constructed from several components. They integrate legacy GIS functions into 3D simulation systems.

An Avalanche Simulation and its Disaster Query

In this section, we describe an example application of our framework. This application shows an avalanche simulation and its disaster query. The scenario is an avalanche hazard evaluation. A risk management expert is analyzing the road damage caused by an avalanche. The analysis process consists of 4 phases: (1) visualizing a 3D map as the simulation base, (2) investigating the highly dangerous slopes where avalanches could easily happen, (3) calculating the avalanche damaged zones from a dangerous slope to the point where sliding snow would stop, and (4) searching for damaged roads within the damaged zones. The avalanche simulation and its disaster query process require four components: a 3D terrain component, a dangerous-slope search component, an avalanche simulation component, and a query component. The 3D terrain component visualizes the 3D terrain data as a 3D terrain model and displays a map of the 2D legacy GIS on its surface. It serves as the basic component for the simulation and visualization. The dangerous-slope search component investigates the dangerous slopes in the specified area and visualizes those slopes on the 3D terrain surface. The avalanche simulation component simulates the avalanche and visualizes the simulation result (avalanche area) on the same 3D terrain. The query component searches for damaged roads within the avalanche area by integrating the query function of the legacy GIS and visualizing the query result in the same 3D simulation environment.

Figures 9 and 10 show an avalanche simulation and its disaster query. Figure 8 (A) shows the application framework, while Figure 8 (B) shows a screenshot. The system consists of a 3D terrain component, a dangerous-slope search component, an avalanche simulation component, and a query component. Using these components, the simulation and query are carried out in four steps.

In the first step, we use the 3D terrain component to visualize the terrain data held in slot #terrain_data as a 3D terrain model and use view integration to visualize a legacy GIS map on the 3D terrain surface. The map range parameter is

Figure 8. An application for an avalanche-simulation system

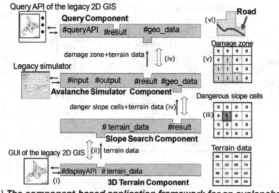

(A) The component-based application framework for an avalanche-simulation system

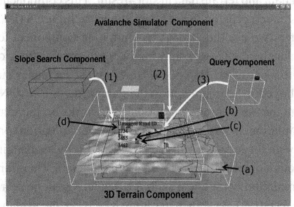

(B) The display hardcopy of an avalanche-simulation system

specified through slot #displayAPI as shown in Figure 8 (A) (i). This generates a 3D map as shown in Figure 8 (B) (a).

In the second step, we use the dangerous-slope search component to look for the high-danger slopes where avalanches could easily happen. In this process, the dangerous-slope search component needs 3D terrain data and a 3D map to visualize the dangerous slopes. Then, we combine the dangerous-slope search component with the 3D terrain component (shown in Figure 8 (B) (1)). The dangerous-slope search component obtains the terrain data from the 3D terrain component through slot #terrain_data shown in Figure 8 (A) (ii). It is generally known that slopes with angles between 35 and 40 degrees are prone to avalanches (K. Maeno, 2000). There-fore, the dangerous-slope search component calculates each slope angle. As shown in Figure 8 (A) (iii), the grid cells of slope angles between 35 and 40 degrees were set as 1 and others were set at 0. The dangerous-slope search component holds the

Figure 9. the avalanche simulation with CONEFALL

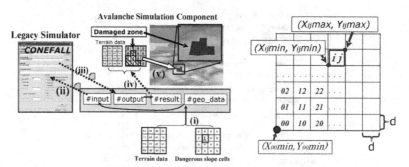

(A) Use of CONEFALL for avalanche simulation   (B) Raster representation of the simulation result

calculation result data and terrain data in slot #result. This component visualizes the dangerous slopes as red cells on the 3D map shown in Figure 8 (B)(b).

In the third step, we use the avalanche simulation component to simulate and visualize the avalanche damaged zones that would occur if the snow slid from a dangerous slope to a predicted stop point. Here, we used a legacy simulator called CONEFALL (Jaboyedoff) for simulating the damaged zones. CONEFALL is designed to estimate the zones prone to rock falls. It works on the same principle as the avalanche simulation. In this process, the avalanche simulation component needs to communicate with the legacy simulator CONEFALL by exchanging files. It also needs the dangerous slope and 3D terrain data as parameters. Therefore, we combine the avalanche simulation component with the dangerous-slope search component (shown in Figure 8 (B) (2)). As shown in Figure 8 (A) (iv), the avalanche simulation component obtains the dangerous slope and terrain data from the dangerous-slope search component through slot #geo_data and slot #result. The files are exchanged with CONEFALL through slot #input and slot #output. The result of this simulation is visualized on the 3D map as shown in Figure 8 (B) (c).

Figure 9 shows the avalanche simulation with CONEFALL. The simulation is carried out as follows. First, the avalanche simulation component obtains the terrain data and the dangerous-slope list from the dangerous-slope search component and keeps these data in slot #geo_data as shown in Figure 9 (A) (i). Then, the avalanche simulation component generates an input I/O file using the data held in slot #geo_data and saves this file in a path specified via slot #input shown in Figure 9 (A) (ii). After that, CONEFALL simulates the damaged zones using the file, and sends the result file of its simulation calculation to a specified file path. The output of CONEFALL (simulation result) is a list of 1s and 0s in which the 1s correspond to the damaged zones. Then, the avalanche simulation component reads in the simulation result file from the path specified in slot #output, as shown in Figure 9 (A) (iii). Finally, the

Figure 10. An application for a flood simulation system

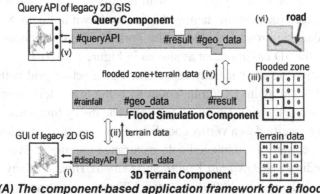

(A) The component-based application framework for a flood simulation system

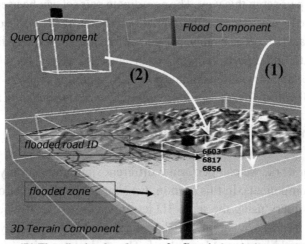

(B) The display hardcopy of a flood simulation system

simulation result is held in slot #result and the simulation result is visualized on the 3D map as shown in Figure 10 (iv) and (v). Moreover, the terrain data is also held in slot #result and can be used for the next simulation or query.

In the fourth step, we use the query component to search for and visualize the damaged roads within the damaged zones. This query process needs the damaged zones data and terrain data to generate query parameters. We combine the query component with the avalanche simulation component to find the damaged roads in the damaged zones as shown in Figure 8 (B) (3). The query component obtains the damaged zones from the avalanche simulation component shown in Figure 8 (A) (iv), and the damaged zones are used to generate the query parameters of the legacy

GIS. The query parameters are held in slot #queryAPI. Using this slot, we integrate the query function of a legacy 2D GIS with the query integration mechanism to search for damaged roads in the damaged zone, as shown in Figure 8 (A) (vi). The query result (damaged roads) is held in slot #result. This component displays the query result in the 3D environment as shown in Figure 8 (B) (d).

The simulation result is usually represented as a set of grid cells (as shown in Figure 9 (B)). The point (X00min,Y00min) is the lower-left corner of cell 00, while the value d is the side length of one cell. The query functions of legacy 2D GIS are usually specified as a vertex coordinate pair, i.e., the lower-left corner and the upper-right corner of a damaged cell, as a range parameter. We can calculate the vertex coordinate pair *(Xijmin,Yijmin)* and *(Xijmax,Yijmax)* of any cell ij by the formulae *(Xijmin,Yijmin)* = *(X00min + i × d, Y00min + j × d)* and *(Xijmin,Yijmin)* = *(X00min +(i+ 1) × d, Y00min + (j+1) × d)*. We can convert all the damaged cells to a coordinate pair set in this way. The coordinate pair set can be used as the range parameter of the legacy 2D GIS query function. Therefore, a query component can use the coordinate pair set as a range parameter for calling the query function of the legacy 2D GIS to find objects in them. For instance, we search for damaged roads, those roads overlapped with the damaged cells, by calling the query function *Sear chForObjects(Within((Xijmin, Yijmin),(Xijmax,Yijmax)), From(road layer))*.

A Flood Simulation and its Disaster Query

Using our framework, we can perform a different simulation simply by changing the simulator components. In this section, we show a flood simulation application and its disaster query using the same 3D terrain and query components. The scenario is a flood hazard evaluation. A risk management expert is analyzing the road damaged that would be caused by a flood. The analysis consists of three phases: (1) visualizing a 3D map as the simulation base, (2) calculating the flooded zone, and (3) searching for damaged roads within the flooded zone. The flood simulation and its disaster query process require three components: a 3D terrain component, a flood simulation component, and a query component. The 3D terrain component visualizes the 3D terrain data as a 3D model and displays a map of 2D legacy GIS on its surface. It serves as the basic component for the simulation and visualization. The flood simulation component simulates the flood and visualizes the simulation result (water surface). The query component searches for damaged roads within the flooded zone by integrating the query function of a legacy GIS and visualizing the query result in the same 3D simulation environment.

Figure 10 shows a flood simulation and its disaster query. Figure 10 (A) shows the component-based application framework, while Figure 10 (B) shows a screenshot of the simulation and the query evaluation. This system consists of a 3D terrain component, a flood simulation component, and a query component. Using these components, the flood simulation and its disaster query are carried out in three steps.

In the first step, we use the 3D terrain component to visualize the terrain data held in slot #terrain_data as a 3D terrain model and to visualize a legacy GIS map on the 3D terrain surface with view integration, as shown in Figure 10 (A) (i). The map range parameter is specified through slot #displayAPI. This generates a 3D map, as shown in Figure 10 (B).

In the second step, we use the flood simulation component to calculate the flooded zone. In this process, the flood simulation component needs 3D terrain data. Therefore, we combine the flood simulation component with the 3D terrain component shown in Figure 10 (B) (1). The flood simulation component obtains the terrain data from the 3D terrain component through slot #terrain_data and keeps it in slot #geo_data as shown in Figure 10 (A) (ii). The flood simulation component changes the height of the water surface based on the simulation results, taking into account the total amount of rainfall. It enables users to visually find the submerged areas of the simulation as shown in Figure 10 (B). The flood simulation result data is a set of 0s and 1s. The cells under the water surface are set as 1, as shown in Figure 10 (A) (iii). So that another query or simulation process can use the same terrain data, the flood simulation component keeps the simulation result data and terrain data in its slot #result.

In the third step, we use the query component to search for damaged roads within the flooded zone. In this process, the query component needs the data for the flooded zone and the 3D terrain. Therefore, we combine the query component with the flood simulation component as shown in Figure 10 (B) (2). As shown in Figure 10 (A) (iv), the query component obtains the data for the flooded zone and the terrain from the flood simulation component through slot #result and keeps it in slot #geo_data. When the query component receives these data, it searches the flooded zone contained geometrically in its cuboids' shape, and the flooded zone is used as a condition of a query to the legacy GIS. We integrated the query function of the legacy 2D GIS with the query integration mechanism as shown in Figure 10 (A) (v). As shown in Figure 10 (B), the query component displays the flooded road IDs (the roads within the flooded zone as shown in Figure 10 (A) (vi)) in the 3D environment.

In addition, using our framework, we can perform the following process simply. We can interactively locate the desired areas by moving the query component or by changing the size of the component. To investigate another area of the 3D terrain, we need simply to change the input data of the 3D terrain component. To search for different objects in the same area, we can also combine another query component with the same simulation component at the same time.

CONCLUSION

In this chapter we have proposed a new component-based 3D geographic simulation framework. Using this framework, component integrators can easily develop 3D geographic simulation systems just by combining the required components and by defining data flow among these components. The end users of this framework only need to replace some component with another of the same functionality, using mouse manipulation, to carry out a 3D geographic simulation integrated with a legacy GIS. Our framework incorporates the fundamental components of 3D geographic simulation systems and two legacy GIS integration mechanisms into an integrated environment. The framework provides a set of 3D visual components required for the development of a new interactive system that can integrate legacy 2D GIS and legacy geographical simulators to make 3D geographic simulation systems. The visual component technology provides a set of 3D visual components required for the development of new interactive 3D visual geographic simulations integrated with GIS functions. In the proposed framework, constructing a new 3D geographic simulation system only requires the component integrators to combine the necessary 3D visual components. To support the integration of a legacy GIS with the simulation system, we also propose two fundamental integration mechanisms: view integration and query integration mechanisms. The view integration technology can integrate the GUI of a legacy 2D GIS on the surface of the 3D terrain used in a 3D visual geographical simulator and then dispatch every event on its surface to the original 2D GIS. The query integration technology can integrate the query function of a legacy 2D GIS by automatically converting each 3D simulation result to a corresponding regional query on a 2D GIS. As a result, our approach enabled us to construct 3D geographic simulation systems interactively, moreover, to integrate the GUI and the query function into a 3D simulation environment simply through the composition with their 3D display objects by direct manipulation on a computer screen. This framework also allows users to integrate a legacy GIS with a legacy geo-simulator that is independently developed and not assumed to integrate with it.

In this chapter we have proposed an integration technique for legacy geographic simulators whose I/O text file formats are open to the public. However, in a future, it will become necessary to propose a new integration technique for various other simulators that do not satisfy this condition. To cope with such integration it is necessary to provide different query components for different GIS APIs. The method of dynamic API slots may become necessary. Such a solution should provide a wizard system to help users to semi-automatically create the required slots from the API list of the legacy system.

REFERENCES

Alves, L. L., & Davis, C. A., Jr. (2006) *Interoperability through Web services: evaluating OGC standards in client development for spatial data infrastructures.* VIII Brazilian Symposium on GeoInformatics, 2006, INPE,193–208. ArcGIS.Retrieved from http://www.esri.com/products.html

GRASS (Geographic Resources Analysis Support System). Retrieved from http://grass.itc.it/

Jaboyedoff, M. & Labiouse. V. CONEFALL: a program for the quick preliminary estimation of the rock-fall potential of propagation zones,. *Computer & Geosciences.*

JCMA.(1988). *Protection Against Snow Handbook.*

Maeno, K. & Fukuda, M. (2000). *Avalanche and Snowstorm.*

Ohigashi, M., Guo, Z. S., & Tanaka, Y. (2006). *Integration of a 2D legacy GIS, legacy simulations, and legacy databases into a 3D geographic simulation,* SIGDOC '06: Proceedings of the 24th Annual Conference on Design of Communication, pp.149–156.

Ohigashi, M., & Tanaka, Y. (2005). *Shadows on 3D: Hosting 2D legacy applications into a 3D meme media environment.* In Leipziger Informatik-Tage 2005(LNI 72, pp. 401–410).

Okada, Y., & Tanaka, Y. (1995). IntelligentBox: A constructive visual software development system for interactive 3D graphic applications. *Proc. of Computer Animation, 95,* 114–125. ·

OpenGIS Standards and Specifications. Retrieved from http://www.opengeospatial.org/standards

Takatsuka, M., & Gahegan, M. (2002). GeoVISTA Studio: a codeless visual programming environment for geoscientific data analysis and visualization. *Computers & Geosciences, 28*(10), 1131–1144. doi:10.1016/S0098-3004(02)00031-6

Tanaka, Y. (2003). *Meme Media and Meme Market Architectures: Knowledge Media for Editing, Distributing, and Managing Intellectual Resources.* IEEE Press, John Wiley & Sons. doi:10.1002/047172307X

Upson, C., & Faulhaber, J. Thomas, Kamins, D., Laidlaw, D.H., Schlegel, D., Vroom, J., Gurwitz, R. & van Dam, A. (1989). The application visualization system: A computational environment for scientific visualization. *IEEE Computer Graphics and Applications, 9*(4), 30–42. doi:10.1109/38.31462

Section 2
Applications and Results

Chapter 5
A Web–Enabled, Mobile Intelligent Information Technology Architecture for On–Demand and Mass Customized Markets

M. Ghiassi
Santa Clara University, USA

C. Spera
Zipidy, Inc., USA

ABSTRACT

This chapter presents a web-enabled, intelligent agent-based information system model to support on-demand and mass customized markets. The authors present a distributed, real-time, Java-based, mobile information system that interfaces with firms' existing IT infrastructures, follows a build-to-order production strategy, and integrates order-entry with supply chain, manufacturing, and product delivery systems. The model provides end-to-end visibility across the entire operation and supply chain, allows for a collaborative and synchronized production system, and supports an event-based manufacturing environment. The system introduces four general purpose intelligent agents to support the entire on-demand and mass customization processes. The adoption of this approach by a semiconductor manufacturing firm resulted in reductions in product lead time (by half), buffer inventory

DOI: 10.4018/978-1-61520-851-7.ch005

(from five to two weeks), and manual transactions (by 80%). Application of this approach to a leading automotive manufacturer, using simulated data, resulted in a 51% total inventory reduction while increasing plant utilization by 30%. Adoption of this architecture by a pharmaceutical firm resulted in improving accuracy of trial completion estimates from 74% to 82% for clinical trials resulting in reduced trial cost overruns. These results verify that the successful adoption of this system can reduce inventory and logistics costs, improve delivery performance, increase manufacturing facilities utilization, and provide a higher overall profitability.

INTRODUCTION

The globalization of businesses and the infusion of information technology (IT) into every aspect of operations have introduced a strong demand for product variety and transformed business environments from a production-centric model to one that is information and customer-centric (Arjmand & Roach, 1999). Although the Internet has strengthened business with its convenience and 24x7global accessibility, it has also dramatically shifted the traditional business model to a new, competitive market space. People can now purchase anything, anywhere, at any time, and both product customization and customer requirements are increasing exponentially, making sales and inventory prediction a challenge. Meeting the wants and needs of such a heterogeneous customer population, in a global market, inevitably calls for product variety, while every efficiency-seeking supply chain prefers to process as few "flavors" as possible.

Mass customization seeks an economical resolution of this fundamental conflict. Taking mass production as a foil implies that a mass customized product should not cost end customers much more than a mass produced near-equivalent, and that the customization process should not create too much of a delay. We believe that this can be realized with consistency and at scale only with a *customer-centric production system*. This is one that enables an end-customer to configure (partially design) the product online and provides real-time visibility of the resulting order directly to the manufacturing floor and throughout the supply chain. In such a production system, businesses focus on their core competencies and outsource activities that are not essential to this core. Improvements in information technology infrastructures and worldwide acceptance of the internet have strengthened this transition. As a result, complex products in the market can be the result of collaborative efforts of many companies (Anderson & Lee, 1999). The auto industry is an excellent example of such a collaborative effort. A car can have over 10,000 parts, with multiple stages of production, many suppliers, high degree of product complexity, and high degree of customization. The manufacturing operation of such a business often requires a high production rate, time and space constraints and often long cycle time. High technology is another example. Fabrication-less firms that design new components are common. These firms now concentrate on their core business of designing a new component and outsource the manufacturing to specialized semiconductor and PC board manufacturing contractors. Transportation and logistics systems are additional examples in which the Internet and online commerce have facilitated rapid movements of products and material in a time-sensitive production environment. Pharmaceutical companies are yet another example in which trials for new drugs are often conducted globally and concurrently and can significantly benefit from an on-demand, real-time production control environment.

The participants in these markets include suppliers, retailers and transportation services providers. The efficient operation of such markets requires extensive collaboration among its many members.

There are several common themes that characterize these markets. The first theme is the time-sensitive nature of the demand in such markets. The order stream for these markets can change in a short period of time. For example, for the semiconductor manufacturing system described later in this chapter, the order stream can arrive multiple times per day creating a turbulent production environment requiring adjustments to production schedules. Similarly, transportation and delivery systems need to account for last minute changes in orders, cancellation of existing orders, addition of new orders, break downs in the actual transportation facilities and complications due to weather or traffic conditions, all within just a few hours (Dorer & Calisti, 2005). Most mass customized production environments are time-sensitive and therefore exhibit such behavior. Traditional production systems cannot efficiently address these needs.

The second theme associated with such markets is the complexity of the supply chain system. The auto industry is an example of such a production environment. The supply chain is often multilayered with complex arrangements. Supporting mass customization of products in these markets can have a major impact on inventory levels for the suppliers that are located upstream from the final production vendor. If timely demand data reflecting the latest change in final product is not available to all suppliers, the inventory bullwhip effect may require upstream suppliers to stock up on the wrong components. The coordination requirements for an efficient operation of such a system are often lacking in traditional production systems.

The third theme present in such markets is the adaptive requirements of such operations. Consider clinical trials for new drugs. The supply chain supporting such operations needs to adapt rapidly to reflect intermediate results from several ongoing clinical trials. As results become available, the supply chain must rapidly adapt itself to support and/or shift operations from one trial site to another and to offer complete visibility in real-time and on-demand.

These themes, associated with on-demand and mass customized markets, clearly introduce additional complexity into the production environment. For these markets, optimal production solutions tend to be order/demand driven, are sensitive to each order quantity, and should account for more frequent changes in order streams. Obtaining optimality in such a production environment requires continuous analysis in very short time intervals. Effective analysis in this environment requires visibility of the changing demand data to all participants in the production system in real-time. The firms participating in such a system often follow a short-term optimization approach to production problems that require coordination and collaborations among local decision makers. The decision making for this environment is often: decentralized and distributed; geographically dispersed; more data driven with less human intervention; benefits from a rule based automated negotiation system; attempts to reach local optimal solutions for the participating firms; and performs final coordination and adjustment of these solutions in a short time interval. In contrast, the traditional production models rely on a centralized decision making process that attempts to optimize a global, central production function representing the primary vendor, to address a longer term production system. We note that agent-based systems allow timely actions and provide optimal response when the rule structure – under which agents act – does not change. However when externalities – i.e. elements not modeled in the system – become effective and change the structure of the decision process, then human interaction becomes crucial to re-establish the optimality of the decision process.

For on-demand and mass customized production environments exhibiting these attributes, an agent-based information system solution can offer improved performance. We present three case studies that show how the implementation of such a system has improved the productivity and profitability for a semiconductor manufacturing company, an automotive firm, and a pharmaceutical company. Actual and simulated results show that for the semiconductor firm, the implementation of our model reduced product lead time by 50%, reduced buffer inventory from five to two weeks, and reduced manual transaction processing by 80%. For the automotive case, our results, using simulated data, show a total inventory reduction of 51%, and an increase in production facilities utilization rates by more than 30%. Results from adoption of this approach has improved accuracy of trial completion estimates from *74% to 82%* for clinical trials while reducing trial cost overruns. Other researchers report similar improvements in cost reduction (by 11.7%), reduced traveled kilometers (by 4.2%), and fewer trucks employed (by 25.5%) in a transportation system utilizing an agent-based transportation optimization system (Dorer & Calisi, 2005), and a 15% increase in revenue with improved profit margin from 2% to 4% in a logistics provider after adoption of an agent-based adaptive transportation network (Capgemini, 2004).

ON-DEMAND AND MASS CUSTOMIZATION BUSINESS ENVIRONMENT

The business environment for successful implementation of on-demand and mass customized markets, thus, requires the establishment of business alliances and partnerships with selected suppliers. Mass customized manufacturing systems need to support a *"demand–driven"* and *"make-to-order"* production system. Such a production system is often component-based and may involve many business partners, suppliers, and other companies that affect the delivery of products to customers (Gilmore & Pine, 2000). Outsourcing exacerbates the challenge of coordination and planning of any such production system. Supporting a mass customized production system, therefore, requires a supply chain paradigm capable of a great degree of synchronization throughout the entire supply chain, including the entire inventory system. In particular, the order and reorder replenishment inventory cycle under this model will be more frequent, involve smaller lot sizes, and require shorter delivery schedules.

Such a synchronized production process will necessitate demand, manufacturing and production information transparency and greater cooperation among the participating members, from the manufacturer to the primary and secondary suppliers (Ghiassi, 2001). Truly successful members of such a manufacturing environment must have stronger alliances and be willing to significantly improve their inter-firm communications. In addition, there is a need for an infrastructure that can:

- Reduce time-to-market for product development, enhancement, and customization.
- Provide end-to-end visibility along the entire supply chain.
- Directly tie order-entry and manufacturing planning systems to speed the availability of demand requirements and to react in real-time.
- Intelligently and selectively communicate with a manufacturer's strategic trading partners.
- Respond expediently to orders, changes in order configuration, and level of demand.
- Support an event-based supply chain management system in a collaborative environment.

Supporting such a production system requires a collaborative, adaptive, and synchronized supply chain management system that spans multiple firms, is event-driven, distributed, and can operate in real-time and across many computer platforms (Ghiassi & Spera, 2003$_a$). Such a synchronized supply chain operation no longer follows a linear model. This system must be a network-based operation that requires timely availability of information throughout the system in order to allow cooperative and synchronized flow of material, products, and information among all participants. The manufacturing environment for this system requires an operational structure and organization that can focus on building and maintaining the capacity to adapt quickly to a changing order stream while minimizing response time. Clearly, the decision making process in this environment needs to shift from a centralized to distributed mode. In this model, operational and strategic decisions may still be driven centrally; however, the responsibility to adapt to a volatile condition needs to be resolved locally. The effects of a response to such events, then, must be communicated to all relevant layers of the organization, including participating suppliers. Obviously, the relationship among the supply chain members of such a production system also must be altered to support this new business paradigm. Transitioning from mass production to mass customization is a complex, enterprise-wide process which affects external supply chain members, which are not typically controlled by the core company, and thus necessitating alliances and collaborations among all supply chain members.

ON-DEMAND AND MASS CUSTOMIZATION IT INFRASTRUCTURE

Implementing such a system would require reliance on an interoperable open system IT structure, a high degree of automation in the decision process, and integration of customers, products and production information across many participants with possibly heterogeneous IT infrastructures.

The technology infrastructure for an on-demand and mass customized production system requires a collaborative and adaptive supply chain management system that can account for the entire system - the customer, manufacturers, entire supply chain and the supporting market structure (Ghiassi & Spera, 2003_b). An effective infrastructure for such a vast domain requires an interoperable open system capable of operating in a multi-firm, heterogeneous IT infrastructure.

In this chapter, we present an IT framework and architecture to support on-demand and mass-customized production system. We report on prototype solutions that have helped firms achieve their mass-customized production strategies. We present an architecture that can manage production resources, perform negotiations, achieve supply chain information transparency, and monitor and manage processes. We use an intelligent agent technology that can tie together resources, parts and process knowledge, in single or multiple locations, to create an agile production system. The system defines *"brokers and infomediaries"* and uses an intelligent, mobile, agent-based trading system that can be utilized in an interactive mode that can react to job streams with customized orders while bringing together buyers and suppliers in an efficient production environment. We have developed scheduling algorithms to balance the "time" vs. "price" trade-off by examining the relations between manufacturers and their suppliers and subcontractors. A multi-agent technology is used to schedule, control and monitor manufacturing activities and facilitates real-time collaboration among design teams. Agents in this environment can provide information about the product development process, availability of resources, commitments to deliver tasks, and knowledge of expected product completion in a distributed platform. These mobile agents are used to reach across organizational boundaries to extract knowledge from resources in order to reconfigure, coordinate, and collaborate with other agents in solving enterprise problems. The agents can interface with a customer, a manufacturing resource, a database, or other agents anywhere in the network in seconds, enabling the supply chain system to continuously adapt to demand fluctuations and changing events. Agents in such an environment can facilitate a decentralized and bottom-up planning and decision making process.

Our IT architecture supports an easily accessible (web-based) order and production management system where customers can:

- Configure a product according to their preferences.
- Monitor progress and obtain status reports.
- Manage changes and gain overall visibility into production.

In this system the firms can:

- Execute and support a demand driven synchronized supply chain system.
- Select suppliers for non-strategic commodity components using mobile intelligent agents.
- Employ intelligent agent technology to support the human stakeholders for strategic sourcing in an expedient manner.

We describe a distributed, Java-based, event-driven system that uses mobile agent technologies over the Internet to monitor multiple production systems, sense exceptions as they occur and dispatch intelligent agents to analyze broken links and offer alternative solutions. The system is designed to improve the coordination and control of the total supply chain network, through the real-time optimization of material movement. This network encompasses all entities of the supply chain, and builds a demand recognition capability that is as close to the demand source as possible, and then uses this information to drive and synchronize the replenishment of all interim raw materials, components and products.

The availability of this system enables all participants to monitor, detect, predict, and intelligently resolve supply chain problems in real-time. Participants can obtain up-to-date, customized visibility into other members of the marketplace and can measure historical supply chain performance activities. This information can lead to a manufacturing operation that supports on-demand or *"make-to-order"* strategy and avoids inventory bloat. In a mature implementation, the supply chain operation can be transformed into a *"demand chain"* operation, in which inventory is reduced to its minimal level throughout the entire system.

OVERVIEW OF THE MODEL

By providing a common communication infrastructure along with intelligent agents and optimization algorithms, we offer a system for transforming static supply chains into dynamic, web-centric trading markets that are closely integrated with the manufacturer's systems. This system formulates the production problem as a set of distributed, decentralized, event-driven optimization sub-problems that can efficiently support an on-demand and mass customized production environment, which are often characterized by high demand variability, fixed capacity, time to market sensitivity, and/or complex supply chain network.

This approach models the supply chain problem as a hierarchical framework and extends it to support a synchronized production system. The framework presented in this chapter partitions the mass customization production environment into hierarchical levels of process, plan, and execution. The framework offers facilities for process monitoring and analysis, short and long term planning capabilities, and efficient, optimized execution of production opportunities. It also provides visibility throughout the system by allowing changes in orders to be communicated to all impacted participants. Each participant in turn reacts to these changes and broadcasts its locally optimized solutions. In the next level of the hierarchy, the local optimum solutions are coordinated and synchronized and discrepancies are broadcasted again to all affected parties. In the final decision making level of the hierarchy, automated and human assisted negotiating agents resolve all production conflicts in support of the final committed production. The responsiveness required for such highly synchronized production systems is significantly higher than those of non-synchronized systems. This requirement necessitates real-time collaboration among all supply chain members. The supporting IT infrastructure and applications presented in this model are able to cope with high demand variability, short product life cycles and tight collaboration and interactions with suppliers.

In this model, information about the entire supply chain system is visible to all authorized members, especially through any device that is Internet enabled. Our system allows the up-to-date demand data to drive the production system following a *"make-to-order"* production policy. In solving the production allocation sub-problems, the up-to-date demand data is used to monitor production allocation at various plants. The fluidity of the demand undoubtedly can create many exceptions to the centrally designed production plan. Decentralized decision-making can allow local players to alter execution plans to satisfy their constraints. To manage such scenarios, a system must be able to detect an exception or unplanned event, identify the players impacted by the exception and its resolution, and develop the models necessary to solve the local sub-problem and to resolve the exception. To be fully effective, such a decentralized decision-making environment requires real-time data running across an intelligent peer-to-peer infrastructure and integrated with contextual understanding of the local production sub-problems.

In the past years, many researchers have examined using "agent technology" to find solutions to problems arising in supporting mass-customized production. (Sundermeyer, 2001 and Wilke, 2002) present an agent-based, collaborative supply chain system for the automotive industry (DaimlerChrysler). These authors identify rapidly changing consumer demands, planning uncertainties, information flow delays, and sequential, batch oriented policies as elements of traditional production systems that contribute to an inefficient production environment. The authors offer an agent-based, web-centric, collaborative solution that integrates the entire supply chain and provides a more efficient production system. They report results from a simulation study which show that using a collaborative, distributed, agent-based supply network management system can reduce production and inventory oscillations, safety stock levels, and working capital. Similarly, (Dorer & Calisti, 2005) report on the integration of an agent-based system into a real-world IT architecture in order to solve and optimize transportation problems facing a major logistics provider. They note that "conventional systems for transportation optimization are limited in their ability to cope with the complexity, and especially with the dynamics, of global transportation business where plans have to be adjusted to new, changing conditions within shortest time frames."

In the following, we describe a Java based software system that uses intelligent agents to constitute a theoretical and practical basis for addressing mass customization markets.

Agent Taxonomy

We define a mobile intelligent agent to be an autonomous software program, capable of achieving goals defined by a set of rules, with learning and adaptive capabilities that are loosely or tightly coupled with other peers. Software agents are often designed to perform a task or activity on behalf of the user and without constant human intervention (Ma, 1999; Adam et al., 1999).

Existing literature lists applications for intelligent agents in a wide array of electronic businesses, including retailing, purchasing, and automated negotiation (Jain et al., 1999; Ma, 1999; Maes et al., 1999; Sandholm, 1999). These software tools are used as *mediators* that act on behalf of their users. Specifically, these agents perform repetitive and predictable actions, can run continuously without human intervention and are often stationary.

The authors in (Singh et al., 2005) present an agent-based model that uses E-marketplaces and infomediaries to register suppliers and consumers of an E-supply chain. This system facilitates purchasing of material by collecting demands from the participants, then locating and matching this demand with suppliers. The proposed system develops supplier profiles based on a satisfaction survey of past performances. When extended to multiple E-marketplaces, a global balancing of supply and demand becomes viable. This system, however, does not include the actual manufacturing operations and relies heavily on the existence of E-marketplaces, infomediaries, and the willingness of all participants to register their demands, capacity and their services.

Researchers have also applied intelligent agent technology to manufacturing and production systems (Kalakota et al., 1998), and mass customized production environments (Baker et al., 1999). Others have used agent technology to support what they have termed *"adaptive virtual enterprises"* (Pancerella & Berry, 1999). They have used mobile agents to extend across organizational boundaries. In their model, these agents extract knowledge from resources in order to reconfigure, coordinate, and collaborate with other agents in solving enterprise problems.

There are many mobile agent systems that provide a platform for agent applications; most of these systems are Java-based. Some examples include "Aglets" from IBM, "Concordia" from Mitsubishi, and "Voyager" from ObjectSpace (Lang & Oshima, 1998).

We have applied agent technology to on-demand and mass customized production problems. We use mobile software agents to support a distributed decision-making process. A mobile agent, unlike a stationary agent, is not bound to one execution environment. A mobile agent can transport itself and its supporting data to other execution environments. It can then begin execution or use data from both sites to perform its tasks. The mobility also allows the agent to interact with other agents or traditional software systems on the new site. Mobile agents additionally offer the opportunity for execution support across heterogeneous computing environments. They can reconfigure themselves to interface with destination environment's libraries, database systems, and other computing components to perform their tasks. Mobile agents introduce a new paradigm to distributed computing. In this paradigm, any host computer in the network can benefit from the *"know-how"*, resources, and processors throughout the network.

We introduce an architecture that deploys mobile agents in the value chain to streamline the efficiency and performance of the entire network under various constraints of materials and time. The agents perform the following primary functions:

1. Distribute and collect data at the right time to process and analyze.
2. Coordinate inter-enterprise business processes and propose the best response to avoid disruptions throughout the supply chain.
3. Tactically and strategically adjust the supply network in an optimal and timely manner to changes in market conditions.
4. Assist the decision-makers in their learning processes.

The four functionalities (monitoring, analyzing, acting, and coordinating) characterize the first dimension of our agent taxonomy, the second being given by the role that each agent assumes in the value chain. We have identified three types of roles:

1. Consumer Assistant.
2. Demand Management.
3. Supply and Resource Management.

The agents performing these roles are mobile and ubiquitous. These agents address the needs of end users, manage product demands, and coordinate supply and resource management continuously. The time-sensitive nature of an on-demand production environment requires the decisions to be made expediently. The mobility of the agents allows the communication between them to occur in real-time. For instance, consider the auto industry case discussed in this chapter. The consumer assistant agent is used by the end user to define product features, place an order, check order processing, and monitor production status of the product all the way through actual delivery. Similarly, in a transportation/package delivery system, the consumer assistant agent can be used to even alter the actual delivery location of a package as the recipient relocates before the final routing of the scheduled delivery of the product.

The demand and supply management agents can also perform their roles in real-time and assist decision makers in resolving conflicts and coordinating operations. In particular, conflict resolutions caused by supply or capacity shortages can be handled more expediently. The mobility of the agents and their real-time connectivity within the production system and with the actual end user is utilized to alter the production schedule and inventory levels. These agents can be pre-programmed to handle some decisions automatically to conduct some negotiations on behalf of their clients. For example, when a product feature is in short supply, the demand management agent can notify the consumer assistant agent of possible delays in delivery and to offer alternative resolutions. At the same time, this agent can negotiate with supply management agents to locate new sourcing of components that are hindering timely production of the final product. Additionally, the mobility of the agents allows managers and consumers to participate in decision making in real-time, using the Internet or even hand-held devices. The technology used to implement these agents and their communication protocols are presented in next section.

The complete Functionality versus Role determining our agent taxonomy is reported below. Agent goals are reported in the corresponding cell.

The entire system uses an event-based architecture (Figure 1). An event in this system is defined as actionable information (an object) that appears as a message in the system. The monitoring agents are registered to listen to certain messages. These messages are interpreted and processed either synchronously (i.e., as soon as they arrive), or asynchronously (pending the agent's reaching of some pre-defined

Table 1. Agent taxonomy and functionality

Functionality vs. Role	Consumer Assistant	Demand Management	Supply & Resource Management
Monitoring	Detect variations of any relevant (for the consumer) product features.	Detect key demand variable changes at product model and location level.	Detect key supply variable changes or resource constraints at product model and location level.
Coordinating	Bring order and semantic structure to the collection of demand and supply events gathered from multiple sources by the mobile assistant.	Bring order and semantic structure to the responses for the mix of demand events that are firing synchronously from multiple sources.	Bring order and semantic structure to the responses for the mix of supply events that are firing synchronously from multiple sources.
Analyzing	Rationalize the follow on actions for comparative analysis based on features and customers' preferences.	Rationalize the follow on actions from excess inventory projections, sub-optimal minimum inventory levels, networked replenishment requirements and multiple shipping alternatives and constraints.	Rationalize the follow on actions from excess/shortage inventory projections, suboptimal minimum inventory levels, networked replenishment requirements and multiple assembling shipping alternatives and production constraints.
Acting	Adjust customers' decisions as their preference changes.	Adjust projected demand through mix of techniques: Optimize base parameters, modify elasticity, adjust for cannibalization and influence demand through dynamic pricing.	Adjust projected supply and production rates through mix of techniques: Optimize base parameters, modify elasticity, adjust price and optimize supply through tight collaboration.

state). An event bus is introduced as a building block that receives, sends and processes messages as objects. The event bus offers an interface that is visible to any component of the system that wishes to send and/or receive events (Figure 1).

The agents presented in this architecture behave dynamically, are rule-based, mobile and respond to events. The behavior of the agents can be in reaction to both internal and external events. For instance, consider an inventory management scenario; the "analyze" and "act" agents can use parameters defined by other agents (monitoring and/or coordinating agents) to determine inventory replenishment policies that reflect up-to-date information about market conditions or even macroeconomic indicators, in addition to specific product parameters such as available sources, lead time information, the supplier's recent behavior profile, and the latest speed of inventory deliveries. The supporting agents (monitoring and coordinating agents) can monitor internal and external events and processes to acquire and coordinate the necessary data that allows the analyzing and acting agents to manage inventory levels dynamically rather than the traditional static models that use predetermined inventory replenishment parameters.

Finally, in production environments for which E-marketplaces exist, this architecture allows the agents to seamlessly interface with these markets to execute procurement activities. When E-marketplaces do not exist, the agents can additionally perform market-making activities, such as identifying candidate suppliers, communicating requirements, and soliciting quotations.

Figure 1. An agent-based architecture for mass customization

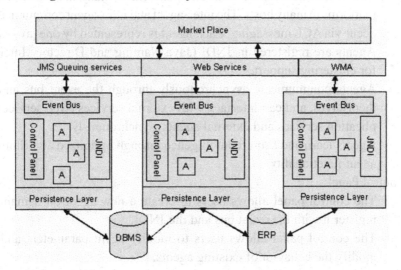

AGENT SERVICE ARCHITECTURE
FOR MASS CUSTOMIZATION

We present an architectural design which is agent-based, supports mass customization, and uses a "cluster model" representation as depicted in Figure 1. This architecture supports the firm's IT infrastructure, and interfaces with existing DBMS, ERP, and other manufacturing support database systems. The architecture uses existing IT networking systems to establish connectivity across participating firms in the marketplace. Clusters of agents can support multiple product lines and/or even different features of a product.

The main features of the above design are:

- Agents Technology and Architecture:
  - Agents are developed using a framework based on the ABLE (Agent Building and Learning Environment from IBM) (Bigus et al., 2002) and JADE-LEAP(Java Agent Development Framework and its extension Light Extensible Agent Platform) (Bellifemine et al., 2003, Bergenti & Poggi, 2001) platforms. The multi-agent system introduced in this architecture uses the ACL language (Agent Communication Language) (ACL, 2006) which complies with FIPA (Foundation for Intelligent Physical Agents) specifications. The architecture employed is distributed, and supports multiple hosts and processes, including mobile systems. Each running instance of the JADE runtime environment is called a "container." A container can include multiple agents (Figure 2). A set of active containers is called a JADE platform which can be distributed across several hosts. The distribution can be from one platform to many hosts and/or many platforms to many hosts. The inter-agent and intra-agent communications occur via ACL messaging. Each agent is represented by one java thread.
  - Agents are registered in JNDI (Java Naming and Directory Interface) for clustering support.
  - Agents communicate asynchronously through the event bus amongst themselves, and can interface with external services (web services, application services and external agents) synchronously.
  - Agents learn and acquire intelligence through optimized algorithms per agent functionality.
- Control Panel:
  - The control panel allows users to create a new agent on demand and register it with the event bus and the JNDI.
  - The control panel allows users to modify agent parameters and thus modify the behavior of existing agents.

- Communication Interface:
  - ◦ The event bus structure is introduced and developed to facilitate fast internal communications among agents.
  - ◦ The JMS (Java Message Services) services are introduced to facilitate communications among agents and external applications including web services interface, WMA (Windows Media Audio) services, agents from other applications, external users and the web environment at large.
- Persistence Layer:
  - ◦ The persistence layer assists agents in interfacing with existing databases and data retrieval systems.

These features offer the necessary elements for supporting visibility across the entire supply chain and allowing the establishment of collaborative efforts in support of a demand driven, mass customized production system. To illustrate these concepts, consider an agent-based system implementation for a manufacturing environment. Figure 2 presents the implementation of this technology for a hypothetical manufacturing system. In this system, agents are implemented as Java container classes that perform the Monitoring, Coordinating, Analyzing and Acting functionalities. The server side of Figure 2 lists five agent containers. The client side shows how users can use mobile phones, PDAs and similar devices to gain access to the system. In Figure 2, the "I/O Container" offers monitoring agents that communicate with data entry systems and provide interface capabilities with existing DBMS, ERPs, and manufacturing databases. Agents from this container communicate and exchange information with the central coordinating agents. Similarly, the "Inference Container," an analyzing agent, stores information about the manufacturing operation for all possible product configurations. It continuously analyzes production schedules, capabilities, and equipment capacities. It also analyzes manufacturing requirements based on production status and the order stream information for new orders to form a batch and to hold them until notified by another agent (the optimizing agent) to release its information. The communications among these agents is in a synchronized mode. The "Optimizing Container" is an acting agent that is invoked upon receiving a new batch of orders from the agents of the "Inference Container." These agents optimize the processing of the orders. The optimization process includes (a) scheduling optimization using tabu search and genetic algorithms, (b) resource planning using linear and integer programming, and (c) inventory optimization using stochastic optimization methods. The "Back-end Splits Container" serves as the interface channel to the client side. The agents in this container receive and record orders from external agents. The orders are filtered and organized according to their manufacturing requirements and are aggregated and presented to the main container for further processing and optimization. The customers and/or external agents can use

Figure 2. An agent-based architecture for a manufacturing system

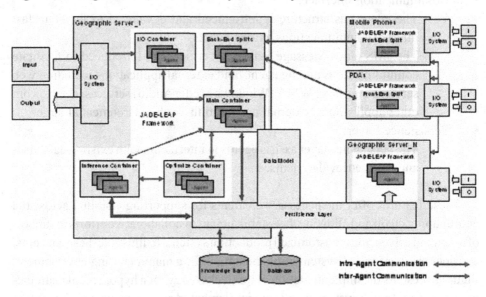

this interface to check the status of their orders. Finally, the "Main Container" serves as the coordinating agent. It interfaces with all other agents, provides supervisory functions to all agents, performs synchronization among processes, and serves as conflict resolution authority among agents. In this architecture, a persistence layer is provided for interfacing with the external database and data retrieval systems. The entire system is Java based and uses the agent technology framework developed by IBM (the "ABLE" technology) (Bigus et al., 2002) and JADE-LEAP framework from the open source software (Bellifemine et al., 2003; Bergenti & Poggi, 2001) and the ACL messaging language. These frameworks are extended and modified to support the mobile technologies that will allow users access to the system via mobile phones, PDAs, and any web-enabled device or interface (Moreno et al., 2005).

The system presented supports the decentralized, distributed decision making model discussed earlier. It is based on a distributed, web-centric, client server architecture in which the server resides at the manufacturing (primary) vendor and the client operates at each supplier site. The clients' implementations are lightly integrated into the suppliers' existing IT architectures. The web-centric nature of the system ensures accessibility across the participating members as depicted in Figure 2. The consistency of the system is ensured by the choice of the communications and the agent frameworks used in this implementation. The use of standard protocols such as XML and the collaborative nature of the environment require each participant to either directly comply with these protocols, or provide converters and translators in support of the communication systems. An implementation of such system may include many geographical servers at various locations. Client installations can also be located at geographically and/or organizationally dispersed sites. Real-time production and consumption data is gathered from the entire supply chain system and distributed throughout the system for decision making (Figure 2).

CASE STUDIES

In this section we will discuss case studies that report on adoption and implementation of our approach by three companies that produce on-demand or mass customized products. The first case study reports on adoption of this system in a semiconductor manufacturing environment, the second case study presents our experience with implementation of the system in the automotive industry, and the third case study reports use of the system by a pharmaceutical company.

The ST Microelectronics System

The first case presents a semiconductor manufacturing firm (STM) that has adopted and implemented our software system. STM is the fourth largest semiconductor company in the world with revenue in excess of eight billion dollars. A large part of this revenue comes from integrated circuits that are heavily customized to STM's customer specifics.

STM is the primary supplier of assembled chip sets to a number of mobile telephone providers. The mobile telephone companies offer a mass customized product line with multiple features (GPS, Camera, and Phone capabilities). There are a number of valid product configurations for consumers to choose. Orders from the phone companies to STM for the various chip sets often arrive daily or even twice per day. STM's production system needs to respond to demands on daily or even shift by shift basis. The order/reorder processing system, defined by the demand at STM centers, requires agile manufacturing facilities capable of supporting a demand-driven supply chain system in real-time. The architecture described here, and its implementation at STM enables the company to operate and manage a manufacturing system far more efficiently than older, batch driven, build-to-forecast alternatives. In July of 2000, STM adopted our software for their mass customized production system. The server side of the software system was installed at STM manufacturing facilities and the clients' side at customers (the telephone manufacturers) and STM suppliers. This implementation has enabled STM to develop collaborative programs with its top customers and has seen notable progress in its delivery schedule, lead time, inventory management, and profit margins.

An important requirement of the project was the ability of STM to connect its IT infrastructure to its customers' existing installed IT systems using mobile intelligent agents. Our software system, sitting on top of STM's existing planning platform, detects the RosettaNet (RosettaNet, 1998) and XML messages, and provides visibility into different inventory scenarios, such as what parts to build and where to hold inventory to meet the highly customized demand. The system offers a set of agent-based coordination tools for extracting and transmitting data across the entire IT infrastructure. This strategy has offered STM a proactive approach for supporting its mass customization strategy. It has allowed STM to connect its long-range plans with short term execution and to optimize the inventory levels and production schedules in order to quickly build the integrated circuits that meet its customers' demands.

STM supplies IC boards (assembled chip sets) to several mobile phone providers. The boards need to be customized according to each customer specification. The challenges facing STM in supporting their customers are to:

- Develop a long-term planning framework for process and systems improvements.
- Implement new demand planning, E-commerce communications, capacity planning, and efficient supply chain execution.
- Roll out E-commerce with supply chain partners, perform end-to-end supply chain planning, and implement an effective available-to-production (ATP) capability.
- Continue to follow a build-to-forecast (BTF) policy in wafer fabrication and probe to maintain a pre-defined level of inventory in the die bank.
- Implement a build-to-order (BTO) policy in the assembly and test phase of the IC manufacturing.
- Develop a financial model to trade-off inventory, manufacturing, and supply chain costs with revenue potentials.

STM adopted the agent-based adaptive supply chain software system described earlier to achieve these objectives. The system is presented in Figure 3 and offers a collaborative supply chain network, supports adaptive demand synchronization and adjustment, provides an adaptive inventory optimization and replenishment policy, and optimizes order, material and flow management systems. In Figure 3 the event management system models supply networks, monitors network input, and triggers events. The agents in the system provide demand synchronization, network inventory optimization, multi-echelon inventory replenishment, delivery and routing planning, and coordination of the final decision resolution. Each of these components includes multiple intelligent agents that perform the monitoring, coordinating, analyzing, and acting functions described earlier. The embedded decision support tools of the system offer performance visibility of suppliers through collection of rankings and metrics, and provides a library of optimization algorithms and learning models.

In Table 2 we provide a comparison of the demand management activities of STM under both the traditional approach and the new agent-based adaptive approach.

Similarly, Table 3 presents the traditional and the new approach for inventory optimization module.

The adaptive replenishment collaboration process, its traditional implementation, and its new implementation are presented in Table 4.

Finally, the routing process used to manage order and reordering of the IC boards, material flow, WIP, and movement of supplies throughout the supply chain and manufacturing plants are optimized to ensure timely availability of supplies and fulfillment and delivery of customer orders. Table 5 presents the new routing processes employed and compares it with the traditional approach used by STM.

Implementation of the agent-based adaptive supply chain management system by STM has resulted in supply chain simplification, logistic process and provider improvements, and better delivery performance. Table 6 summarizes these improvements.

The agent-based system presented offers an effective infrastructure that enables and encourages updated demand data to be distributed among members of the production environment on daily or even shift-by-shift bases. In the traditional system, demand data was often only updated weekly. Clearly, accurate information offered by our solution allows decision makers to optimize their operations throughout the system. The distributed nature of this system allows STM to validate orders for

Figure 3. STM adaptive supply chain system

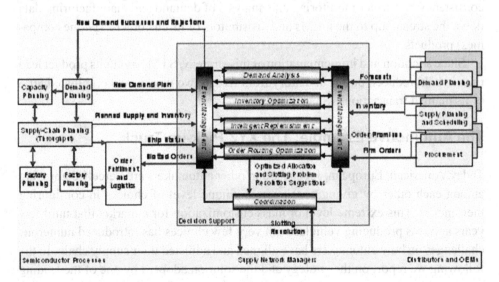

Table 2. Demand management activities for STM

Traditional Approach	Agent-Based Demand Management Approach
Forecast sharing is not traditional, but if occurs, follows a passive process like the following: 1. Semiconductor supplier receives forecasts and firm orders from Distributor and OEM on a weekly/daily basis by ship-to location and SKU. 2. Preprocess data to adjust for standard customer request dates, and account for uncertainty. 3. New forecast and firm order data are updated in demand planning system. 4. Supply chain planners use new demand data to reevaluate and adjust production plans.	Agent-based adaptive solution is driven by demand changes that impact as far upstream the supply network as possible. 1. Semiconductor supplier receives forecast or actual sales data from Distributors and OEMs on a daily/weekly basis. This will depend on cycle for forecast updates. If actual sales are given, then forecast from Distributor and OEM is also provided as it changes. 2. Semiconductor supplier receives changes to firm orders from OEMs and Distributors on a daily basis 3. Event management system triggers a "New Demand" event whenever a new forecast or firm order is received into the system. 4. MONITOR agents are listening for any demand event and will apply the appropriate business rules to adjust the input streams and trigger the required ANALYZE agents to check for any trending anomalies. 5. ANALYZE agents perform the following actions: a. ANALYZE "Order Synchronize" is designed to detect inconsistencies with transition from forecasted to firm orders. b. ANALYZE "Volatility" is designed to check for excessive volatility between successive forecasts. c. ANALYZE "Forecast Error" is designed to check for significant error between forecast and semiconductor shipments. d. ANALYZE "POS Sales" is designed to check for significant error between customer forecast and daily/weekly sales from source location in supply network. In this case that is the OEM's and Distributor's. 6. ANALYZE agents will coordinate with ACT agents to engage demand synchronization actions a. ACT "Rationalize Error" agents deduce root cause actions from analysis results. b. ACT "Optimize Parameters" agents adjust forecasting model parameters to minimize forecast error. c. ACT "Forecast" agents create and recommend new forecasts.

consistency by further monitoring and analysis of demand and manufacturing data down the stream, up to the OEMs and distributors of its customers' (phone companies) products.

Since adoption and implementation of this strategy, STM has cut its product lead time in half, reduced buffer inventory from five to two weeks, and eliminated 80% of its manual transactions (Shah, 2002).

The Automotive Example: The XYZ Pick-up Truck

Today, American, European, Japanese and other automakers are fiercely competing among each other by giving consumers a unique level of choices in configuring their model. This extreme level of mass customization for a market that until few years ago was producing vehicles with very few choices has introduced numerous challenges on how automakers have aligned and adjusted their supply chain. In the following we report on the strategy and the solution adopted by one of the leading

Table 3. Inventory management activities for STM

Traditional Approach	Agent-Based Inventory Management Approach
1. Inventory performance is reviewed on a periodic basis. 2. Viewed from a single enterprise perspective. 3. Review of safety stock levels based on expected demand and variability, general service level targets, lead-times, lead-time variability.	1. Inventory management is driven from a network perspective. 2. Event management monitors demand trending, demand error trend, lead time trending, supply error trending, inventory level trend and service level performance. If there is a threshold violation, an event is created. 3. MONITOR agents deduce the semantic value of the mix of events and will trigger the appropriate ANALYZE agents. 4. The ANALYZE agents will focus on the following: a. ANALYZE "Stock Up" agents deduce where and why average inventory is increasing. b. ANALYZE "Stock Out" agents deduce where and why stock-outs are excessive. c. ANALYZE "Min Buffer" agents compute the minimum for all key buffers in network. 5. ANALYZE agents will coordinate with ACT agents to engage inventory optimization actions. a. ACT "Balance Network" agents will be used to adjust inventory positions and levels via ACT "Replenishment" agents to adjust for both inventory shortage and excess scenarios. b. ACT "Set Level" agents make the appropriate safety stock parameter adjustments at all buffers.

Table 4. Replenishment management activities for STM

Traditional Approach	Agent-Based Replenishment Approach
1. Long-term forecasts are created by customers for up to 3 months lead-time. 2. Forecast is frozen and used to negotiate for capacity from Semiconductor company. 3. Semiconductor company incurs significant manual process costs to continually match capacity to expected customer demand. 4. Semiconductor company is required to keep high levels of inventory to protect against high variability of demand. 5. Customers replenish inventory by continually placing orders with Semiconductor company.	1. Updated demand plan is provided for target replenishment customers on a daily basis. 2. Event management system monitors the demand plan changes and inventory buffer changes. If a threshold limit is violated an event is created. 3. MONITOR agents capture such events and engage the appropriate ANALYZE agent. 4. The ANALYZE agents are of the following two types: a. ANALYZE "Buffer" agents compute the threshold values for all of the demand buffers for a new demand plan. b. ANALYZE "Shortage" agents evaluate the shortage situation when inventory is low. 5. ACT agents optimize replenishment over a targeted horizon in order to minimize costs and realize targeted service levels established by Semiconductor supplier and all OEM/Distributor customers. a. ACT "Replenishment" agents create an optimized (min cost flow) replenishment plan for all items over supply/demand map and within targeted plan horizon. b. ACT "Shipment" agents coordinate with "Replenishment" agents to create and trigger shipments, with the goal of minimizing shipment costs over target shipping horizon.

car manufacturers in addressing the challenges related to customization of one of the components of the pickup truck: the engine block.

Table 5. Order routing process management activities for STM

Traditional "Commit" Approach	Agent-Based Routing Optimization
Whereas replenishment is used to support the indirect sales process, the "Order Commit" process supports direct sales. 1. Orders are entered and booked with a temporary Scheduled Ship Date and are localized in multiple offices. 2. Within 24 hours the centralized Sales Planning team determines the initial commit date. 3. Sales orders are continuously revisited to bring the Schedule Date closer to the Customer Request Date. 4. Management of sales order rescheduling is usually very manual, with limited ability for managing changes and exceptions.	Adaptive Order Routing dynamically adjusts the slotting of orders to fulfillment routes that best meet the sales, service level and supply chain cost goals across a network. 1. Event management system is designed to monitor, new orders, inventory, customer request date changes, goods in transit. Significant changes trigger events. 2. MONITOR agents recognize such events and trigger the appropriate ANALYZE agents. 3. ANALYZE agents interpret changes and recommend the best actions: a. ANALYZE "Order" agents use order prioritization and current supply/demand state to correct order slotting. b. ANALYZE "Supply" agents use change prioritization and current supply/demand state to correct order slotting response. 4. ACT agents are engaged by ANALYZE agents to continuously drive order schedule dates to the customer request date: a. ACT "Simple Slotting" uses heuristics to slot or change an order to respond to a critical supply event. b. ACT "Allocation Optimization" optimizes order slotting, given the user selectable weightings for sales, service levels and cost or profit goals subject to available material and capacity constraints.

Table 6. Overall improvements for STM manufacturing processes

Process	Results
Supply Chain Simplification	1. Non-value-added movement of wafers or packaged part is reduced. 2. Redefined the testing process to increase offshore testing. 3. Reduced end-to-end cycle time by 8 to 10 days.
Logistic Improvements	1. Identified root cause of long transit between Asia and the US. 2. Changed sourcing activities from multiple freight forwards to single 3PL (third party logistic providers). 3. Reduced inter-company door-to-door cycle times from 7 days to 2 days. 4. Reduced total logistic costs by $2M/year.
Delivery Performance	1. Identified the root causes of the poor delivery performance. 2. Used inventory monitoring and optimization for allocating supply in capacity-constrained environments. 3. Improved delivery performance to first commit by more than 35% within five months on pilot product line.

This customization introduces a high degree of variability in the cylinder machining operation at Engine Plant A, the coating process at the Coating Plant B, and the block casting process at the Casting Plant C. The mass customization process can often result in excessive inventory, which is not tolerable financially.

The objectives of the automaker were:

Figure 4. Supply chain model from Plant B to Plant A

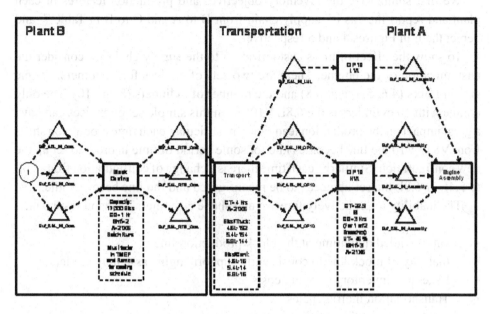

1. To increase the responsiveness to high customized demand.
2. To reduce the inventory level in the supply chain.
3. To improve control of managing the overall material flow to the target performance levels.

Table 7. Plant inventory objectives and production features

Location	Inventory Objectives	Production Features
Plant A	1. Supply material needs for engine assembly, which is driven by end demand needs. 2. Buffer against short supply from Plant B for the very near-term JIT windows.	1. Unstable machine capability. 2. Low schedule stability.
Plant B	1. Supply scheduled material needs (JIT schedule) at Plant A. 2. Supply unexpected material needs at Plant A, which may be caused by end demand shift, high scrap rate or material consumption, overtime production, etc. 3. Buffer against short supply from Plant C, which may be caused by high changeover rate, unexpected machine downtime at Plant C, etc.	1. Batch production. 2. High demand uncertainty from Plant A. 3. High supply uncertainty from Plant C.
Plant C	1. Supply scheduled material needs (JIT schedule) at Plant A. 2. Buffer against short material supply from internal or external suppliers.	1. Long changeover time. 2. Batch production. 3. Inflexible product switch.

We first summarize the inventory objectives and production features of each plant and report the "as is" supply chain from B to A and C to B in Table 7, and depict them in Figures 4 and 5 respectively.

To show the effect of mass customization to the supply chain we consider the customization of the engine. There are two sets of choices for customers: engine size in Liters (4.6, 5.4, and 6.8) and the number of cylinders (8 and 10). The only engine with 10 cylinders is the 6.8L V10. Even this simple set of choices can have a great impact on the production lead time. In particular, each time production shifts from V8 to V10 the line becomes idle for some period of time in order to set up the new configuration. Similarly, each time there is a change of configuration from 4.6L to 5.4L or 6.8L the set up needs to be reconfigured and the line becomes idle.

The inability to proactively forecast and shape customers' demand results in:

- Unscheduled downtime at the block production line
- Inability of block line to consistently support engine assembly at Plant A
- Excessive inventory carrying costs
- Transportation inefficiencies
- Unplanned overtime at all the plants
- Scheduling instability

To support this degree of mass customization, we have applied the "agent-based adaptive supply chain model" presented in this chapter to the manufacturing processes at the three plants. Since the auto industry's supply chain is complex and

Figure 5. Supply chain model from Plant C to Plant B

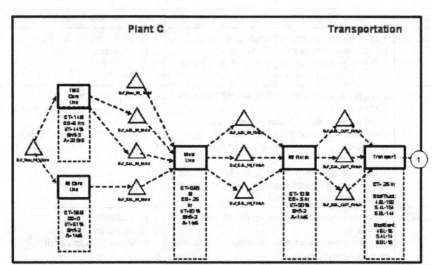

often includes many tiers, the agent-based solution provided in this model can make changes in the demand data to be simultaneously visible throughout the system. The propagation of this up-to-date information will allow production and inventory level adjustments for all participants, including the entire supply chain members. This model minimizes downtime, reduces inventory throughout the production system, and offers a more efficient transportation system while achieving a more stable scheduling and delivering option. This model is presented in Figure 6.

There are seven components of this adaptive model:

1. **The Event Management:** The Event Management Framework is a foundational capability of the Adaptive Supply Chain solution. Its primary purpose is to monitor events and orchestrate the adaptive response to the significant event changes that occur in the supply chain. An event is any supply chain variable that represents some key dynamic in the operation of the supply chain process, e.g. demand or inventory level. Throughout the supply chain a change in an event can trigger one of two possible paths. If the change is considered within the normal variability, it will trigger the Changeover Optimization Engine, Pull Replenishment Engine or both. If the change is outside a preset tolerance limit it will trigger an exception and notify the appropriate user.

2 – 3. **Optimal Changeover Sequence and Target Inventory:** The Optimal Changeover and Target Inventory (OCTI) is an intelligent engine that will calculate both the optimal sequence of product runs and target inventory buffer levels for any series of product changeover constrained operations in the supply

Figure 6. The adaptive supply chain model for engine assembly

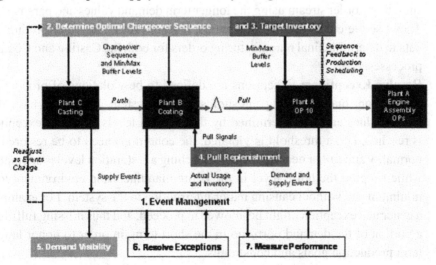

chain. The engine uses a mixed integer programming model to minimize the total supply chain costs subject to demand, inventory, and transportation and production constraints. The OCTI engine is used to calculate both the optimal block sequence for each of the supply chain operations and adjust the associated min/max buffer levels. The supply chain system uses a push/pull control strategy for coordinating the material flow, with a pull replenishment buffer established at the ready to ship buffer in Coating. The OCTI results are used as input to both Casting and Coating stages to drive the build schedules that are used to push the engine blocks through Coating to the pull buffer. The min and max levels of the interim buffers are adjusted as needed. On the Plant A OP 10 side, the OCTI results are used as input to the OP 10 pull scheduling process to develop production runs that best support the actual engine assembly usage and the calculated optimal block sequence. When the event of the OP 10 input buffers reaches the reorder levels, it will trigger the Pull Replenishment engine to pull in blocks from the Coating replenishment buffer

4. **Pull Replenishment:** The Pull Replenishment is an intelligent replenishment engine designed to trigger and control the "Pull" replenishment from any two entities in the supply chain. It also has a look-ahead capability, driven by forecasted demand that will assess the synchronization viability of the source supply. Plant A supply chain uses the Pull Replenishment engine to coordinate the pull signals between the OP 10 input buffer and the Coating ready to ship buffer.

5. **Demand Visibility:** The demand forecasting module offers intelligent agents that are invoked by the event management component. These agents use the longer term demand values and parameters as guidelines and receive up-to-date demand information from the actual customer base. The agents revise and smooth the order stream using the longer term demand values and parameters. They use the current production status, buffer values, and other production data to determine final manufacturing orders for both the Casting and Coating processes.

6. **Resolve Exceptions:** Exceptions are defined to be violations of production values from manufacturing thresholds. In this system, thresholds have dynamic values and are determined by the demand levels. Once an exception is reached, i.e., a threshold is violated, the conditions need to be restored to normality and full or near optimality. Reaching a restoration level is attempted while keeping the noise level in the entire manufacturing environment to a minimum and without causing major interruption to the system. For example, a generated exception might be allowed to proceed, and thus missing fulfilling a portion of the demand portfolio in the short term, in order to honor longer term production goals and constraints.

7. **Measure Performance:** This module uses intelligent agents to monitor key performances of the system through the event management component. It can measure performance of any event, both internal and external, by collecting statistics dynamically. Examples of internal events include inventory buffer levels, number of changeovers, production line throughput, and total inventory in the pipeline. Similarly, customer satisfaction and supplier performance, external events, can also be monitored and measured by this module.

Implementation of this system has used several features of the model, described in this chapter, in the engine manufacturing process. The data requirement of the system necessitated an information technology infrastructure based on the agent technology for decision making, JDBC for data storage, and XML for interfacing and data access. The concept of synchronization was used to ensure sequencing of the steps. The system allowed for interaction with auto dealers, partners, and suppliers. This visibility brought demand information and fluctuation to the manufacturing floor and broadcasted manufacturing status, alerts, and exceptions to the affected targets. Finally, a graphical user interface was produced to allow authorized users to view, input, or edit the entire system information.

Prior to the implementation of the system, a simulation model was developed to assess the effectiveness of the proposed system and compare its performance to the existing one. The objectives of the simulation were to measure inventory levels, changeover time, and utilization of the manufacturing facilities for given demand values. The demand information represented a dynamic stream of customized orders and reorders recorded daily over a 90 day period. The objective function used represented total production costs while allowing for switching among the different configurations. The constraint set included the various buffer limitations for inventory, changeover capacity and its opportunity cost, maximum throughput capacity, and equipment availability and maintenance constraints. The results of the simulation showed improved performance as measured by the two key indices (inventory levels and utilization rates) for the three plants. Table 8 shows that total inventory level for the system was reduced from 27,000 units to 13,283 units (a 51% reduction). The utilization rate for plant A increased from 60% to 90% and the combined utilization rate for plants B and C was improved from 41% to 61%. These improvements have increased the automaker's responsiveness and its competitive edge in meeting customers' demand.

The Pharmaceutical Company Example Clinical Trials

Development of a new drug is a complex process that is difficult to manage, and includes a lengthy cycle lasting often years or even decades. These projects have

Table 8. Simulation results for the engine manufacturing plant

Models	Total Inventory	Utilization (Plant A)	Utilization (Plants B & C)
Existing System	27,000	60%	41%
Proposed System	13,283	90%	61%

several variables, many stakeholders with differing interests, and are closely scrutinized because of the urgent need to bring new treatments to market. Study managers and their teams try to control a process that is largely outside of their sphere of influence and scope of control.

A typical drug development cycle begins with laboratory research and animal experimentation (pre-clinical phase) and it is followed by five testing phases. Phase zero trials are also known as the "human micro-dosing studies" and are designed to speed up the development of promising drugs. Phase one of the trials usually involves few volunteers (less than 50). Phase two of testing involves larger numbers of volunteer patients with advanced diseases that might benefit from such a new treatment. This is often affiliated with a hospital and a team of research medical doctors. Phase three, the most costly and time consuming phase, involves a much larger number of patients (between 300 -3000) and must follow the FDA (or similar regulatory bodies) guidelines. The results of this phase are submitted to the FDA for final approval. Once the approved drug reaches the market, development enters phase four of the cycle. This phase addresses any anomalies or unforeseen adverse effects that might become present.

This research focuses on phase three. As mentioned earlier, this phase is the most elaborate, costly, and time consuming phase. In today's global market, most international pharmaceutical companies prefer to conduct this phase over geographically dispersed locations often expanding many countries. Clearly, conducting such clinical trials over multiple sites, spreading over many locations can significantly benefit from existence of an advanced IT infrastructure that will enable coordination, monitoring, analyzing, and acting in a timely manner. Adoption of the architecture described in this paper by pharmaceutical firms meets the requirements of this phase of the clinical trials and is described below.

A typical phase three of a clinical trial consists of the following steps.

- Since phase three of the clinical trial requires meeting regulatory guidelines, the first step is the approval of the study protocols by the FDA. This approval can range from medical considerations to approval of the sample size for the clinical trials such as the number of patients to be recruited for the study.

- The next step involves selection of the sites for the trial including location of hospitals, clinics, and doctors' offices.
- Once the total number of patients and sites are defined, allocation of patients to sites is determined.
- In the next step the actual patient recruitments by the local health sites is attempted. The recruitment follows two stages: in stage one, patients are screened for appropriateness of the study. The second stage is the randomization of patients who have successfully passed stage one. In this stage a patient is either assigned to a treatment at a site or is assigned to a placebo group.
- Once groups are designed, patient monitoring begins. For clinical trials patients must follow a pre-defined visitation and monitoring plan. During this step necessary data are collected and transmitted from the investigators' sites to a central location in the pharmaceutical company for analysis.
- Today's clinical trials follow an advanced approach called *"multi-arms."* In this approach a drug may contain many ingredients or components. Trials are designed to test multiple combination of dosage for each version of the drug. This approach results in many configurations of the medicine, allowing the pharmaceutical company to simultaneously evaluate the most effective combinations. Therefore, at each site multiple independent dosages (versions) are being evaluated. Patients are assigned to each drug version following a uniform distribution. The prescribed dosage of the drug for each version is administered to members of the group following the pre-defined procedures for the pre-defined period of the treatment.
- An added complexity of these trials is the globally distributed nature of the trial. Clearly, logistics, management, coordination and visibility of the entire system requires an information architecture that enables all participants to have real-time access to all the necessary information.
- Once trials have begun, partial results are analyzed to determine whether a particular dosage is a promising one or not. When there is enough evidence that a particular dosage is not effective, that specific configuration (version) is stopped and patients from this group are re-assigned to begin taking other dosages from the beginning cycle of the new dosage. The process continues until the pre-determined trial cycles for all dosages (versions) are complete.

Managing the Supply Chain for Distributed Clinical Trials

The supply chain management for distributed clinical trials is very complex and includes many steps. Recent advances in medical science have increased introduction of new drugs. However, developments cycles have become more complex, exclusive patent timelines have shrunk, and costs have skyrocketed. Companies look for ways to reduce these costs and to find an answer to the *"costs more, takes longer"* problem. Monitoring clinical trial cycles, managing the supply chains, and accurately predicting the end date for recruitment are of great interest to pharmaceutical companies. We first discuss a pharmaceutical company's traditional supply chain system for distributed clinical trials and then present a new approach based on the architecture outlined in this research and show how adoption of this new paradigm has reduced cost of the trials and shortened the completion time.

The current landscape for distributed clinical trials for the pharmaceutical firm in this study is presented in Figure 7. The process begins with identification and acquisition of raw material, processing, packaging, delivery, administering, investigation, and drug accounting. Existing system has used forecasting techniques, inventory control, Manufacturing Resource Planning (MRP), Intelligent Voice Recognition Systems (IVRS), and Electronic Data Communications (EDC) systems.

The traditional approach follows the "make-to-stock" production policy. In this approach once the dosages (versions) are defined, the entire demand for all versions and all sites are produced in batches and are shipped to the sites. Clearly, in this approach when the trials reveal a dosage not to be promising the associated dosage and its supporting material and clinical and support staff are no longer useful and must be discarded or disbanded. The costs associated with the non-promising dosages are significant and the firm cannot reuse the dosage for other versions.

Once "multi-arms" and globalization of the clinical trials are added, complexity of the system increases. Managing this complex system can significantly benefit from visibility, monitoring, coordinating, analyzing, and acting features of the architecture described earlier.

Figure 7. The traditional supply chain for clinical trials

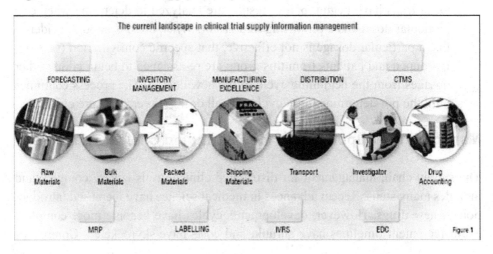

One of the most important factors driving the cost and length of phase three of the clinical trial is recruitment time. Recruitment time is defined as the time needed to recruit a pre-determined number of patients for the entire study. In a multi-arms system, the recruitment problem is significantly more complex. The study managers must recruit sufficient number of patients for each dosage of the drug. The traditional approach uses a batch or "make-to-stock" policy, in which the numbers of sites, number of patients per site and per dosage (version) are first defined and then the supply of drug for each site is produced, packaged, and shipped to each site.

As depicted in Figure 7, raw materials are converted into compounds or drug ingredients. A dosage or version uses a pre-defined portion of each ingredient per its recipe. In the traditional drug production approach, once the number of patients per site and per version is determined, a complete set of dosage for the recipients is produced, packaged, and distributed to each site. Additionally, clinical and support staff as well as instructions, guidelines, and administering procedures are defined and organized for each version proportionally.

This approach is neither cost effective nor timely. The process begins with patient arrivals and administration of specific dosage and monitoring of the patients. The traditional approach does not provide a timely support structure for immediate analysis of the results and immediate termination of the less promising dosages. This in turn limits re-use of the ingredients and re-assignment of patients from failed dosages to the ongoing promising ones thus lengthening the entire process or even missing crucial deadlines. Cost overruns for this system are observed in all stages of the process, from wasted dosages (for the less promising versions) to costs associated with recruitment and administration of the trials.

We next describe a system that follows the "on-demand" or "make-to-order" policy that with its supporting IT infrastructure can reduce the cost of the trials while simultaneously shortens the trail length.

An Adaptive, Agile, Agent-Based, Intelligent Supply Chain System

We present a new paradigm to manage supply chain for distributed clinical trials and show how our solution architecture can reduce cost of trials and shorten time to market. The paradigm applies the concepts of visibility, monitoring, coordinating, analyzing, and acting presented in this architecture to create an adaptive environment for trial management. The agent technology introduced earlier is combined with web services technology and the RFID technology to track and trace the elements of the trials (dosage, packages, team status, etc.). The system offers agility that allows the company to respond to changes in trial environment in the short term without compromising long term (strategic) goals. This architecture uses agent-based technology to support a distributed decision making environment. The system ensures optimal service to the patients, offers an integrated network, provides visibility into patient recruitment and treatment, and coordinates recruitment and trial program rate forecasts with drug and treatment availability at local trial sites. Figure 8 presents the overall optimal supply chain design based on this paradigm. In this paradigm, a plan consists of a set of activities and processes are event driven. We acknowledge recruitment strategies as a driving force for the entire clinical trial. The recruiting strategy has been a subject of many studies. Literature in this field offer simulation and stochastic modeling as the two most widely used approaches for managing recruitment policies. Patel, et al. (2009) offer simulation modeling and tools for managing drug supply chains. Anisimov & Fedorov (2007) recommend stochastic solutions for recruitment management of a clinical trial. We use a stochastic modeling approach to dynamically manage patient recruitment for the trials.

The primary objective is to complete the recruitment of patients within the defined time of the study. Specifically, project objectives are:

- To enroll the required number of subjects within the specified timeframe, and
- To manage to the allocated budget for the study.

To achieve these goals, study managers must be able to quickly monitor changes, analyze the new information, decide on corrective course of actions and act expediently. We have introduced intelligent agents that use pre-defined algorithms as a means for providing the needed insights for making intelligent decisions. Essentially, study managers want the algorithms to define:

Figure 8. Optimized supply chain system for clinical trials

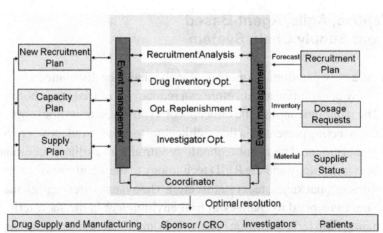

- The distribution of productive sites, showing when they become active and when they are forecast to screen their first patients, and
- The distribution of screened and randomized/enrolled patients.

These two interdependent time series are distributions of stochastic variables over a time horizon and therefore represent two interlinked "stochastic processes." The ability to accurately predict these stochastic processes is the key for a study manager to define and maintain a predictable study plan.

Many existing analytical tools for such systems have focused on the use of simulation to address this problem (Patel et al., 2009). The system described in this research, however, provides an intelligent user interface with predictive capabilities that eliminates the need for users to deeply understand the framework, yet still apply it when developing plans and managing recruitment. Our solution effectively visualizes these two interdependent time series across all phases of the enrollment process and provides proactive alerts for projected violations of the trial's business goals. We have examined both deterministic and stochastic model frameworks. A deterministic model framework assumes the patient arrival rate that follows a known pattern or estimated deterministic linear or non-linear function, whereas a stochastic model framework allows the definition of probability functions with expected mean values and variance. Our results show that the stochastic framework delivers superior results. Under the stochastic model framework the user is able to define instances of the model by specifying the recruitment problem parameters (expected initial recruitment estimates, by countries and across centers, as well as the rules for recruitment: competitive, balanced, or restricted recruitment). The advantage of this approach is that the model framework remains invariant and multiple instances can be generated and tested. The instanced model can now be solved using an "efficient" algorithm. Efficiency is characterized mainly by two factors: time and accuracy of the result. Because our stochastic model framework allows us to define algorithms that provide closed form solutions, accuracy and time are optimal and outperform existing simulation techniques utilized in traditional models.

In modelling the recruitment problem we consider the following:

- **Uncertainties during the recruitment period.** There are uncertainties (unpredictable events) in patient recruitment over the time horizon. Because of this, recruitment rates generally fluctuate over time and centers may delay screening patients due to unexpected events;
- **Expected recruitment mean and confidence boundaries**. To correctly model the uncertainties outlined above, we characterize the expected recruitment average for mean and its confidence boundary value. This will allow

the algorithm to generate the expected number of randomized patients and its confidence bounds over the defined time horizon;

- **The minimum number of centers required.** The model determines the minimum number of centers needed to complete recruitment by a certain date at a given confidence.
- **Estimated future performance of centers.** Information about the future initiation of centers and estimated performance is factored in to improve the significance of the prediction.

The above characteristics are the driving assumptions of the model. Literature on patient recruitment (Senn, 1998, Anisimov & Fedorov, 2007, Cox, 1955) offer guidelines for patient arrivals and assignments to the centers. We follow the same two general assumptions:

- Given the stochastic fluctuations of recruitment over time, patients arrive at centers following the distribution of a Poisson process.
- Variations in recruitment rates between centers are estimated as samples from a gamma distributed population.

Additionally, we add some extensions to these assumptions. They are:

- The minimum number of centers required to complete the recruitment by the target date.
- Knowledge of the information about future performance of centers.
- Capacity of the centers and their constraints (facility constraints, maximum number of patients).

We use these assumptions to extend the Cox stochastic forecasting model to develop a specific algorithm to determine the distribution of the patient arrival rate for each center. Figure 8 presents the proposed approach based on the outlined architecture to manage the supply chain for such clinical trials, including the multi-arms approached used in this study and uses the extended algorithms for its patient arrival forecasting.

Results from adoption of this approach show significant improvements in cost and time to completion. The savings are the consequences of the "visibility, monitoring, coordinating, analyzing, and acting" features of the system. Specifically, the de-centralized framework of the system and the intelligent agents combine to realize the improvements. This architecture uses a de-centralized production policy. In this approach, instead of the finished drug dosage used in the traditional system, ingredients (drug components) and recipes are sent to each site and the actual dosages are produced on an on-demand or "make-to-order" bases at each site and upon patient arrivals. In this strategy once a dosage is deemed non-promising, the production of that dosage immediately stops and the remaining ingredients (drug components) are re-used for more promising dosages using their recipes. Clearly, in this de-centralized production system, expensive drug components are not wasted thus reducing the overall costs of the trial. Similarly, the predictive algorithms used in this study form the intelligence of the system allowing the study managers to forecast events accurately, specially the patient recruitments events, and manage the entire process more efficiently. These features have resulted in faster decision making, allowing less promising trials to end sooner and re-assignment of patients and clinical and support staff to more promising cases, thus, completing the trials faster. The production, packaging, shipment, and administration of the dosages are based on on-demand or "make-to-order" policy, are done more expediently, and result in cost reductions and faster completion time of the trials.

Study Results

The pharmaceutical company referenced in this study leverages a store of previously completed clinical studies—classified by therapeutic area and organized according to features (such as target number of subjects, number of sites and cycle time)—to test and refine the implementation of the model and its associated algorithms. Studies are sorted by category values from High (+), Medium (O), to Low (-) in order to better understand and analyze possible pattern behaviors, similarities, and differences.

To arrive at the results presented in the examples outlined here, a "post-mortem" analysis was conducted to compare our results with the traditional approach. In the traditional approach, before the trials begin, the study manager offers his projection for the Last Subject Randomized (LSR) based on his past experiences. This input is a very rough estimate and is grounded on the manager's intuition and earlier similar studies. His estimates are used for budgetary purposes, design of the trial framework, and to define system's parameters. These parameters consists of (i) the number of countries in the study, (ii) the number of centers per country, and (iii) the total recruitment per center. and are used to create the initial recruitment plan. Clearly, these rough estimates need to be revised and corrected as soon as real data from the field becomes available. In the traditional approach, once the process begins and some information from the field is collected, the LSR projections are revised. In this approach, the revision is deterministic and is triggered when 25% of the sites are operational and are actively recruiting. The study manager uses the field data to revise its LSR projections. Therefore, in a post-mortem analysis, the projection error in this approach can be computed by subtracting the LSR projections @ 25%

from the actual completion date. We will use this error rate to compare with our corresponding error.

We introduced a stochastic approach to compute the LSR projections. To be able to compare our results with the traditional approach, we also choose the 25% site activation metric as our trigger point. The projected LSR values based on this approach, on the other hand, uses the stochastic process described in this section. Therefore, in a post-mortem analysis, the projection error can be computed by subtracting the LSR projections @ 25% from the actual completion date based on the stochastic algorithm used in this approach. The improvement in the process can be computed by comparing these two error values.

Table 9 describes the study features of three sample studies, followed by the results demonstrated by our methodology.

The results presented below are illustrated through the use of two performance functions: "Absolute Time Error" and "Relative Time Error." The "Absolute Time Error" measures the difference between the model estimates at the 25% trigger point and the actual end day the last patient was enrolled. The "Relative Time Error" measures the per cent error relative to model estimates at the 25% trigger point. The simplicity of these metrics provides for an immediate normalized comparison of our results across different studies as well as an immediately measurable understanding of the tangible economic impact of proper and accurate forecasting.

The actual recruitment completion date for the oncology study was 1-Feb-2007, which was 129 days before the originally forecasted plan (based on the traditional approach). Using the stochastic model described in this research, at 25% centers active, the projections would have been within 23 (8-Jan-2007) days of the actual completion time. The improvement rate of the stochastic algorithm over the traditional deterministic approach is 82%.

The actual recruitment completion date for the immunology study was 8-Jan-2007, which was 27 days later than the originally forecasted plan (based on the traditional approach). Using the stochastic model described in this research, at 25% centers active, the projections would have been within 6 days. The improvement rate of the stochastic algorithm over the traditional deterministic approach is 78%.

The actual recruitment completion date for the respiratory study was 3-Aug-2007, which was 127 days later than the originally forecasted plan (based on the traditional approach). Using the stochastic model described in this research, at 25% centers active, the projections would have been within 33 days. The improvement rate of the stochastic algorithm over the traditional deterministic approach is 74%.

The web-enabled, intelligent, agent-based system with specialized patient recruitment algorithms presented offers a more accurate trial progress forecast. Better accuracy improves and impacts the entire process, from dosage production, distribution, delivery, and administering, to drug version monitoring, information

Table 9. Study features of three trials

Study Features	Study 1: Oncology	Study 2: Immunology	Study 3: Respiratory
Number of patients	O/-	+	+
Number of centers	O	-/O	+
Estimated recruitment rate	-	+	+
Expected # of active centers	-	O	O

Table 10. Oncology study targeting 680 patients

Study Start		Projected Last Subject Randomized		
Planned First Site Initiated	Planned Last Subject Random-ized	Deterministic Model – 25% Sites Active	Stochastic Model – 25% Sites Active	Actual – Study Completed
3-Jan-2004	3-Jan-2006	10-Jun-2007	8-Jan-2007	1-Feb-2007

analysis, and site management. The cost savings in this system are spread throughout the supply chain and are the results of reduction in expensive dosage production (by immediate stoppage of non-promising versions) to patients' assignment and drug administration.

The stochastic model presented serves as the "intelligent component" of the agent technology. The stochastic model can determine the best and worst case scenarios for trial completion times. The agents can use these parameters to determine the feasibility of achieving projected goals. When these goals are deemed to be

Table 11. Immunology study targeting 2000 patients

Study Start		Projected Last Subject Randomized		
Planned First Site Initiated	Planned Last Sub-ject Randomized	Deterministic Model – 25% Sites Active	Stochastic Model – 25% Sites Active	Actual – Study Completed
1-Jan-2006	21-Nov-2006	5-Feb-2007	2-Jan-2007	8-Jan-2007

Table 12. Respiratory study targeting 2600 patients

Study Start		Projected Last Subject Randomized		
Planned First Site Initiated	Planned Last Sub-ject Randomized	Deterministic Model – 25% Sites Active	Stochastic Model – 25% Sites Active	Actual – Study Completed
1-May-2005	30-Dec-2006	28-Mar-2007	30-Jun-2007	3-Aug-2007

infeasible, a new trigger point is generated. A second agent can then use this trigger point and re-evaluate the LSR values using the latest available information. In the above examples, we used the 25% center activation metric as the trigger point only to allow us to compare our results with the traditional approach. In our model, the value of the trigger point is dynamically computed by the agent technology.

Finally, the system presented here has been recently adopted by a pharmaceutical company and early actual results are very promising and are in line with the experimental values. Since such a system brings significant cost reduction, the savings might translate to further research for drugs targeted to specific customer needs, thus allowing the pharmaceutical company to move toward a "personalized medicine" model.

CONCLUSION

The goal of an on-demand and mass customization strategy is to deliver customized products at costs that are near-equivalent to their mass produced versions without significant delays. To achieve this goal, we presented a web-enabled information system model that uses mobile intelligent agent technology and can be interfaced with the firms' existing IT infrastructures. Successful implementation of any mass customized strategy requires a collaborative environment that follows a build-to-order production strategy. In such an environment, customers can configure their orders online and monitor the orders' status at any time, suppliers can view demand stream dynamically in real-time, and the manufacturers can react to changing orders efficiently and expediently. We presented a distributed, Java-based, mobile intelligent information system model that is demand driven, supports a build-to-order policy, provides end-to-end visibility along the entire supply chain, allows for a collaborative and synchronized production system, and supports an event-based manufacturing environment. The system introduces an agent-based architecture with four general purpose intelligent agents to support the entire mass customization process. Experiences with implementations of this approach at a semiconductor manufacturer, an automotive company, and a pharmaceutical company show the effectiveness of the proposed architecture in enhancing the *'velocity of execution'* of supply chain management activities, including order management, planning, manufacturing, operations, and distributions. Results verified that successful adoption of this system can reduce inventory and logistics costs, improve delivery performance, increase manufacturing facilities utilizations, and provide a higher overall profitability.

REFERENCES

ACL. Agent Communications Language. (2006). Retrieved from http://www.fipa.org/repository/aclspec.html.

Adam, N. R., Dogramaci, O., Gangopadhyay, A., & Yesha, Y. (1999). *Electronic Commerce*. Upper Saddle River, NJ: Prentice Hall.

Anderson, D. L., & Lee, H. (1999). The New Frontier. In *Achieving Supply Chain Excellence Through Technology. Montgomery Research* (pp. 12–21). Synchronized Supply Chains.

Anisimov, V. V., & Fedorov, V. V. (2007). Modeling, Prediction and Adaptive Adjustment of Recruitment in Multicentre Trials. *Statistics in Medicine*, *26*(27), 4958–4975. doi:10.1002/sim.2956

Arjmand, M., & Roach, S. (1999). Creating Greater Customer Value by Synchronizing the Supply Chain. *In Achieving Supply Chain Excellence Through Technology*, Montgomery Research, 154-159, also in http://arjmand.ascet.com.

Baker, A.D., Van Dyke Parunak, H., & Kutluhan, E. (1999). Agents and the Internet: Infrastructure for Mass Customization. *IEEE Internet Computing*, Sept.-Oct., 62-69.

Bellifemine, F., Caire, G., Poggi, A., & Rimassa, G. (2003). JADE: A White Paper. *Exp 3(3), 6-19.*

Bergenti, F. & Poggi. A. (2001). LEAP: A FIPA Platform for Handheld and Mobile Devices. *In Proc. Eighth International Workshop on Agent Theories, Architectures, and Languages (ATAL-2001)*, Seattle, WA, 303-313.

Bigus, J. P., Schlosnagle, D. A., Pilgrim, J. R., Mills, W. N. III, & Diago, Y. (2002). ABLE: A Toolkit for Building Multi-agent Autonomic Systems – Agent Building and Learning Environment. *IBM Systems Journal*, (September): 1–19.

Capgemini. (2004). A Collection of Agent Technology Pilots and Projects. Retrieved from http://www.capgemini.com/resources/thought_leadership/putting_agents_to-work/

Cox, D. (1955). Some Statistical Methods Connected with Series of Events (with Discussion). *Journal of the Royal Statistical Society. Series B. Methodological*, *17*, 129–164.

Dorer, K., & Calisti, M. (2005). An Adaptive Solution to Dynamic Transport Optimization. *In Proc. Of the Fourth International Joint Conference on Autonomous Agents & Multi-agent Systems, AAMAS '05, Utrecht, The Netherlands. Also at:*http://www.whitestein.com/pages/downloads/publications.

Ghiassi, M. (2001). An E-Commerce Production Model for Mass Customized Market. *Issues in Information Systems, 2*, 106–112.

Ghiassi, M., & Spera, C. (2003). $_a$). Defining the Internet-based Supply Chain System for Mass Customized Markets. *Computers & Industrial Engineering Journal, 45*(1), 17–41. doi:10.1016/S0360-8352(03)00017-2

Ghiassi, M., & Spera, C. (2003$_b$). A Collaborative and Adaptive Supply Chain Management System. *Proceedings of the 31st International Conference on Computers and Industrial Engineering.*, San Francisco, Ca., 473-479.

Gilmore, J. H., & Pine, B. J., II. (2000). Markets of One: Creating Customer-Unique Value Through Mass Customization. *A Harvard Business Review Book.* GPRS: General Packet Radio System. Retrieved from http://www.gsmworld.com/technology/gprs/index.html

JADE. http://jade.cselt.it & http://jade.tilab.com

Jain, A. K., Aparicio, M. IV, & Singh, M. P. (1999). Agents for Process Coherence in Virtual Enterprises. *Communications of the ACM, 42*(3), 62–69. doi:10.1145/295685.295702

Kalakota, R., Stallaert, J., & Whinston, A. B. (1998). Implementing Real-Time Supply Chain Optimization Systems. *Global Supply Chain and Technology Management*, POMS, 60-75.

Lange, D. B., & Oshima, M. (1998). *Programming and Developing Java Mobile Agents with Aglets*. Reading, MA: Addison-Wesley.

Ma, M. (1999). Agents in E-Commerce. *Communications of the ACM, 42*(3), 79–80. doi:10.1145/295685.295708

Maes, P., Guttman, R. H., & Moukas, A. G. (1999). Agents that Buy and Sell. *Communications of the ACM, 42*(3), 81–91. doi:10.1145/295685.295716

MIDP. Mobile Information Device Profile. Retrieved from http://java.sun.com/products/midp/index.jsp

Moreno, A., Valls, A., & Viejo, A. (2005). Using JADE-LEAP to Implement Agents in Mobile Devices *(Research Report 03-008, DEIM, URV).Retrieved from*http://www.etse.urv.es/recerca/banzai/toni/MAS/papers.html Pancerella, A., & Berry, N. (1999). Adding Intelligent Agents to Existing EI Frameworks. *IEEE Internet Computing*, Sept.-Oct., 60-61.

Patel, N. R., & Tourtellotte, E. (2009). Drug Supply for Adaptive Trials. http://www.cytel.com/Knowledge/stimulating_adaptive_1_08.pdf

RosettaNet. (1998). http://www.rosettanet.org

Sandholm, T. (1999). Automated Negotiation. *Communications of the ACM, 42*(3), 84–85. doi:10.1145/295685.295866

Senn, S. (1998). Some Controversies in Planning and Analysing Multi-centre Trials. *Statistics in Medicine, 17*(15-16), 1753–1756. doi:10.1002/(SICI)1097-0258(19980815/30)17:15/16<1753::AID-SIM977>3.0.CO;2-X

Shah, J. B. (2002). ST, HP VMI Program Hitting Its Stride. *Electronics Business News (EBN), 42,*http://www.ebnonline.com.

Singh, R., Salam, A. F., & Iyer, L. (2005). Agents in E-Supply Chains. *Communications of the ACM, 48*(6), 109–115. doi:10.1145/1064830.1064835

Sundermeyer, K. (2001). Collaborative Supply Net Management. In Baader, F., Brewka, G., & Eiter, T. (Eds.), *KI:2001, Advances in Artificial Intelligence* (pp. 467–470). doi:10.1007/3-540-45422-5_35

Wilke, J. (2002). Using Agent-Based Simulation to Analyze Supply Chain Value and Performance. *Supply Chain World Conference and Exhibition, New Orleans, La.*

Chapter 6
Enhancing Video Viewing Experience

Akio Takashima
Tokyo University of Technology, Japan

ABSTRACT

In this study, the authors have considered video viewing style to be a type of knowledge medium. Video viewing styles, which are considered to be habitual behaviors during video viewing, are used to externalize one's viewing skills or know-how about video viewing; they allow users to experience videos through these skills. In order to allow users to experience videos in various viewing styles, the authors have developed a system called the video viewing experience reproducer (VVER), which determines the user's viewing styles and reuses them. To determine these styles, the system extracts associations between the user's manipulation of videos and the low-level features of these videos. In this chapter, the authors describe the notion of reusing the video viewing styles and composing them. After discussing examples of utilizing this concept, preliminary user studies have been reported.

DOI: 10.4018/978-1-61520-851-7.ch006

INTRODUCTION

People often undertake similar actions for a particular situation in everyday life. In these habitual behaviors, although there are some general actions that can be used for collaborative filtering, most of them are very personal because these actions are selected based on the individual's empirical knowledge. We believe that intelligent systems can assist users in their habitual behaviors in their daily lives.

In this study, we have focused on the habitual behaviors encountered during the video viewing process. Video viewing is increasing in popularity for novices and the relationship between videos and the users who watch these videos has been gradually changing. We used to watch TV programs passively; now, with the advancement in technology, we can watch videos more actively by skipping commercials, zooming into an important object in a certain video frame, examining a particular scene at various playing speeds, and so on. This notion, which is called "active watching," represents the rich interactivity between videos and users; it also represents the importance of the influence of changing appearances in video data (Takashima et al., 2003). As more concrete examples, in the video of a football game, in order to understand the positioning of a particular player or the formation shift of the entire team, these sequences can be better presented at a faster speed. Conversely, in order to understand the ball rotation or the shooting motion of a player, a slower playing speed would be more suitable. Therefore, we assume that users create their own video viewing style, which is a set of habitual behaviors formulated during video viewing by the user; these involve exploring or skipping certain scenes according to the user's requirements. The goal of this study is to design and build a system that assists users to reuse their video viewing styles and creating novel viewing styles by composing several viewing styles.

Hereafter, we first discuss the techniques to assist video viewing for users, and then, we explain our approach that considers video viewing styles to be a type of tacit knowledge. We then present several scenarios that utilize the video viewing style. Following sections describe the system developed by us, and the result from preliminary user studies.

ASSISTING PEOPLE IN VIDEO VIEWING

To support the video viewing process, numerous studies focusing on content-based analyses for retrieving or summarizing videos have been reported (Nakamura & Kanade, 1997; Ekin et al., 2003). These studies assume that content-based knowledge may include the semantic information of video data; in other words, it includes generally accepted domain knowledge. For example, people tend to pay additional attention to goal scenes during football games or captions during news programs that describe the summary or location of the news topic. Therefore, these approaches are applicable only for specific purposes (e.g., extracting goal scenes from football games as important scenes), which are assumed beforehand. However, it is difficult to determine the scenes of interest for a particular user. Some users might like to watch a summarized video, which focuses particularly on the goal scenes in a football game video, whereas other viewers might want to watch the scenes in which a particular star player appears. Further, in the case of a weather forecast video, users might want to watch the scenes showing the area in which they reside (Figure 1). Therefore, it is difficult for systems using content-based knowledge to satisfy the needs of users because the users' intention or knowledge, which determines what they want to watch, is not entirely predictable, and occasionally, the users themselves cannot distinctly describe their viewing requirements.

As described above, intelligent systems can be considered as systems that can assist users in their habitual behaviors in their daily lives. From this point of view, studies on recommendation systems can be considered as related works. Information recommendation based on the extraction of the user's preference is widely used for selecting items on an online shopping Web site such as Amazon.com. The process of information recommendation can be roughly categorized into two types: explicit methods and implicit methods. In the former, the systems inquire about the information that interests the user. On the other hand, in the latter method, the systems predict the users' interests according to their actions. In this method, which is also the method employed in this study, several researches have been reported for

Figure 1. It is difficult for systems using content-based knowledge to satisfy the needs of users because the users' intention or knowledge, which determines what they want to watch, is not entirely predictable, and occasionally, the users themselves cannot distinctly describe their viewing requirements

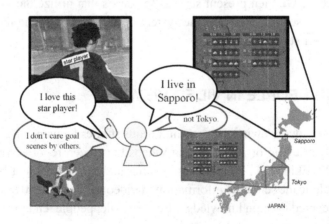

the Web browsing process. Seo and Zhang (2000) described a method for an information filtering agent to understand the users' preferences by analyzing their Web browsing behaviors such as time taken for reading, book marking, scrolling, and so on. Sakagami and Kamba (1997) developed a system that extracts the user preferences during the reading of online news by monitoring ordinary user operations such as scrolling and enlarging articles in an Internet browser. In the field of video viewing, a few studies have been reported. Yu et al. (2003) proposed an algorithm named ShotRank, which is similar to the PageRank system developed by Google (Brin & Page, 1998); ShotRank is used to measure the interestingness and importance of segmented video scenes by using the data of how many times the users selected and watched each video shot. Syeda-Mahmood & Ponceleon (2001) modeled the users' viewing behaviors using the hidden Markov model (HMM) and developed a system that generates video previews without any prior knowledge of the video content. Although both these studies employ the implicit method, they investigate only the summarizing of a particular video; no study has attempted to combine the user preferences encountered during the video viewing process.

In this study, we employ the user's behavior analysis (and not semantic content analysis) and the implicit method for extracting the user's preferences (and not the explicit method); we then assist the users in reusing their habitual behaviors and combine them.

VIDEO VIEWING STYLE AS KNOWLEDGE MEDIA

As mentioned in the previous section, many researches on video viewing have aimed toward summarizing the videos such that they can be watched briefly. However, the way to watch videos is gradually changing: summarization is just one type of video viewing style. The manner in which people interact with videos during their everyday lives involves complex knowledge-construction processes and not simple naïve information-receiving processes. Further, we have a large number of opportunities to use videos in increasing our knowledge, such as monitoring events, reflection on physical performances, learning subject matter, or analyzing scientific experimental phenomena. In such ill-defined situations, the domain knowledge about such contents is insufficient; hence, the users interact with videos according to their viewing styles (Yamamoto et al., 2005). However, such type of tacit knowledge, which is acquired through user experiences (Polanyi, 1983), has not been effectively managed.

Many studies have been reported in the area of knowledge management systems (Alavi & Leidner, 1999). As media for editing, distributing, and managing knowledge (called knowledge media), Tanaka (2003) introduced the meme media architecture and framework for reusing and combining such knowledge media by means of direct manipulation. In this framework, however, the target objects for reusing or sharing have been limited to the resources that are easily describable such as functions used in software (Fujima & Tanaka, 2007) or services provided by Web applications (Sugibuchi & Tanaka, 2004). In this study, this approach has been extended to be more user-friendly, which considers indescribable resources such as know-how or skills of human behavior (i.e., tacit knowledge).

In this study, we consider video viewing styles as a type of knowledge media. Video viewing styles, which are considered as habitual behaviors in video viewing, are used to externalize one's viewing skills or know-how of video viewing; it allows the users to experience videos in various viewing styles. "To experience videos in various viewing styles" stands for to watch video which are automatically played based on the viewing skill (Figure 2). In this case, experience is re-produced by watching automatically playing videos.

APPROACH

To allow users to experience videos through video viewing styles, our approach employs extraction of relationship between video and human. In addition this extraction, we introduce three types of profiling to utilize users' video viewing styles.

Estimating Relationship between Human and Video

In this chapter, we describe the notion of extracting, reusing, and composing the users' video viewing styles to enhance users' video viewing experience. We assume the following characteristics during video viewing:

Figure 2. Video viewing styles, which are considered as habitual behaviors in video viewing, are used to externalize one's viewing skills or know-how of video viewing; it allows the users to experience videos through these skills by automatically playing videos

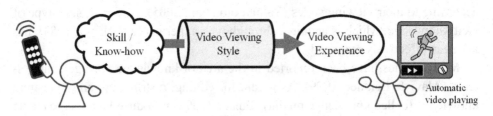

- People often browse through videos in consistent and specific patterns
- User interaction with videos can be associated with the low-level features of such videos

While the user's manipulation of a particular video depends on the meaning of the content and the thought process of the user, it is difficult to observe these aspects. In this study, we attempted to estimate these associations between the video features and user manipulations (Figure 3). The low-level features (e.g., color distribution, optical flow, and sound level) have been associated with user manipulations, which reveal the changing speeds (e.g., fast-forwarding, rewinding, and slow playing). The identification of the associations from these aspects, which can be easily observed, implies that the user can possess a video viewing style even without the domain knowledge of the video content.

Three Types of Profiling

In order to utilize video viewing styles, we introduce three types of profile: manipulation profile, viewing profile, and composition profile.

Figure 3. While the user's manipulation of a particular video depends on the meaning of the content and the thought process of the user, it is difficult to observe these aspects. In this study, we attempted to estimate these associations between the video features and user manipulations

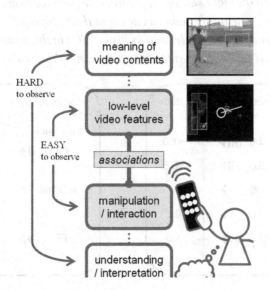

Manipulation Profile

Manipulation Profile distinguishes viewing manipulations such as fast forwarding, rewinding, and slow forwarding. This profile is manually determined by a user. This profile also defines the score of importance (SOI) for each manipulation. Figure 4 indicates two examples of manipulation profile. In the left side of the figure, a profile defines five manipulations for changing play speed. As for SOI for each manipulation, in this case, the slowest play speed is defined as the highest score and the fastest play speed is defined as the lowest score. In the right side of the figure, a sequential manipulation is defined. Re-examine means rewinding some scenes and then playing the scene at a slower speed, and this manipulation is defined as higher SOI in this example. Manipulation profile can be used for both reusing and composing video viewing styles.

Viewing Profile

Viewing profile represents a user's video viewing style. If a user has his/her habitual behavior in video viewing process, it could be relating low-level video feature; and behaviors should be described in a manipulation profile. In other words, a setting for a tool to classify low-level video features as a playback manipulation is called

Figure 4. In the left side of the figure, a profile defines five manipulations for changing play speed. As for SOI for each manipulation, in this case, the slowest play speed is defined as the highest score and the fastest play speed is defined as the lowest score. In the right side of the figure, a sequential manipulation is defined. Re-examine means rewinding some scenes and then playing the scene at a slower speed, and this manipulation is defined as higher SOI in this example. Manipulation profile can be used for both reusing and composing video viewing styles.

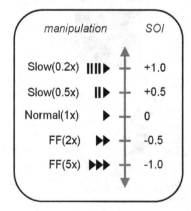
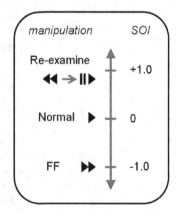

viewing profile. Viewing profile is defined automatically by using some machine learning algorithms. More detail about how to classify the relationship is described in the system overview section.

Composition Profile

Composition profile defines the manipulations for composing viewing styles. In this study, we employ the notion that composition is executed independently in each video frame. This means that when a user tries to combine each viewing style of several users, at first, manipulations of the same number of viewing styles should be estimated for one video frame through each viewing profile. These are the candidate manipulations. And then one manipulation will be selected as a result of considering the candidate manipulations by using a composition profile.

Composition profile is categorized into two types; manipulation based composition and SOI based composition.

The manipulation based composition selects one manipulation by using a selection rule which is based on statistical number of candidate manipulations. For example, one rule may select the most frequent manipulation in the candidate manipulations as the estimated manipulation (majority vote). Another example of manipulation based composition may select the slowest manipulation in the candidate manipulations so as not to miss important parts (if an important frame tends to be played at a slower speed).

The SOI based composition selects one manipulation by calculating SOI (which is defined in a manipulation profile) of the candidate manipulations. This type of composition allow users to experience the video frames through, for example, the manipulation that has the average SOI of the candidate manipulations, or the manipulation that has the highest SOI of them. One example of an average type composition profile is that the composition selects a manipulation which is based on the calculated average SOI such as ($\sum$ (SOIn)/n). In this situation, if the average SOI is near to slow (0.5x) manipulation, the composition result make the video frame be played at a slow (0.5x) speed.

Various types of compositions can be defined in the same way into one composition profile. These profiles are defined manually by users.

SCENARIO

In this section, we illustrate several examples for reusing and composing various video viewing styles.

Reusing Scenarios

Once a particular video viewing style is extracted, this video viewing experience can be reproduced. Here, we describe the reusing of scenarios that utilize the user's video viewing style as well as those of others.

Reusing the User's Video Viewing Style

By using the user's video viewing style, the user can experience unknown videos through personalized efficient playback.

If the user is the coach of a particular football team, the video viewing style of the coach for the videos of football games may be distinguishable from the styles of novices. When a coach analyzes a particular game video of an opponent team, the coach may try to determine the weaknesses of the team by judging the positioning of the players or the formation shift of the entire team. In order to achieve this, if the coach repeatedly watches zoomed-out scenes, this habitual behavior will be included in the video viewing style. For a diligent football player, the video viewing style might include behaviors that explore scenes, including tricky techniques, at a slower speed. On the other hand, novices tend to skip to scenes that excite them, such as goal scenes, to save time. This is also a type of video viewing style.

Several sports (e.g., American football, golf, Japanese sumo wrestling, and so on) include frequent interval scenes (out-of-play scenes). Skipping such scenes is a practical video viewing style that ensures efficiency in time spending.

For checking the weather report just before leaving one's home, weather forecasts from other areas might be a waste of time. If the weather report for a particular town is frequently watched (and the other areas are skipped), the weather information related to that particular town is included in the video viewing style.

Reusing Others' Video Viewing Styles

In addition to reusing one's own video viewing style, videos can be experienced through various types of video viewing styles produced by others.

The video viewing style of a particular famous head coach of a football team may have some special characteristics and a film reviewer may have a different video viewing style. By using such types of specialized video viewing styles, a particular video can be experienced in an unusual manner, leading to some serendipitous findings about the video.

Composing Scenarios

One of the features of this study is the introduction of the notion of the composition of video viewing styles. These compositions will be utilized for experiencing both general and personal video viewing.

Composition for Experiencing General Video Viewing

As described in the section on reusing scenarios, novices may tend to skip to the scenes that excite them, such as goal scenes, to save time. If most people skipped the same scenes based on their own respective video viewing style, these habitual skipping behaviors can be composed (i.e., pick up the same behaviors) and the scenes that are generally assumed to be attractive can be experienced. That is, making a digest video or summarizing the video is one of the practical applications of the composition of video viewing styles. Further, this composition can achieve social filtering without any domain knowledge about the video content.

Similarly, people can re-edit some lengthy home video with the recording of a playing child. After the video has been played by skipping unwanted scenes, the video would transform into a digest version of the original video. If the video is viewed by many people, another viewer will find the clue to view a video effectively. This resembles a book that has been read repeatedly and has dogs-ears, finger marks, and stains left by the readers.

Composition for Comparing Personal Video Viewing Experiences

One practical application obtained by comparing a particular video viewing experience with others is collaborative filtering. People with similar video viewing styles can experience video viewing through the others' video viewing styles, which may lead to a serendipitous way to watch the video. Collaborative filtering indicates, for instance, that "the viewers who have replayed this scene also replayed another particular scene," which is similar to Amazon.com's recommendation system in which "customers who bought this item also bought..." is mentioned.

Further, the user's video viewing style can be compared with a particular person's style, such as a famous head coach of a football team or a film reviewer, for learning their strategies in video viewing. These compositions help in the sophistication of the user's video viewing style.

VIDEO VIEWING EXPERIENCE REPRODUCER

In this section, we describe a system that extracts the user's video viewing style and allows the users to reuse and compose these styles.

System Overview

To extract the associations between users' manipulations and low-level video features and to reproduce the viewing styles for other videos, we have developed a system called the video viewing experience reproducer (VVER). The VVER consists of the "association extractor" and "behavior applier" blocks (Figure 5).

The association extractor block identifies the relationships between the low-level features of videos and the user manipulation of these videos by using machine learning. This block requires several training videos and viewing logs of a particular user for these training videos for supervised learning. In order to record the viewing logs, a user views the training videos using a simple video browser, which enables the user to control the playing speed. The viewing logs possess pairs of the video frame numbers and the speed at which the user actually played the video frames. As low-level features, the system analyzes more than eighty properties of each frame such as color dispersion, mean of the color value, number of moving objects, optical flow, sound frequency, and so on. Then, the association extractor generates a classifier that determines the speed at which each frame in the video should be played by using the viewing logs and low-level features. In generating

Figure 5. VVER consists of association extractor and behavior applier blocks. The association extractor generates a classifier that determines the speed at which each frame in the video should be played by using the viewing logs and low-level features. The behavior applier block plays the frames of the target video automatically at each speed in accordance with the play schedule that is produced by the classifier.

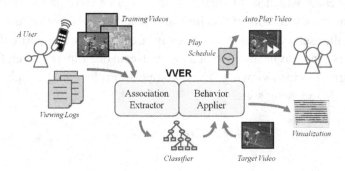

the classifier, we use the C4.5 algorithm implemented in the WEKA engine, a data mining application (WEKA). Using more features leads to a more accurate classification result although the calculation time increases.

The behavior applier block plays the frames of the target video automatically at each speed in accordance with the play schedule that is produced by the classifier. This play schedule possesses the pairs of the video frame number and estimated speed for the frame. The behavior applier can remove the outliers from a sequence of frames that should be played at the same speed, and it can visualize all the behaviors applied to each frame of the video. In addition, the behavior applier allows the users to compose several play schedules, which will be described later.

Now, we describe the association extractor and behavior applier in greater detail.

Association Extractor

The association extractor identifies the relationships between the low-level features of a video and the user manipulation of the videos and it then generates a classifier. In this section, we elaborate upon the low-level features of videos and their user manipulations in greater detail, which are employed in the association extractor.

Low-Level Features of Videos

Video data possess a lot of low-level features. Currently, the system can deal with more than eighty features. These features are categorized into the following five aspects:

- Statistical data of color values in a frame
- Representative color data
- Optical flow data
- Number of moving objects
- Sound levels

Statistical Data of Color Values in a Frame

As the simplest low-level feature, the system considers the statistical data of color values in each frame of a video, for example, the mean and standard deviation of the hue, saturation, and value (brightness).

Representative Color Data

The system uses the statistical data of the pixels painting a representative color. The representative color is a particular color space set selected beforehand (e.g., $30 < H <= 50$, $80 < S <= 90$, $75 < V <= 95$). The system counts how many representative color pixels exist in a particular frame and calculates the mean of the X and Y positions for the pictorial frame and their standard deviations (Figure 6 (a)). Currently, the color space is manually specified; however, it can be automatically specified by calculating which colors are the most frequently used throughout the entire video.

Optical Flow Data

As the dynamic data of video, the system calculates the optical flow of moving objects in a video. For example, first, the system detects the distinguishable pixels such as contours of the human body or the corners of a goalpost in football games. Then, the system calculates the vector data of the optical flow at each point and then calculates the mean angle and vector magnitudes in twelve rectangular sub-areas (Figure 6 (b)). These values may represent not only the states of the moving objects

Figure 6. System makes associations between users' viewing speeds and low-level video features such as representative color data (a), optical flow data (b), number of moving objects (c), and sound levels (d)

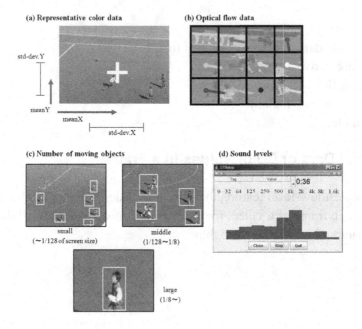

but also the camera movements. The combination of values of twelve rectangular sub-areas can be used for distinguishing camera movements.

Number of Moving Objects

The system first detects the moving objects and then counts the number of such objects according to their sizes (Figure 6 (c)). In order to detect the moving objects, the system employs Motion Template technique (Davis & Bradski, 1999) implemented in OpenCV Library (OpenCV). In a video of a football game, if the video consistently records the same objects, all the detections of a small object imply that it may have been recorded at a wide angle and vice versa for a large object.

Sound Levels

Sound levels are divided into ten groups based on the sound frequency (e.g., 0–32 Hz, 32–64 Hz,..., 8000–10000 Hz) and used as a low-level feature (Figure 6 (d)). If the video includes sound data, it can be one of the better features of a video.

User Manipulations

To record the viewing logs, the user views the training videos using a simple video browser, which enables the user to control the playing speed. For making a manipulation profile, we categorized the patterns of changing the playing speeds into three types based on the patterns frequently used during an informal user observation (Takashima et al., 2003). The three types are as follows:

- Skip
- Re-examine
- Others

Skip

We regard the viewing at a speed higher than the normal playing speed (1.0x) as skipping behavior.

Re-Examine

When exploring a video, the user can re-check and focus on a particular frame that has just passed during viewing. When the pattern is arrived at by forwarding at less than the normal speed after rewinding, we regard it as re-examining behavior.

Others

The speeds that are not described above are categorized into this particular type of behavior.

To avoid any conflicts during reusing and composing, we set priorities for selecting the order of re-examining, skipping, and other behaviors.

Behavior Applier

The behavior applier automatically plays the frames of a target video at each speed in accordance with the play schedules. This allows the users to compose the video viewing styles such that the users can experience videos in different ways.

Mapping from User Manipulation to Automatic Playback Speed

User manipulations are categorized into the three types described above, and the classifier tries to associate each video frame of the target video into these three types.

We designed the mapping from the three types of behaviors into specific speeds (Figure 7). The skipping behavior could be reproduced by playing at a faster speed (5.0x). The other behavior could be reproduced by playing at normal speed. The re-examining behavior could be reproduced by playing at a slower speed (0.5x).

Figure 7. This visualization shows how a target video will play at various speeds. The three belts indicate the video data, i.e., the accumulated video frames from the left to the right. The first belt indicates the viewing log of the training video used for the classifier. The second belt shows the estimated behaviors of the target video. In this figure, the same video is used as the training as well as the target video for confirmation purposes. Therefore, the first and second belts should ideally be the same. The third belt indicates the noise-reduced version of the second belt. The target video will play at each speed indicated at the bottom of the figure.

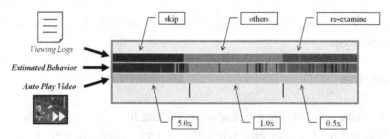

Composing Video Viewing Styles

As described in the previous section, user manipulation was associated with the video features; in other words, the video viewing style was decomposed into rules. Then, each rule was composed so that other video viewing styles could be created. The "timing" when a particular composition is executed is after the generation of the play schedules (Figure 8). As described earlier, a play schedule is a list of associations between each video frame in a video and the user's behavior. A single play schedule is generated by a classifier of the behavior applier; therefore, for Figure 8, two classifiers are formulated in order to generate two play schedules.

To compose the video viewing styles, the system composes the play schedules via several operations. In other words, this process for making operation rule indicates a setting of composition profile. We defined a few simple operations in a composition profile, such as intersection $A \cap B := \left\{ x \mid x \in A \text{ and } x \in B \right\}$, complement $A \setminus B := \left\{ x \mid x \in A \text{ and } x \notin B \right\}$, and union $A \cup B := \left\{ x \mid x \in A \text{ or } x \in B \right\}$, where A and B are sets of video frames that are associated with specific behaviors such as fast forwarding or re-examining and x is a specific video frame.

Some examples made by using these operations are as follows:

Figure 8. A single play schedule is generated by a classifier of the behavior applier; therefore, in this figure, two classifiers are formulated in order to generate two play schedules. A composition is executed after the generation of the play schedules for composition purposes

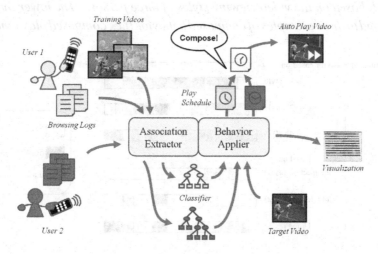

$$S_{USER1} \cap S_{USER2} \cap S_{YOU} \text{ (ex.1)}$$
$$(S_{USER1} \cap S_{USER2}) \setminus S_{YOU} \text{ (ex.2)}$$
$$(S_{USER1} \cap S_{USER2}) \cup S_{YOU} \text{ (ex.3)}$$

Figure 9 shows these examples. The upper three belts in this figure indicate the estimated behavior of the video through the VVER based on the video viewing styles of three persons. For instance, the first belt shows that User1 may initially browse through the video at normal speed and later skip (fast forward) the second part, re-examine the subsequent scenes, skip the fourth part, and then normally browse through the last part. The second and third belts can be described in a similar manner. The lower three belts correspond to three examples of composed behavior (i.e., composed play schedules). The details are as follows:

- ex.1 describes the intersection of the three video viewing styles. In this case, the system estimates that these three persons will skip the earlier scenes. This operation detects meaningful manipulations for all the users. In other words, the operation functions as a social filtering system if the number of users is sufficiently large.
- ex.2 shows the complement of SYOU in the intersection of SUSER1 and SUSER2. This operation determines the habitual behavior of other users that do not tend to be selected by a particular user. This operation can be regarded as an active help system (Fischer et al., 1985).

Figure 9. Examples of estimated viewing behaviors and their composition. The upper three belts in this figure indicate the estimated behavior of the video through the VVER based on the video viewing styles of three persons. The lower three belts correspond to three examples of composed behavior (i.e., composed play schedules).

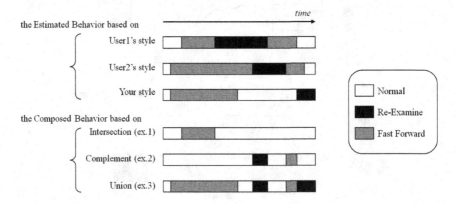

- ex.3 describes the union of SYOU and the intersection of SUSER1 and SUSER2. The user can experience his/her habitual behavior while taking into account the habitual behaviors of other users. (It should be noted that this union operation needs to determine the priority in order to avoid conflicts between the behaviors.)

These examples show that the simple compositions of the associations between a video frame and the viewing behavior can create other meaningful viewing styles.

USER STUDY

We conducted two preliminary user studies. The first study involved observing the users' impression when they extract and reuse their video viewing styles, and the second one involves the composition of these two viewing styles by the users.

Setting

In these two studies, we used ten 5-min. football game videos for training a classifier and two 5-min. football game videos for applying the viewing style and automatic playing. The number of recorded football games is three and the training videos comprise several fragments of these recorded games. The target videos are not included in the training videos. Two subjects were being observed. Each subject is a typical computer user who is asked to explore the training videos and find interesting scenes in the football games. After the system generated the classifiers for each user, the users watch two target videos that play automatically through each classifier; they were later asked about their impression of the reusing study. In the composing study, two subjects were subjected to three types of compositions, namely, intersection, complement, and union compositions.

Result of Reusing Video Viewing Styles

In the training phase, subjectA tried to re-examine (rewind and then play at a speed less than the normal speed) particular scenes, which showed players gathering in front of a goalpost or showed a player kicking the ball toward the goal. In addition, the subject skipped the out-of-play scenes and scenes that did not display the goalpost. SubjectB tended to skip the out-of-play scenes of the games.

Figure 10 shows the visualization of one result generated by using subjectA's video viewing style and the target video. This visualization corresponds to the estimated play schedule of the target video. Further, the upper belt on each thick

Figure 10. Visualization of one result generated by using subjectA's video viewing style and the target video. This reveals the estimated play schedule for the target video. Further, the upper belt on each thick line indicates the estimated behavior (corresponds to the second belt in Figure 7) and the lower belt indicates the smoothed version of the upper belt (corresponds to the third belt in Figure 7).

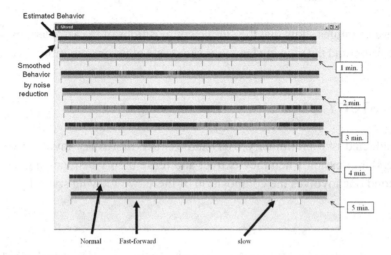

line indicates the estimated behavior (corresponds to the second belt in Figure 7) and the lower belt indicates the smoothed version of the upper belt (corresponds to the third belt in Figure 7). It can be seen that some part of the estimated video was played at various speeds; in fact, the system estimated that the scenes that include the goal area should be played at a normal or slower speed, and the other scenes should be skipped.

By using the behavior applier, the target videos were played automatically for each subject in accordance with their own viewing styles. In the trial for subjectA, nearly 80% of the important (for subjectA) scenes were played at a slower speed. In the trial for subjectB, nearly 70% of the out-of-play scenes were skipped. These percentages were calculated by manually measuring the duration of these scenes. The results of the informal interview reveal that both these subjects were satisfied by the automatically played target videos.

Result of Composing Video Viewing Styles

In the study for composing the video viewing styles, the same classifiers described in the previous section were used. SubjectA and subjectB saw two target videos. Each video was automatically played in accordance with the three types of manipulation based compositions described as follows:

Figure 11. User can select three types of compositions from the menu bar in the video viewer, and the automatic playback directly changes its play schedule according to the selected composition. The first belt of each thick line in the visualization indicates the estimated play schedule by using subjectA's video viewing style, and the second belt indicates that for subjectB's style. The third belt is the result of the composition of the two styles. In this figure, the result of cmp.1 is shown.

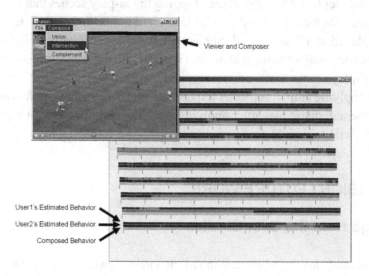

$$S_{SubA} \cap S_{SubB} \qquad\qquad\qquad\qquad\qquad (cmp.1)$$

$$S_{SubB} \setminus S_{SubA} \text{ or } S_{SubA} \setminus S_{SubB} \qquad\qquad\qquad (cmp.2)$$

$$S_{SubA} \cup S_{SubB} \qquad\qquad\qquad\qquad\qquad (cmp.3)$$

In this study, the user could select any of these three compositions from the menu bar; the automatic playback directly changed the play schedule according to the selected composition (Figure 11). The users could verify the play schedule from the visualization. In the visualization shown in Figure 11, the first belt of each thick line indicates the estimated play schedule by using subjectA's video viewing style, and the second belt indicates that for subjectB. The third belt is the result of the composition of these two viewing styles.

As described earlier, subjectA tended to re-examine scenes that showed the goalpost and skip the out-of-play scenes. SubjectB tended to skip the out-of-play scenes in the games.

When cmp.1 was applied, the system fast-forwarded the scenes that were expected to be skipped by both the subjects and played the other scenes at normal speed. This automatic playback became almost similar to the video viewing style of subjectB. In the interview given after viewing the videos, subjectA said that "although some scenes (in-play scenes that he wanted to skip) were played at normal speed, the overall viewing style was acceptable." SubjectB regarded this composition as almost the same as his own viewing style.

After applying cmp.2, the result of $S_{SubB} \setminus S_{SubA}$ was shown to subjectA and vice versa for subjectB. As a result, each subject experienced only others' viewing behaviors. Subject B did not appreciate skipping the in-play scenes that did not show the goalpost. On the other hand, he was interested in exciting scenes (for subjectA) that are played at a lower speed. SubjectA did not appreciate skipping the replay scenes that he usually browsed at normal speed. Both the subjects were irritated by the out-of-play scenes that were not skipped by the system.

After applying cmp.3, subjectA felt that the video viewing style was acceptable because the automatic play after applying cmp.3 was similar to his video viewing style. SubjectB said "it looks like a digest video of a football game."

DISCUSSION / FUTURE WORK

Findings from the User Studies

In our user study involving the reusing of the video viewing styles, we attempted to quantize the number of scenes that were meaningful for the user. Although it was difficult to describe whether the applied viewing behavior by the system constituted a perfect fit for the user's particular requirements or not, it was possible to reuse the video viewing styles without any domain knowledge of the contents.

The results obtained from this user study can be considered as extremely speculative for two reasons. First, the data used for training the classifier and playing the target video are not sufficiently large. Although these videos are not the same, the videos are recorded by one TV station; therefore, the low-level features might not be very different. Second, the viewing styles were very consistent because both the subjects had their own video viewing styles at least for the football games. If the viewing by the subjects had been inconsistent, the results could have been worse.

In the composition study, several positive aspects, such as accepting other users' video viewing styles, were found. However, there were negative aspects caused by the forced unexpected viewing behaviors.

It was proposed that offering a person's video viewing style to the person was possible; on the other hand, offering a person's video viewing style to others requires some mechanism that is less than the cost of employing unknown video viewing styles. The mechanisms should allow users to obtain an overview of the video viewing styles when they reuse or compose their own styles.

Preciseness of a Classifier

In this study, we use the C4.5 algorithm for generating a classifier implemented in WEKA engine. We tested classifiers quantitatively to investigate how the classifiers precisely reuse video viewing style to unknown target videos. The approach of this test is to compare a sequence of manipulations thorough an Intentional viewing style with a sequence of manipulations through an Intentional classifier. Intentional viewing style is achieved by forced viewing process, and Intentional classifier is generated by using the logs of several forced viewing process. The concrete method to generate a sequence of manipulations with Intentional classifier is as follows: (1) defining a relationship between scenes and manipulation, for example, goal scene of a football game video had to be re-examined; (2) analyzing several training videos manually, then using the result as viewing logs; (3) generating an Intentional classifier by using the viewing logs; (4) recording a sequence of manipulation; and this sequence is called Classifier set. On the other hand, for generating a sequence of manipulations through Intentional viewing style, we forced a user to view and control the training videos in a specific manner such as the goal scenes had to be re-examined. This sequence is called Human set.

We call the sequence of manipulation through the Intentional classifier the Classifier set, the one through the Intentional viewing style the Human set, and the sequence of manipulations which is manually extracted with the defined relationship the Answer set. Ideally, for a specific user, both the Classifier set and Human set should be the same as the Answer set of a target video.

To figure out gaps between the Classifier set or the Human set and the Answer set, we introduce SOI described in the right side in Figure 4 as a major. For instance, when a specific video frame is associated with re-examine as the Answer set, it is possible to give a difference between wrong estimations. More concretely, if the wrong estimated manipulation were normal, the gap from the Answer set is better than one of skip. The error value (i.e. the gap from the Answer set) is formulated as follows:

$$error_{classifier} = \frac{1}{nm} \sum_{i=1}^{n} \sum_{j=1}^{m} (A_{ij} - C_{ij})^2$$

$$error_{human} = \frac{1}{nm} \sum_{i=1}^{n} \sum_{j=1}^{m} (A_{ij} - H_{ij})^2$$

In these expressions, n indicates the number of target videos; m is the number of frame of each target video, A means the Answer set, C means the Classifier set, and H means the Human set. By using this method, we tested an Intentional classifier that is generated with football game videos. Three 5min. videos were used for generating the classifier, and another three 5min. videos were used as target videos to produce three Classifier sets. These three target videos were also used for producing Human sets by four subjects through the Intentional viewing style. Each subject produced three Human sets. The result of calculation error value of the Classifier set is 0.142 on the average. The error values of the Human set of four people are 0.201, 0.098, 0.120, and 0.103 on the average. As a result, the error value of the Classifier set is similar to the values of Human sets. This result shows VVER can reproduce a user's video viewing style at the same level of precision as ones by a human.

Timing of Composing

In this chapter, although we used play schedules for composing, other options can be employed. We plan to compose viewing logs or classifiers of each user as other types of composition. The timing of the composition can yield much better results.

Type of Attribute for Association

In this study, the association extractor considered more than eighty features for generating a classifier. Video data has a large number of features that can be observed; we suggest that the results will be much better if the system can employ more features.

On the other hand, we categorized the users' manipulations into some meaningful patterns such as skipping and re-examining and we used only three categories for associating the large number of possible low-level features. This is because the system may not generate any association if both user behavior and video features have a large number of attributes. Estimating several patterns of viewing behaviors (Syeda-Mahmood & Ponceleon, 2001) is a future work in which users' manipulations can be regarded as low-level actions.

In addition to this, other types of data can be considered as features of the users. For example, data about eye gazing might include some information related to the user's video viewing style.

Additional User Study Using Videos of Other Genres

The user studies described above were conducted with football game videos. As an additional user study, we conducted the same user study with videos of other two genres to explore differences depending on type of video content. The two genres used in this user study were TV program of Japanese wrestling (Sumo) and recording data from surveillance camera which is set up at entrance of a building.

TV program of Japanese wrestling includes the program editor's viewpoints such as camera motion (zooming, panning, and tilting) and replay scene as well as football game video. On the other hand, the recording data from surveillance camera include neither camera motions nor sound. This non edited type video was chosen supposing video analyzing situation.

The setting of this user study was the same as the one described in the previous, however, the subjects were not the same. In this user study, four subjects participated. The classifiers were made for each genre and each subject respectively, and five videos were used to make one classifier. In the reusing video viewing style phase, three unknown videos were used for automatic playback. For composing video viewing style, we employed manipulation based composition. Each unknown video was automatically played in accordance with the three types of compositions described as follows:

$$S_{SubA} \cap S_{SubB} \cap S_{SubC} \cap S_{SubD} \qquad \text{(cmp.1')}$$

$$\left(S_{SubA} \cap S_{SubB} \cap S_{SubC} \right) \setminus S_{SubD} \qquad \text{(cmp.2')}$$

$$S_{SubA} \cup S_{SubB} \cup S_{SubC} \cup S_{SubD} \qquad \text{(cmp.3')}$$

These compositions are revised version of cmp.1, 2, and 3 described in the user study section. Cmp.1' and cmp.3' produce the same result for SubjectA, B, C, and D. The expression of cmp.2' is only for SubjectD. This expression means that the composition allows users to experience the habitual behaviors of subjectA and B and C which do not tend to be selected by SubjectD.

In viewing the videos of Japanese wrestling match, all users tended to skip out of play scenes. They also tended to play in-play scenes and replay scenes at a normal speed. This tendency is similar to the result of viewing football game video. The results of the interviews held after the reusing phase reveal that these subjects were satisfied by the automatically played target videos produced by reusing their video viewing style to three unknown videos of football game. In the result of composition of video viewing styles, all subjects mentioned that they could not figure out the difference between their own viewing style and the result through cmp.1', because they did similar manipulation (i.e. skipping out of play scenes). Positive opinions that the automatically played videos look like some digest videos were obtained through the result of composition with cmp.3'. All subjects were irritated by the out of play scenes that were not skipped by the system by composition through cmp.2'. These opinions about three types of composition are almost the same opinions as in the result of composition phase with foot ball game videos. TV programs of the sports game seem to have a common viewing style.

In viewing the recording videos of surveillance camera, all subjects tended to skip the scenes that have no human or moving object in the frame. When a human or a moving object enters the frame all subjects tended to play these scenes at a normal speed to check the detail. Two of them sometimes tried to re-examine the scenes. Through an interview after the reusing phase, we found that all subjects were satisfied very much by the automatically played videos produced by reusing process because the result of reusing process marks high performance (i.e. the automatically played video is very similar to the subject's video viewing style). This is because the low level features of surveillance video are simpler than sports video and then the classification was not so difficult. The features of optical flow data seem to have worked effectively though it is not verified. For the same reason, the results of video composition phase with cmp.1' and cmp.3' obtained positive opinions. On the other hand, the result through cmp.2' made all users irritated as was the result with sports game videos. Most scenes which are estimated as ones that all subjects will play in the same manner were played at normal speed. This means all subjects had to watch the boring scenes without any change at a normal speed. Although cmp.2' is designed to allow users to find out habitual behaviors of other users that do not tend to be selected by themselves, no subjects needed to know others' habitual behavior in these user studies.

Additional User Study with SOI Based Composition

The user study described in Section 7 employed the manipulation based composition. We conducted an additional user study by using SOI based composition.

The subjects were not the same as the ones of the previous study. In this user study, four subjects were asked to view and control five videos of 5-min. football game so that these video were used as training videos for generating their classifiers. The manipulation profile in the right side of Figure 4 was used. In viewing these videos, all four subjects tended to skip (i.e. fast forwarding) the out of play scenes. Two subjects sometime tried to re-examine (i.e. forwarding at less than the normal speed after rewinding) the goal scenes. Two subjects tended to skip in-play scenes which have no goal posts in view. Though three subjects tended to play the replay scenes at a normal speed, one subject tended to skip these replay scenes. After generating their classifier, they watched another three 5-min. football game videos with composition profile. The composition profile used here was the average type composition profile described in the approach section. The composition selects a manipulation which is based on the calculated average SOI ($\sum$ (SOIn)/n). Because the manipulation profile in the right side of Figure 4 includes three types of manipulation (Re-examine, Normal, Skip), if the average SOI is less than -0.333, the video frame should be played at a faster speed, while if the average SOI is from -0.333 to +0.333, the video frame should be played at a normal speed. In the same way, the video frame will be played at a slower speed (or re-examine the video frame) when the average SOI is more than +0.333.

The subjects were asked to watch the other three 5-min. football game videos which are not used for training classifiers. Figure 12 shows one example of video with the average type composition. The visualization in Figure 12 consists of normal and skip manipulation. Although there were several goal or shoot scenes in the video, the composition result does not estimate the scenes as ones which should be played at a slower speed. Through an interview asking subjects' impression after watching composed videos, they felt the composed videos are like digest videos.

All subjects agreed with the fact that the composed video they watched is the average type viewing style. However, one of them mentioned that it is little bit puzzling because the results never try to play some scenes at a slower speed. This may be caused by the design of the manipulation profile. In the design of the left side profile in the Figure 4, linear SOI is corresponds to linear playback speed. On the other hand, the design of the right side profile in the Figure 4 associates linear SOI with non linear playing manipulations such as re-examine and skip. This design and the composition results based on this design might not fit the subject's intuition. Although the manipulation profiles were defined by the author in these user studies, it is better to allow users to edit their own manipulation profile by themselves.

Figure 12. One example of video with the average type composition. This visualization consists of normal and skip manipulation. Although there were several goal or shoot scenes in the video, the composition result does not estimate the scenes which should be played at a slower speed.

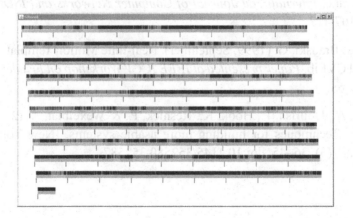

CONCLUSION

In this chapter, we describe the notion of reusing the video viewing style; we present examples of composition using these styles to create new video viewing styles.

Contrary to researches that employ content-based domain knowledge, little has been reported about the composition of tacit knowledge such as video viewing styles in knowledge studies. It is well known that video data essentially have temporal aspects that might make users view the videos more passively than other media such as text or images. On the other hand, the fact that we have increasingly more opportunities to use videos for our knowledge might facilitate the active browsing of videos. We believe that novices might be able to operate videos more freely and develop their own video viewing styles. To support these users, we need to clarify not only the semantic understanding of the video content but also the habitual behavior of each user.

It is suggested that the social navigation technique for supporting the user's activity by using past information is useful [19]. The contributions of our study are the provision of not only the notion of reusing past information but also the creation of new video viewing styles. In this chapter, we present three types of composition manipulations; composition manipulations have a greater possibility of generating new and meaningful video viewing styles. Refining composition manipulations can be considered as future work.

REFERENCES

Alavi, M., & Leidner, D. E. (1999). Knowledge management systems: issues, challenges, and benefits. *Journal of Communications of the AIS, 1*(2es).

Brin, S., & Page, L. (1998). The Anatomy of a Large-Scale Hypertextual Web Search Engine, *International Journal of Computer Networks and ISDN Systems, 30*, (1-7) 107-117.

Davis, J., & Bradski, G. (1999, September). Real-time Motion Template Gradients using Intel CVLib. *Paper presented at IEEE ICCV Workshop on Framerate Vision*, Kerkyra, Greece

Dieberger, A., Dourish, P., Höök, K., Resnick, P., & Wexelblat, A. (2000). Social navigation: Techniques for building more usable systems. [New York: ACM.]. *Interaction, 7*(6), 36–45. doi:10.1145/352580.352587

Ekin, A., Tekalp, A. M., & Mehrotra, R. (2003). Automatic soccer video analysis and summarization. *IEEE Transactions on Image Processing, 12*(7), 796–807. doi:10.1109/TIP.2003.812758

Fischer, G., Lemke, A. C., & Schwab, T. (1985). Knowledge-Based Help Systems. In L. Borman, & B. Curtis (Eds.), *Proceedings of CHI'85 Conference on Human Factors in Computing Systems* (pp. 161-167). New York:ACM.

Fujima, J., & Tanaka, Y. (2007). Web-application composition through direct editing of Web documents and multiplexing of information access scenarios. *Journal of Systems and Computers in Japan, 38*(12), 1–13. doi:10.1002/scj.20861

Nakamura, Y., & Kanade, T. (1997). Semantic analysis for video contents extraction—spotting by association in news video. *Proceedings of the fifth ACM international conference on Multimedia* (pp.393-401). New York: ACM Press.

Open, C. V. retrieved December 22, 2009, from http://opencv.willowgarage.com/

Polanyi, M. (1983). *Tacit Dimension*. Gloucester, MA: Peter Smith Pub Inc.

Sakagami, H., & Kamba, T. (1997). Learning Personal Preferences on Online Newspaper Articles from User Behaviors., *International Journal of Computer Networks and ISDN Systems, 29,*(8-13) 1447-1456.

Seo, Y., & Zhang, B. (2000). Learning user's preferences by analyzing web-browsing behaviors. *Proceedings of International Conference on Autonomous Agents* (pp.381-387). New York: ACM.

Sugibuchi, & T., Tanaka, Y. (2004). Integrated Framework for the Visualization of Relational Databases and RelatedWeb Content. *Proceedings of Fourth IEEE Pacific-Rim Conference On Multimedia* (CD-ROM). Tokyo, Japan.

Syeda-Mahmood, T., & Ponceleon, D. (2001). Learning video browsing behavior and its application in the generation of video previews. *Proceedings of the ninth ACM international conference on Multimedia* (pp.119-128). New York: ACM Press.

Takashima, A., Yamamoto, Y., & Nakakoji, K. (2004). A Model and a Tool for Active Watching: Knowledge Construction through Interacting with Video. *Proceedings of INTERACTION: Systems, Practice and Theory* (pp.331-358). Sydney, Australia: Creativity and Cognition Studios Press.

Tanaka, Y. (2003). *Meme Media and Meme Market Architectures: Knowledge Media for Editing, Distributing, and Managing Intellectual Resources*. Hoboken, NJ: Wiley-IEEE Press. WEKA. retrieved December 22, 2009, from http://www.cs.waikato.ac.nz/ml/weka/

Yamamoto, Y., Nakakoji, K., & Takashima, A. (2005). The Landscape of Time-based Visual Presentation Primitives for Richer Video Experience. In Costabile, M. F., & Paterno, F. (Eds.), *Human-Computer Interaction: INTERACT 2005* (pp. 795–808). Heidelberg, Germany: Springer Berlin. doi:10.1007/11555261_63

Yu, B., Ma, W. Y., Nahrstedt, K., & Zhang, H. J. (2003). Video Summarization Based on User Log Enhanced Link Analysis. *Proceedings of the eleventh ACM international conference on Multimedia 03* (pp. 382-391). New York, NY: ACM.

Chapter 7
Utilisation of Expert Online Retrieval Tools:
An Exploration of Barriers and Added Values

Roberta Sturm
Saarland University, Germany

Christoph Igel
Saarland University, Germany

ABSTRACT

This chapter focuses on analysing system utilisation patterns, in connection with the use of the "Movement and Training" knowledge management system. Developed with the aim of supporting teaching courses at university level, or more precisely their preparation, realisation and follow-up, this web-based system is free of charge and has been available to a general educational audience since 2005. The authors present an analytic approach, which, in the first instance and from the user's perspective, illustrates whether the intended utility and added values for instructors and learners have been achieved. A further intention was to identify any potential barriers that would obstruct utilisation of the system. In combination with basic theoretical principles and empirical findings relating to knowledge management, the authors derive implications for modifying the system with the aim of facilitating its future use.

DOI: 10.4018/978-1-61520-851-7.ch007

INTRODUCTION

With the rapid dissemination of new technological possibilities in all areas of society, the utilisation and application of new information and communication technologies (ICT) is also increasingly becoming a focus of attention in the education sector. The Federal Ministry of Education and Research (Bundesministerium für Bildung und Forschung – BMBF) postulates that computers and the Internet can even be considered as commonplace tools in the education system. This applies equally to schools, vocational training and further education, as well as to higher education. In this connection, the focus on the path to a globalised economy and knowledge society also applies to the "reorganisation and redefinition of learning processes that have so far been dominated by social interaction through the increased use of [Electronic Data Processing (EDP)] technology as a teaching and learning medium" (Heine & Durrer, 2001, 2 (translated)). But to what extent has the use of digital information and knowledge objects in fact already become part of everyday teaching and learning activities at German institutes of higher education? In this chapter we aim to explore this question, taking as an example the discipline of sports science, based on a specific systems development project.

Two perspectives are anchored within the scope of the project "eBuT – eLearning in der Bewegungs- und Trainingswissenschaft" (eLearning in Movement and Training Science), supported by the BMBF: the perspective of the learner and of the teacher. For pragmatic reasons, teaching-learning modules were developed for learners, and separately a multimedia database was designed to store the digital material to support lecturers during their apprenticeship. While teaching-learning modules cannot be used according to their original purpose during a seminar, a lecturer can use elements of the database as a fallback within a face-to-face seminar, to act as a cognitive anchor for the students.

With the development and implementation of the "Bewegung und Training" (Movement and Training) knowledge management system (KMS), a web-based application was created that offers instructors (e.g., lecturers in lectures, or students presenting papers in a seminar) digital information or knowledge objects that can be integrated into conventional presentation tools such as Microsoft PowerPoint at no cost. In accordance with the project application, the conceptual design embodied the following goals relating to the utility and added value of the KMS for teaching in movement and training science (Igel & Daugs, 2002):

- Time- and place-independent access to digital information and knowledge objects,
- Enhancement of conventional teaching offers,

- Support of innovative teaching concepts, and
- Distribution of teaching materials to a wider educational audience.

The whole discussion about learning and teaching technologies is not new, but has its origin in programmed instruction, where teaching and learning machines were common. Indeed, neither the teaching-learning modules nor the multimedia database should be, according to Cube (1968), seen as a "learning or teaching machine" to replace or substitute the teacher. The classical attempts by Pressey, Skinner and Crowder had the purpose of assisting the teacher, enabling him or her to devote attention to "real" teaching duties (Daugs, 1979, 34).

From the technological perspective, the "Movement and Training" KMS is based on a Windows 2000 server equipped with a MySQL database and Active Server Pages; its front-end is designed for a connection with a data rate of 56kb/s. According to the "pull principle", so-called digital information and knowledge objects can be retrieved and selected, collected in a separate download domain and, where required, archived and downloaded. Alternatively, users can make digital information and knowledge objects that they have created themselves available to the (scientific) community via the "push principle". The two functionalities "search" and "submit" characterise the exchange platform. After the registration process, the user accesses the search mask (Figure 1). Now he can narrow his search to specified object areas and different search parameters (e.g., subject areas, file formats and file dimensions). Afterwards the user receives a hit list. The more precise the search query – in other words, the more parameter specifications it includes – the more narrowly will the hit-list results be chosen. If a hit meets the user's demands, he transfers it to his e-book, where hits can be stored permanently. Objects can be downloaded from the eBook as a zip file.

The digital information and knowledge objects include multimedia assets [1] and text and literature files, including full texts. In addition, a trilingual movement and training-science thesaurus is available via the Internet. Goal-directed retrieval is assured through markup based on an application-specific adaptation of the meta-data standard Dublin Core including integrated, multilingual thesauri. The KMS has a differentiated rights and roles management. The download of the digital in-

Figure 1. The "pull principle"

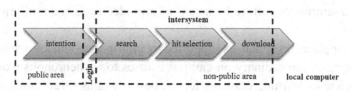

formation and knowledge objects takes the requirements of the German Copyright Act[2] into account, on the one hand through declarations of assignment of temporally and spatially unrestricted rights of use by the authors and programmers, on the other hand through the digital signature of the stored digital information and knowledge objects, plus the archiving and documentation of their respective development files.

Literature files, assets and texts can be uploaded via the "push principle". Before they are published they have to pass a quality-assurance stage. In close consultation with the educational network's content experts the following steps are taken:

- The quality of the new object and its attached information are examined.
- Positive classification leads to allocation to a subject area; if necessary the subject area is extended.
- The object gets an ID which acts as a primary key in identifying the database object.
- If a new object is published, the users will be informed via newsletter.

For clarification, two possible application scenarios are described here, including their expected added value. A course similar to a seminar is described. Multimedia-based assets in on-campus courses are supposed to be used in the framework of this teaching/learning scenario. Both lecturers and students who are expected to give presentations about certain topics have to consider the following steps in terms of their preparation time:

- KMS registration
- Goal-oriented search (influenced by intention and competence)
- Topic-related number of hits and their upload to the e-book
- Downloading the e-book to the client computer
- Integration of selected assets into a PowerPoint presentation

Besides multimedia-based enrichment of courses, the KMS can support students in their preparation and analysis of seminars or lectures. This will be addressed further in the second application scenario. As soon as a lecturer has provided information and knowledge objects in the framework of a seminar, for example, students can download them from any place at any time. Students can reflect on lesson materials used in a seminar or lecture by means of provided texts and multimedia-based elements.

Possible application scenarios supported by information and knowledge objects of a KMS range from ordinary on-campus courses to asynchronous work such as targeted review of learning contents for upcoming exams ("revision courses"). A further differentiation of application possibilities is caused by thematically strongly diverging study regulations at universities. Furthermore, the protagonists do not play a minor role. The added value achieved by use of the KMS depends on the degree of factors of the opened pedagogical space (see also Daugs, 1979, p. 55).

PROBLEM AND OBJECTIVES

High expectations are attached to the application of new ICT at all levels of education, and especially for teaching and learning purposes. Kerres (2001) summarises three dimensions of potential improvement possibilities for different teaching and learning scenarios:

1. Added-value dimension "distance": Information can be made available regardless of place and time.
2. Added-value dimension "multimedia": Multimodal Information can be provided.
3. Added-value dimension "interaction": Information can be exchanged; interaction with computer (human-computer interaction) and communication between teacher and learner via computer (human-computer-human interaction).

There is currently no adequate answer regarding exactly what form teaching and learning with new media is supposed to take, or what kind of use is to be expected. Although there are numerous attempts in almost all scientific disciplines to force the use of multimedia-based applications, the existing projects and attempts do not go beyond the status of single isolated activities (Keil-Salwik et al., 1997, p. 73).

Taking application-oriented interests into account, this chapter focuses on the impact analysis of the system. We focus on the one hand on the question "How is the KMS utilised?", and on the other hand on the question "What reasons do users have for not (or no longer) utilising the system?".

The theoretical utilisation possibilities of a KMS as a time- and place-independent online distribution platform for teaching materials have already been described. But are they in fact actually used? How is the KMS used in day-to-day scientific work?

The utilisation of new ICT technologies is jeopardised by barriers[3]. The scientific literature postulates various kinds of barriers: material barriers, institutional barriers, socio-cultural barriers, mental and psychical barriers, fundamental barriers, natural barriers, intentionally generated barriers (see also Ortner, 2002). According to Adelsberger et al. (2002, p. 531) two approaches can be isolated:

The object of the empirical approach is to identify barriers based on studies, and to develop suitable measures to overcome them (see also Bullinger et al., 1997). On the other hand, various systematization approaches for identifying knowledge and learning barriers have been proposed. In either case, however, it is unclear what measures should be taken in order to prevent the barriers from arising.

Based on this state of affairs, we aim to provide a second step that identifies, with the help of a theory-based analysis, concrete phenomena that hinder added-value utilisation of information and knowledge management systems (see also Sturm & Igel, 2005). The literature available in this field is, for the most part, restricted to a corporate context. Enhanced by the sparse empirical findings relating to the difficulties encountered in utilising new media in the education sector, we draw up a system of personal and non-personal determinants that influence teaching and learning with the help of new ICT technologies, and hence also the potential use of the KMS (see also Figure 2).

Figure 2 shows several sub-dimensions assigned to each branch of the main dimension. Human barriers belong to the section of personal barriers and can be divided into two parts. The first is the area of skills, and the second the area of volition. Skills are taken as summarising all aspects of competence. Anxiety, efficacy, liking, awareness and usefulness are just a few of the motivational factors that influence voluntary use of a system. Non-personal barriers can be ascribed to system-related or organizational aspects, such as a lack of access to the Internet.

Figure 3 illustrates the different approaches before and during the use of the KMS. Non-personal barriers inhibit usage completely, while personal barriers impede it to a greater or lesser degree.

It goes without saying that the literature, mostly based on empirical values, also cites numerous intervention measures that counteract the various barriers. One common practice when introducing new systems or software is to offer training courses, although empirical studies of their effectiveness tend to be rare (see also Siepmann, 1993). The findings, for the most part from pedagogical psychology and human-computer interaction research, are taken up and incorporated into the concept of a training course for system novices in the form of guidelines oriented towards Carroll's (1990) principles of minimal instruction.

Figure 2. Personal and non-personal barriers prior to and during the utilisation of new ICT technologies

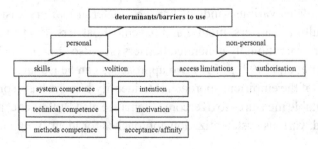

The factors that are obligatory in terms of training for end users remain uncertain. Therefore, the following questions also remain unanswered:

- What degree of competence requires training?
- When should training be recommended in terms of an EDP product, and what is the determining factor in this regard: design aspects or new functionalities?
- What does a good training course look like, and how can success be evaluated?
- What kind of training is most successful? (Which instructional design is more suitable: constructivist, cognitive, behaviouristic or action theory-based? With or without instructions? With or without instruction materials (manuals)? Optimal group size for training courses? etc.).
- How long are training courses supposed to take, and how extensive should they be in order to compensate any missing applied knowledge?

METHOD OF MEASUREMENT

Utilisation analyses[4] can be employed either to sound out the demand for new offerings prospectively or to evaluate retrospectively the adequacy of the contents and design of existing structures. Such analyses study the users of a system or a website and the way they utilise the system or navigate within the website. In addition to questionnaires and log-file analyses, more complex exploratory methods can also be applied, notably from the field of human-computer interaction research (e.g., registering eye movements). Based on the findings obtained, recommended actions can be formulated in order to increase the efficiency of working with the system, for example in the form of software-ergonomics proposals. Utilisation analyses are therefore used, among other things, to determine the information demand on the basis of utilisation correlations and user typologies, to analyse user potential and to identify utilisation barriers, with the aim, where applicable, of introducing suitable measures to reduce these barriers and evaluate user acceptance.

Figure 3. Contact points of barriers before and during the use of the KMS

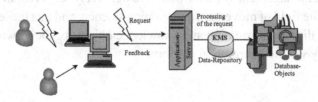

The present chapter focuses on the retrospective analysis of the adequacy of the contents and design of the "Movement and Training" KMS; the design aspect is thus not solely restricted to the design of the user interface, but first and foremost encompasses the functionalities of the KMS as such (Tröger, 2004). The following sections describe the analytical approach to examining the questions formulated above.

Methodical instruments are necessary tools for analysing real user behaviour given certain parameters and usage barriers. These instruments are supposed, on the one hand, to illustrate usage behaviour, and on the other to elicit user-typical correlations of human-computer interaction. Therefore,

- Server-side system-log-files were used to record usage behaviour;
- Standardized questionnaires were used to assess computer and Internet literacy, attitudes to computers and the Internet, and to software and hardware and Internet connectivity, and thus to get information about the cause variable and usage barrier "personal know-how" and "non-personal know-how" ("technology questionnaire").
- One standardized questionnaire including questions about intention and affinity with the Internet concerning system usage ("added-value questionnaire") was used to assess usage and added value of the "Movement and Training" KMS.
- Finally, factors that influence individual usage behaviour were identified by means of a partly standardized Delphi method.

The analysis consists of two successive phases:

Phase 1. Exploratory Study

The first, exploratory study aimed to establish the suitability of the KMS for daily use in a real-life scenario, and to analyse this use with the help of qualitative and quantitative methods from empirical social research. In addition to identifying typical behaviour patterns and search strategies, we looked for difficulties in use and attributed them to the identified personal and non-personal barriers.

The data collection for the exploratory study covered the period from October 2005 to March 2006, while the university's winter semester was in session. It was expected that during this period the digital information and knowledge objects of the knowledge management system would be extensively retrieved, in particular by instructors in the field of movement and training science, and that these users would perhaps make digital information and knowledge objects of their own available to the community via the distribution platform.

Phase 2. Quasi-Experimental Study

In the second phase, the aim was to determine the impact of utilisation barriers on usage patterns in relation to the "Movement and Training" KMS, and possibly to identify the level and direction of impact.

We aimed to document whether a prior course of training proved to be the most suitable means of minimising the barriers identified in the exploratory study. Furthermore, a central purpose of this study was to make the impact of IT qualification on system-specific know-how more transparent, and to stimulate more intensive research in this field.

ANALYSIS APPROACH AND SELECTED RESULTS OF THE 1ST STUDY

Since the KMS is available free of charge via the Internet to a broad educational audience, and our exploratory study aimed to map real use of the system, we made no attempt to purposefully select the sample group. The fact that during the survey period the system was only accessible in German restricted the sample group to German-speaking users. The primary target group comprises domain experts in the field of movement and training science, as well as aspiring experts, and can be roughly quantified as follows:

The 75 German-speaking sports science institutes and universities are made up of 66 sports science institutes and universities in Germany, 4 sports science institutes and universities in Austria, and 5 sports science institutes and universities in Switzerland. Movement and training science in itself comprises around 51 fields, employing more than 128 members of staff. In any one semester, almost 350 courses (218 seminars, 98 lectures and 28 exercise/practical courses) are held on selected topics relating to movement and training science, which are attended by roughly 28,000 students. Added to these are Internet users from organised sport: from around 70 professional associations and sports federations with 87,000 clubs totalling 27 million members, of whom in a given year some 550,000 (exercise leaders etc.) require training at some level.

From an application-oriented point of interest the investigation of user-KMS interaction is a particular emphasis of this exploratory study. The answer to the overall question "How is the KMS used?" implicitly includes many further questions, including the following:

- Who uses the KMS and when?
- Which functions are mainly used?

- What are the predominant search strategies?
- What do people look for?
- Which hits are selected?
- Are there technological or system specific reasons to avoid using the KMS?

Due to the variety of the data, the results presented within this chapter can be no more than a selected extract of those available.

Most of the users were students and young scientists between the age of 20 and 35; students make up the majority of these two groups. This corresponds with the expected age distribution of Internet users. As far as a clear assignment was possible, there were 70% male and 24% female users. This result shows that there are still gender-specific differences in the use of new ICT technologies. After the activation of the KMS was announced in October, there were nearly 140 logins from the beginning of the second week of the semester. In December there were nearly 190 logins; thereafter logins fell back to an average of around 50 per month. Most accesses were made during working time or lecture periods (i.e., between 9am and 5pm), and lasted until late evening. This suggests that in terms of teaching and learning purposes the system was being used for preparation and analysis of lessons, and does not exclude the use of the KMS in university courses.

Summary results:

- The respondents of the added-value questionnaire used the KMS as teaching support, as well as an independent learning aid.
- 17% of the people agreed that the KMS was very supportive in teaching, in that necessary materials were available to course participants at a glance without the lecturer having to distribute them to each participant.
- 96% of the students agreed that the KMS would be a helpful learning support for them in the future, the main reasons being the ability to revise unclear aspects frequently and independently, and the convenience for getting information for presentations and term papers.
- Since nearly 90% of the actions in the log files were registered in "Search" and "eBook", the main focus was put on this aspect throughout the subsequent investigation.
- The main search strategies were narrowing down the topic area or entering keywords.
- Very often people looked for digital information and knowledge objects in general – preferably assets – and would accept a big result list.

Selected usage events are the focus of further consideration. Besides investigating user typologies, the first visit is analyzed in detail in terms of its orientation role, and the last visit in terms of usage timidity.

There are certainly countless other possibilities for identifying typical behaviour patterns by analysing the system log files. Within this chapter, we (1) examine the logs of each user's first session, in the hope of identifying patterns that reveal how users acquaint themselves with a new system, and (2) focus on the last session, in the hope that this will reveal some reasons for no longer utilising the system. From both of these perspectives we hope to gain insights into aspects that impede the smooth handling of the system, and in particular retrieval.

The First Session

We start by directing our attention to the first session of 200 users, which we assume is a time of "familiarisation with the new system". Learnability is a fundamental aspect of usability, characterized by the time that needs to be invested in training before a user can work productively with a system. It is important that this time be short, since "users are busy people trying to accomplish tasks" (Dumas & Redish, 1999, p. 5). Users should be able to achieve their goals with the product simply, effectively and satisfactorily after a relatively short period of training.

It may be that usage patterns emerge from this time that allow inference of recommended actions for a training course aimed at counteracting initial reservations in utilising the system. To select representative users, a multi-stage procedure was carried out. Selection criteria were – depending on the context of the questions – the number of sessions, the length of the sessions, and the number of clicks in study-relevant domains of the KMS.

At first glance, the histories of the sessions do not suggest that the users have very much in common. The frequency distribution as an indicator for particularly frequented domains in the KMS shows that of the 454 actions of the analysed data records, 25% are retrieval actions and as many as 64% occur in the e-book. The chronological histories reveal that the user profile is called up relatively promptly after login, although only 50% actually make changes there. The subsequent actions take place in the parent search domain. In 80% of the cases, a successful search is carried out by entering individual search terms or by narrowing down the subject area, but without subsequently selecting any of the hits, which suggests that such searches in the first 25 to 35 actions were "exploratory". Concluding that none of the hits corresponded to what the user was looking for seems unjustified, due to the short time span (<4sec.) between subsequent searches, and the failure to browse in the displayed hit lists. In those cases where the help function was called up, it was equally for the categories "e-book" and "submit". This provides some first indications of what should be dealt with in the context of a training course for system novices in order to assure, optimise or stimulate the use of the system as intended by the project.

The Last Session

Schüppel (1996) and Lewin et al. (1996), among others, list a large variety of reasons that could deter users from utilising information and communication technologies. In this section, we attempt to identify motives that discourage users from further utilisation of the KMS. To this end, we considered in isolation the last sessions of the 200 test users.

The data records were categorised, with respect to their content, into successful and failed sessions[5]. In this section we investigate the latter, as they are deemed to be more meaningful for the present analysis. Successful sessions as a rule generate a new login. We also include in this category those sessions that show, among their last actions, the uploading of a hit into the e-book following a successful search, or the downloading of the e-book to the local computer. Sessions that do not meet these criteria are categorised as failed. 92 users' last sessions fell into the "failed" category; 65 of these users furthermore showed no record of downloading the e-book. Contrary to our assumptions, the distribution with regard to the used functionalities hardly differs from the other data records analysed, with the exception of the number of actions in the e-book, which at 22% lies significantly below the percentage otherwise recorded. In parts, the data records of the sample demonstrate striking similarity with the first session. Most of the aborts occur directly after a successful parent search, which, despite narrowing down the subject area and entering search terms, led to a comparatively high number of hits (>50). It can be seen as more informative that many successful searches culminate in the upload of several hits, which are subsequently saved together in the e-book as a zip file. Contrary to our assumption that downloading the e-book would mark the end of a session, users repeatedly called up the help pages before ending. These phenomena could point to barriers in working with the system relating to the handling of the hit pages, the e-book, or the offered system help.

Usage Barriers from the Respondents' Perspective

According to respondents who took part in a study carried out by the Hochschul-Informations-System GmbH in 1996 concerning multimedia-based support in university teaching, there were obstacles in terms of using the KMS that still exist today. This is sobering news, but may also refer to sport science as cultural science and Geisteswissenschaft. [6]

The idea that there are various aspects that prevent existing as well as potential users from using all capabilities offered by the KMS was confirmed within the exploratory study. A number of results are given below to illustrate this.

Having complete technical equipment, network-connected computers or Internet access does not automatically guarantee a new level of quality in teaching and learning.

Personal know-how is one determining aspect, which among other things contributes in terms of system competency.

Table 1 summarises EDP skills of the random sample. The figures are a result of self-assessment.

In summary, the majority of users reported that they had a significant level of computer and Internet literacy, but that their competence declines with the growing specificity of the application.

In their study, Kleinmann et al. (2005) investigated the influence of familiarity with particular computer applications on the use of eLearning offerings. Based on the HISBUS results it was confirmed that besides basic competencies regarding computer handling, familiarity with the Internet and communication applications is a prerequisite for unproblematic use of eLearning offerings.

Noting that "search tools" and "submission tools" (tools to submit digital information and knowledge objects) were predominantly marked "bad" or "still OK", one might recommend a training course. The respondents consider subject and methodological skills as important in terms of an actionable and multi-valued use of online distribution platforms. Aspects assigned to the factor "volition" can only partly be regarded as inhibitory, since KMS users consider themselves as technophile (according to the "Computer Attitude Scale" developed by Loyd & Gressard in 1984), as motivated and curious, and with particular enthusiasm for working with computers. Following the model of Behaviourism, we considered cognitive aspects such as individuals' working-memory-dependent information-processing abilities, which influence both "skills" and "volition", as being a form of "black box" and therefore not part of the exploratory study or quasi-experiment. Non-personal barriers influence the use of information/knowledge management systems only

Table 1. Self-assessment concerning EDP-skills

Know-how [%]	PC-Handling	Web	New Media	KMS	search tools	submission tools
very good	21,1	10,5	5,3	-	-	5,3
good	42,1	57,9	89,4	10,5	26,3	15,8
still ok	36,8	31,6	5,3	63,2	47,4	68,4
bad	-	-		26,3	26,3	10,5

marginally. Support provided by external institutions and people is very popular but not essentially necessary. Given the intended improvements of basic conditions at universities, and increasingly favourable conditions concerning the use of the Internet, those obstacles should soon be a thing of the past.

ANALYSIS PROCEDURE AND SELECTED RESULTS OF THE 2ND STUDY

Although the "acquisition of extensive EDP competences and the habitualised use of computers" (Heine & Durrer, 2001, p. 2 (translated)) among the current generation of graduates is undisputed – they accord it a similar elementary status to basic skills such as reading, writing and arithmetic – the results of our quasi-experimental study of sports-science foundation students' use of a KMS as an online retrieval tool do not paint such a positive picture. Following the results of the exploratory study, in the quasi-experiment we decided to focus on the identified "system competency" usage barrier, in the hope of reducing it in future by means of suitable intervention strategies. The follow-up study was aimed at identifying the degree and direction of influence on this "system competency".

In addition, part of the study addressed the question of whether a system training course[7] attended before using the KMS for the first time could have a decisive positive influence. The following statements are limited to use of the KMS as an online search system, because of the small number of accesses to the submission function.

Prior to the quasi-experimental study, the impact of the "digital literacy" utilisation barrier and the effect of the "system training" intervention measure on application and utilisation patterns with respect to the KMS were formulated as follows:

- System users with a high level of system competence solve set tasks faster and more efficiently than system users with a low level of system competence.
- System training helps system users to solve set tasks faster and more efficiently.
- System training improves task solving knowledge, more so for users with a low level of system competence than for those with a high level of competence.

Tying in with gender-sensitive studies, we further pursued the heuristic goal of eliciting the influence of gender and system training on the solving of tasks using the KMS.

The above-mentioned hypotheses were to be verified or refuted by means of a "classical test". With the use of classical control-group arrangements to control all confounding variables (i.e., those that cannot be eliminated or held constant), the main goal is to examine changes of dependent variables concerning the effect of confounding variables, whether these changes (in part) had been emerged without treatment (intervention measure: training course to handle the system). The influences of the other barriers recognizable in Figure 2 are controlled, as far as possible, by selecting a random sample and by the laboratory-like experiment procedure. The access barrier "non-personal factors", which predominantly depends on the hardware and software being used, is ruled out because all participants performed all parts of the experiment with one computer in a closed room. This computer will be described in more detail in a further concretisation of the experiment procedure. Furthermore, high Internet costs and long waiting periods concerning downloads of files were not an issue, since the laboratory computer is connected to the Internet via the university's LAN. Also the second factor of influence, which was assigned to the non-personal category "authorization", does not play a major role concerning students as a target group, since neither university policies nor any other restrictions prevented them from using the system. By presenting the users with tasks that are to be completed, "intention" as a course variable is almost completely regulated, since different individual intrinsically or extrinsically motivated approaches are limited. The remaining factors, which are predominantly assigned to the personal aspect "volition", show different results (including pleasure-of-use, stress, fear, liking, usefulness, curiosity).

After the study, students were asked to fill out an evaluation form referring to these aspects. Figure 4 shows the plan of the two-random-sample experiment, which was realized as design without previous measurement. The system novices were first divided into two groups to relate a more effective and more efficient use of the KMS to the training courses on the system. One group consisted of system novices with a high degree of system competencies, the other with low competencies. These groups were again divided into a treatment group and a control group.

Of 125 sports students on the foundation course, 48 were divided according to their digital literacy into two extreme groups with either high or low level of system competence. Within these two groups, matched samples were formed on the basis

Figure 4. Experimental design of the quasi experiment

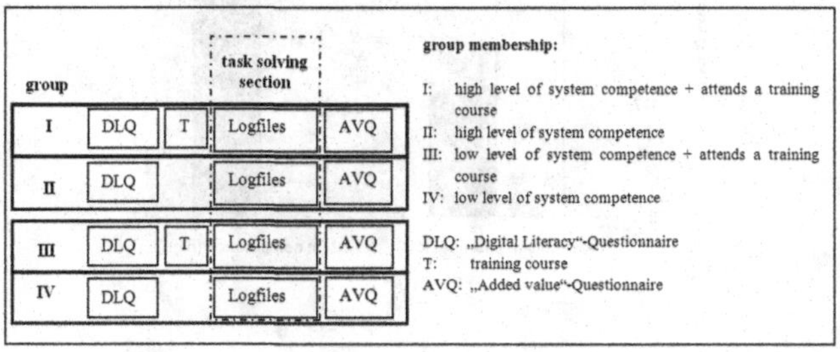

of digital literacy, gender and age. One student from each pair attended a training course, while the other taught him/herself the retrieval functionalities of the KMS. In order to permit conclusions about the effectiveness of the training, tasks were designed that when successfully solved covered the entire set of program function-alities taught in the training course. The design of the tasks took account of the fact that in a real utilisation context users have different intentions and expectations when working with the system. A procedure scheme, which was developed before-hand, was used to assess the solutions of specific tasks. A catalogue of criteria, validated beforehand by two domain experts, reflected the features of an optimal search strategy regarding so-called unspecific tasks. This catalogue reliably as-sesses the search process up to task solution, as well as the result of the task repre-sented by the number of downloads of information and knowledge objects.

With respect to their central tendency regarding the quality of task completion, the comparison between the groups produced a significant interaction effect for one task type and for the gender factor. It appears that system training helps sys-tem novices with a low level of system competence in terms of their task-solving knowledge when completing specific, detailed set tasks more than it does system novices with a high system competence (see also Figure 5).

Male participants in the training course perform considerably better than their untrained counterparts. For women, by contrast, participation in a training course has an influence that is even negative. The most significant differences can be identified for the solving of unspecific tasks (see also Figure 6)[8].

The calculated p-values substantiate, for the remaining hypotheses, the insig-nificant difference between the identified middle ranks of both extreme groups.

Figure 5. Task solving knowledge regarding specific tasks

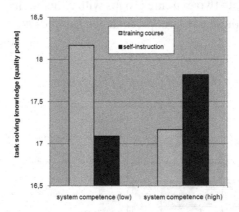

The results of the questionnaires provide an initial basis of explanation. Even though assessed as critical in training science, the subjective appraisal of the training participants is pulled up as a criterion for success for the training objective due to the lack of substantiated alternatives. By logging all data transmissions from the various steps taken by users in solving a specific task it is possible to objectively assess whether a positive course rating correlates with efficient utilisation of the system. According to the estimates of the training participants, the performed treatment only had a limited effect in dispelling prejudices and fear of contact with the computer, with the Internet and especially with the KMS. This result was not in accordance with the self-assessment of the participants before taking the course. 78% of the course participants certify an improvement in handling the KMS. 68% of the participants argue that they could not have assessed the system more quickly on their own.

Course participants with a low system expertise tend to be more motivated and focused, and therefore probably handle tasks more conscientiously. They ask more questions in the scope of the system training and assure themselves of the fact that their user identification is still active at the end of the test phase. According to their own estimation they use their identification to access and research texts for exam preparation, and for assets used to visually enhance presentations. Unspecified emotionally motivated reasons could explain the performance of the training participants with high system competency, perhaps resulting from not being challenged enough, but this finding is speculative.

There are still gender-specific differences between sport students regarding expertise and know-how in handling a personal computer. By separately observing computer and Internet skill, the formulated statements from past analyses are underlined to the disadvantage of female sport students.

Figure 6. Task solving knowledge regarding low system competency

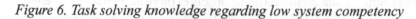

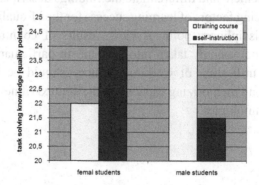

CONCLUSION

For the further development of the system, approaches from AI research relating to adaptive systems could help to improve user friendliness. One might, for example, draw on the procedure proposed by Nebel & Paschke (2004) "with the help of which domain-specific knowledge about users is integrated into user profiles [...]" (Nebel & Paschke, 2004, p.264 (translated)), that contributes to earlier, qualitatively better and quantitatively richer inference processes. Within the scope of the exploration, intrapersonal search strategies were observed. The adaptation could, for example, take the form of organising the hit list according to user-specific preferences. One could also work to avoid the frustration caused by text-field entries that produce no hits: following the example of Google, orthographical errors could be handled by offering a "Did you mean...?" prompt with the correct spelling, while keyword entry could be supported by offering automatic completion using terms filed according to the entry field's metadata.

While the utilisation of information technologies in the tertiary education sector can almost be considered commonplace[9], impact research in this field is restricted principally to the question of the effectiveness of new media from the perspective of learners. Little attention has been given so far to the acceptance of using information technology in teaching from the perspective of university instructors. Within the scope of the exploratory study we were able to confirm that there are aspects that deter existing as well as potential users from tapping the full capabilities associated with the KMS. Although computer training courses are taken for granted in practice, and the need for them is undisputed by experts, there are very few well-grounded models and studies in this field. The relevance of this topic ultimately becomes clear not only given the importance of computer skills for the labour market, but also in light of the impossible-to-ignore discussion about "lifelong learning". We therefore believe future research should more closely explore the behaviour-oriented approach and supplement and differentiate the findings described here, taking into account the influencing factors of learning success for the IT qualification of adults.

From an interdisciplinary point of view, results of cognitive-psychological studies should be increasingly taken into account. In particular, the influence of cognitive-capacity utilisation of working memory should be investigated with regard to teaching and memorizing capacity in the context of new information and communication technologies.

REFERENCES

Adelsberger, H. H., Bick, M., & Hanke, Th. (2002). Einführung und Etablierung einer Kultur des Wissensteilens in Organisationen. In M. Engelien & J. Homann (Eds.), *Virtuelle Organisationen und Neue Medien* (pp. 529-552). Köln: Eul.

Bannert, M. (1996). *Gestaltung und Evaluation von EDV-Schulungsmaßnahmen. Eine empirische Studie zur Effektivität und Akzeptanz. Landau.* Empirische Pädagogik.

Bower, G. H., & Hilgard, E. (1984). *Theorien des Lernens.* Stuttgart: Klett-Cotta.

Bullinger, H.-J., Wörner, K., & Prieto, J. (1997). *Wissensmanagement heute.* Stuttgart: Fraunhofer-Institut für Arbeitswirtschaft und Organisation.

Carroll, J. M. (1990). *The Nurnberg funnel: designing minimalist instruction for practical computer skill.* Cambridge, Mass: MIT press.

Cube, F. v. (1968). *Kybernetische Grundlagen des Lernens und Lehrens.* Stuttgart: Klett.

Daugs, R. (1979). *Programmierte Instruktion und Lerntechnologie im Sportunterricht.* München: Minerva.

Dix, A., Finlay, J., Abowd, G., & Beale, R. (1995). *Mensch Maschine Methodik.* München: Prentice Hall.

Dumas, J. S., & Redish, J. C. (1999). *A practical guide to usability testing.* Norwood, NJ: Ablex.

Gagné, R. M. (1969). *Die Bedingungen des menschlichen Lernens.* Hannover: Schroedel.

Heine, C. & Durrer, F. (2001). Computer und neue Medien in der Schule. Erfahrungen mit EDV-gestützten Lernprogrammen und Erwerb von Computerkenntnissen während der Schulzeit. Befunde aus der Befragung der studienberechtigten Schulabgänger 1999. *HIS-Kurzinformation A5/2001.*

Igel, C., & Daugs, R. (2002). Mehrwertpotentiale internetbasierter Lehre. In Jantke, K. P., Wittig, W. S., & Herrmann, J. (Eds.), *Von E-Learning bis E-Payment* (pp. 8–19). Berlin: Akademische Verlagsgesellschaft.

Keil-Slawik, R., Beuschel, W., Gaiser, B., Klemme, M., Pieper, C., & Selke, H. (1997). Multimedia in der universitären Lehre. Eine Bestandsaufnahme an deutschen Hochschulen. In I. Hamm & D. Müller-Böling (Eds.), *Hochschulentwicklung durch neue Medien* (pp. 73-122). Gütersloh: Verlag Bertelsmann-Stiftung.

Kerres, M. (2001). *Multimediale und telemediale Lernumgebungen. Konzeption und Entwicklung*. München, Wien: Oldenbourg.

Kleimann, B., Weber, S., & Willige, J. (2005). *E-Learning aus Sicht der Studierenden. 10. Kurzbericht der HIS – Hochschul-Informations-System GmbH*. Retrieved February 22, 2007, from http://www.his.de/pdf/24/HISBUS_E-Learning10.02.2005.pdf

Klix, F. (1971). Information und Verhalten. Kybernetische Aspekte der organismischen Informationsverarbeitung. Einführung in naturwissenschaftliche Grundlagen der Allgemeinen Psychologie. (1. Aufl.). Berlin: Verlag der Wissenschaften.

Lewin, K., Heublein, U., Kindt, M. & Föge, A. (1996). Bestandaufnahme zur Organisation mediengestützter Lehre an Hochschulen. *HIS Kurzinformationen 7/96*.

Loyd, B. H., & Gressard, C. P. (1984). The effects of sex, age, and computer experience on computer attitudes. *Association for Educational Data Systems Journal, 18*(4), 67–76.

Nebel, I.-T., & Paschke, R. (2004). Integration domänenspezifischer Informationen in Benutzerprofile für adaptive e-Learning-Systeme. In K.P. Fähnrich, K.P. Jantke & W.S. Wittig (eds.), *Conference Proceedings of the Leipziger Informatiktage '04 - LIT'04* (pp. 264-272).

Ortner, J. (2002). Barrieren des Wissensmanagements. In M. Bornemann & M. Sammer (Eds.), Anwendungsorientiertes Wissensmanagement: Ansätze und Fallstudien aus der betrieblichen und universitären Praxis (pp. 73–114). Wiesbaden: Gabler.

Schründer-Lenzen, A. (1995). *Weibliches Selbstkonzept und Computerkultur*. Weinheim: Deutscher Studienverlag.

Schüppel, J. (1996). *Wissensmanagement: Organisatorisches Lernen im Spannungsfeld von Wissens- und Lernbarrieren*. Wiesbaden: Gabler.

Siepmann, B. (1993). *Effektives EDV-Training*. Doctoral dissertation, University Bochum.

Søby, M. (2003). *Digital Competence: from ICT skills to digital "bildung"*. Oslo ITU, University of Oslo.

Sturm, R. (2008). *Internetbasiertes Wissensmanagement in Sportwissenschaft und Sport: eine empirische Studie zur Nutzung des Knowledge-Management-Systems „Bewegung und Training*. Retrieved December 1, 2009, from http://scidok.sulb.uni-saarland.de/volltexte/2008/1510/

Sturm, R., & Igel, C. (2005). Überlegungen zur empirischen Analyse des Nutzungs-verhaltens des Knowledge Management Systems „Bewegung und Training". In U. Lucke, K. Nölting & D. Tavangarian (Eds.), Workshop Proceedings DeLFI 2005 and GMW05(pp. 103-112). Rostock, 13-16 September 2005. Berlin: Logos Verlag

Tröger, B. (2004). Nutzungsanalysen im Blick auf fachliche und interdisziplinäre Webportale – Ergebnisse und Konsequenzen. *B.I.T.online brochure 1/2004*. Retrieved October 30, 2006, from http://www.b-i-t-online.de/hefte/2004-01/troeger.htm

ADDITIONAL READING

American Association of University Woman. (2000). *Tech-Savvy: Educating Girls in the New Computer Age*. Retrieved July 3, 2007, from http://www.aauw.org/research/girls_education/techsavvy.cfm

Anderson, M. D., & Hornby, P. A. (1996). Computer attitudes and the use of computers in psychology courses. *Behavior Research Methods, 2*, 341–346.

Bannert, M. (1999). Design und Evaluation von EDV-Schulungen. In Arend, U., Eberleh, E., & Pitschke, K. (Eds.), *Software-Ergonomie '99. Design von Informationswelten* (p. 385). Stuttgart: Teubner.

Bannert, M. & Arbinger, R. (1994). *Geschlechtstypische Zugangsweisen zum Computer Ergebnisse einer Befragung von Schülerinnen und Schüler der Sekundarstufe I in Rheinland-Pfalz*. (Bericht des Zentrums Nr. 1). Landau: Empirische Pädagogik.

Batinic, B., Bosnjak, M., & Bereiter, A. (1997). Der "Internetler". Empirische Ergebnisse zum Netznutzungsverhalten. In L. Gräf & M. Krajewski (Eds.), *Soziologie des Internet. Handeln im elektronischen Web-Werk* (pp. 196-215). Frankfurt/Main: Campus.

Baumgartner, P., & Kalz, M. (2005). Wiederverwendung von Lernobjekten aus didaktischer Sicht. In Tavangarian, D., & Nölting, K. (Eds.), *Auf zu neuen Ufern! Elearning heute und morgen. Medien in der Wissenschaft* (*Vol. 34*, pp. 97–106). New York, München, Berlin: Waxmann.

Beckers, J. J., Wicherts, J. M., & Schmidt, H. G. (2007). Computer Anxiety: „Trait" or „State"? *Computers in Human Behavior, 23*, 2851–2862. doi:10.1016/j.chb.2006.06.001

Dickhäuser, O., & Steinsmeier-Pelster, J. (2002). Erlernte Hilflosigkeit am Computer? Geschlechtsunterschiede in computerspezifischen Attributionen. *Psychologie in Erziehung und Unterricht, 49,* 44–55.

Dittler, U. (Ed.). (2003). *E-Learning. Einsatzkonzepte und Erfolgsfaktoren des Lernens mit interaktiven Medien.* München: Oldenbourg.

Döring, K. W., & Ziep, K.-D. (1989). *Mediendidaktik in der Weiterbildung.* Weinheim: Deutscher Studienverlag.

Garaven, T. N., & McCracken, C. (1993). Introducing end-user computing. The implications for training and development – part 1. *Industrial and Commercial Training, 25,* 8–14.

Gerbig, C., & Gerbig-Calcagni, I. (1998). Moderne Didaktik für EDV-Schulungen: ein praxisorientiertes Handbuch für Trainer, Ausbilder, Lehrkräfte und Qualifizierungsverantwortliche. Weinheim, Basel: Beltz.

Groebel, J., & Gehrke, G. (Eds.). (2003). Internet 2002: Deutschland und die digitale Welt. Internetnutzung und Medieneinschätzung in Deutschland und Nordrhein-Westfalen im internationalen Vergleich. Schriftenreihe Medienforschung der LfM (Vol. 46). Opladen.

Harley, D. (2002). Investing in educational technologies. *Journal of Studies in International Education, 6,* 172–187. doi:10.1177/1028315302006002006

Haussmann, M., & Hettich, C. (1995). *Geschlechterunterschiede beim Zugang zu Neuen Technologien. Eine empirische Studie zur Gestaltung von Schulungsmaßnahmen am Personalcomputer.* Doctoral dissertation, University Tübingen.

Hugger, K.-U. (2004). Neue Medien und Hochschullehrer: Zu Hinderungsgründen und Widerständen. In Bett, K., Wedekind, J., & Zentel, P. (Eds.), *Medienkompetenz für die Hochschullehre. Medien in der Wissenschaft (Vol. 28,* pp. 269–273). New York, München, Berlin: Waxmann.

Jerusalem, M., & Pekrun, R. (1999). *Emotion, Motivation und Leistung.* Göttingen: Hogrefe.

Kulik, J. (1994). Meta-analytic studies of findings on computerbased instruction. In Baker, E. L., & O'Neil, H. F. Jr., (Eds.), *Technology assessment in education and training.* Hillsdale, NJ: Lawrence Erlbaum.

Lang, N. (1998). Medienkompetenz in der Informationsgesellschaft. In *M. Ockenfeld, J. Lave, & E. Wenger, (1991). Situated learning. Legitimate peripheral participation.* Cambridge, UK: Cambridge University Press.

Lehmann, K. (1999). *Studieren 2000. Medien in der Wissenschaft (Vol. 8).* Münster, Germany: Waxmann.

Lehnert, U. (1992). *Der EDV-Dozent - Planung und Durchführung von EDVLehrveranstaltungen- Ein Leitfaden für Dozenten, Trainer, Ausbilder, Instruktoren.* Haar: Markt & Technik Verlag.

Norman, D. A. (2002). Emotion and design: Attractive things work better. *Interactions Magazine, ix*(4), 36–42.

Rümler, R. (2001). Wissensbarrieren behindern effektives Wissensmanagement. *Wissensmanagement, 5*, 24–27.

Shashaani, L. (1994). Gender-Differences in Computer Experience and it's Influence on Computer Attitudes. *Journal of Educational Computing Research, 11*(4), 347–367.

Siepmann, B. (1993). *Effektives EDV-Training.* Dissertation an der Universität Bochum.

Stine, W. D., & Wildemuth, B. M. (1992). The training of microcomputer users: Insight from two disciplines. *Journal of Education for Library and Information Science, 33*, 100–109.

Streitz, N.A. (1988). *Psychologische Aspekte der Mensch-Computer-Interaktion* (Arbeitspapier der GMD 344). Sankt Augustin: Gesellschaft für Mathematik und Datenverarbeitung mbH.

Taprogge, R. (1996). *Internet-Nutzung durch Studierende geistes- und sozialwissenschaftlicher Studiengänge in Deutschland.* Retrieved February 14, 2006, from http://www.uni-muenster.de/Publistik/MAG3/ifp/taprogg.html

von Papstein, P., & Frese, M. (1988). Training und Transfer im Mensch-Computer Bereich - ein arbeitspsychologischer Ansatz. In Ruppert, F., & Frieling, E. (Eds.), *Psychologisches Handeln in Betrieben und Organisationen. Aktuelle Aufgaben in Fallbeispielen* (pp. 69–90). Bern: Huber.

Whitley, B. E. Jr. (1996). Gender Differences in Computer-Related Attitudes: It Depends on What You Ask. *Computers in Human Behavior, 12*, 275–289. doi:10.1016/0747-5632(96)00007-6

ENDNOTES

1. Under the term "assets", multimedia developments (incl. stills, animations, simulations, videos, VRML models) in any technological format (incl..swf,. rm,.png,.gif,.pdf) are subsumed.

2. Further information about the German Copyright Act can be found on http://bundesrecht.juris.de/urhg/index.html

3. As a synonym to obstacles, resistance or difficulty, the term barrier, negatively connoted, stands for a wide range of influences that impact or even prevent the unrestricted use of systems or their accessibility.

4. "User behaviour" and "analysis of usage behaviour" are widely used terms. Therefore, there are no general definitions in the scope of scientific usage. Following the paradigm of human-computer interaction an operational definition is used, which focuses on the interaction of people and computers (and browser and Internet regarding the Knowledge Management System "Movement and Training") and makes them the object of empirical analysis.

5. Tying in with the comments of Schründer-Lenzen (1995, p. 44), in which to explain low female computer affinity they recommend primarily questioning the success or failure attribution and the consequences arising from this for self-esteem and self-assessment as far as computer literacy and use are concerned, success attribution is classified as a factor for the individual intention to work with the system.

6. Lacking EDP skills and vague commitment regarding modern ways of teaching, unsatisfying spatial and technological preconditions as well as gaps concerning the implementation of media-based ways of teaching in the curriculum are just a few of the reasons, which can be looked up in detail in Sturm (2008).

7. Systematically planned teaching-learning process for computer users, which aims at independent handling of specific program functions of computer systems (Bannert, 1996, p. 4 (translated)).

8. Unspecific tasks, as representative for browsing, accord the user a high degree of freedom for completing tasks using the KMS. In contrast to specific tasks, here only the topic outline is set; the individual user is free to decide on the approach and the selection of appropriate hits.

9. See also: High-tech strategy of the Bundesministerium für Bildung und Forschung (Federal Ministry of Education and Research). Retrieved April 12, 2007, from http://www.bmbf.de/de/equalification.php

Chapter 8
Software Agents for Human Interaction in Social Networks

Christian Erfurth
Friedrich Schiller University Jena, Germany

Volkmar Schau
Friedrich Schiller University Jena, Germany

ABSTRACT

Social networks like Facebook or MySpace have become very popular in recent years. The number of users visiting these networks on a regular basis is already very high and still increasing. The integration of users into such networks is typically achieved via web interfaces. In addition, modern mobile devices have been developed to support the "reachable everywhere" mentality. They feature up-to-date communication and web interfaces, offering the capacities of small computer systems. By combining these capacities with so-called mobile software agents, a seamless integration of users in on-line communities can be reached. This chapter highlights the potential of software agents for sophisticated interaction in ubiquitous, mobile applications by utilizing the example of social networks as a practical scenario.

INTRODUCTION

Today, the Web is the most popular communication channel for accessing and sharing information. At the beginning, and to a certain extent even today, the Web was highly unorganized. The start-up period of Web 1.0 was primarily characterized

DOI: 10.4018/978-1-61520-851-7.ch008

by data assembling. Information organization followed no general standard. Today we operate a more standardized Web, enhanced by semantic metadata and network services. Using network services, the entire media spectrum is becoming available in a standardized manner and is displacing the conventional browsing of common Web pages. Network services open up a new crop of opportunities to retrieve and combine data items into new media and information aggregates.

As a matter of course we are on the starting blocks to integrate and share our daily life within the context of web communication channels. That is the new understanding of mobile access and modern life. Thereby, mobile communication devices and applications are primarily designed to increase efficiency and productivity, as well as to manage our rapid way of life. For many people, particularly younger users, interaction functions of cell phones, smart phones, and other handhelds are paramount (Eagle & Pentland, 2005). A few small companies are beginning to exploit the growing demand for social mobile applications and start a new market of mobile software services. The seamless integration of mobile devices into daily life is, however, still challenging. Typically the usage of a mobile device happens on the spur of the moment. Therefore, social-mobile applications must be simple to use.

Facing additionally the continuously changing web and the enormous quantity of resources, humans are no more able to conceive the possibilities and to utilize available services efficiently. We need a kind of intelligent broker which is able to translate a human's requests into suitable service calls which will finally result in prepared information. Moreover, we need assistance to target a smooth integration of the virtual and the real world – of internet resources and daily life. With modern mobile devices and next generation communication techniques we are already able to realize this integration at a high level of quality. Mobile software agents are in addition well suited to provide essential support in this matter, due to their autonomous nature.

BACKGROUND

Social networking and community interactions have been the global consumer phenomenon of 2008. Nielsen Online points out that social network and blogging sites are now the fourth most popular activity on the internet ahead of personal emails (The Nielsen Company, 2009). The story is consistent across the world and dates back to the early days of computer networks. Following the SixDegrees.com experience in 1997, the doyen of social network sites that allowed its users to create profiles, invite friends, organize groups, and surf other user profiles, hundreds of social networks burst into life (Acquisti & Gross, 2006; Goble, 2009). From 2003 onward (see Figure 1), many new social network sites were launched (Boyd

& Ellison, 2007), prompting social software analyst Clay Shirky (Shirky, 2003) to coin the term YASNS: "Yet Another Social Networking Service". All services, as a definition for social network sites, consist of a web-based service that allow users to construct a public or semi-public profile within a delimited system, set up a list of other users with whom they share a connection, and view and traverse their list of connections and those made by others within the system.

When joining a social network site and building up a social profile, users are invited to identify others in the system with whom they have a potential relationship. The tag for these relationships differs depending on the site, e.g. "Friends", "Contacts" or "Fans". Most social network sites require bi-directional confirmation for friendship. Some sites use only one-directional friendships, labeled as "Fans" or "Followers", and call these "Friends" as well. So the term "Friends" can be mislead-

Figure 1. Launch dates of social network sites (Boyd & Ellison, 2007)

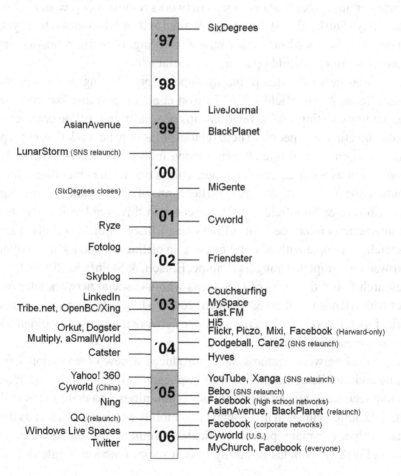

ing, and to have a connection on the Web does not necessarily mean to have a friendship in the usual context (Boyd, 2006). Beyond profiles, friends, and public or private messaging, social network sites vary greatly in their features and user basis. Some sites provide sharing of photographs or videos, and others have built-in blogging and instant messaging technology. Others are true mobile or mobile-enabled social network sites, like Dodgeball or match2blue, or support other types of limited mobile interactions (e.g. Facebook, MySpace and Cyworld). Furthermore some social network sites are designed with specific ethnic, religious, political, or other identity-driven categories. They target very specific social groups, e.g. for dogs (Dogster) and cats (Catster), although it is still the human owner who manages the profile in this case. While social network sites are often designed to attract a homogeneous population, it is still not unusual that groups use exactly these sites to differentiate themselves by means of age, educational level or other typically segmenting social factors. Most social network sites focus on growing broadly and exponentially, though others (such as aSmallWorld and BeautifulPeople) explicitly seek narrower audiences, because social networks require a degree of exclusion to work properly (Shirky, 2003). Creating a limited and small community, anyone can thus create a niche social network site, e.g. on Ning, a platform hosting services that encourage users to build up their own social sites.

Most social network sites primarily support pre-existing social relations. In (Lampe, Ellison, & Steinfield, 2007) Ellison et al. suggest that Facebook is used for maintaining existing offline relationships or solidifying offline connections, as opposed to meeting new people. These relationships may be weak ties, but typically there is some common offline element among individuals who set themselves up as friends, such as a shared time together. This is one of the chief dimensions that differentiate social network sites from earlier forms of communities like newsgroups (Lampe, Ellison, & Steinfield, 2007). Research in this area has investigated how online interactions interface with offline ones. Ellison et al. found that Facebook users search for people with whom they have an offline connection more often than they browse for complete strangers (Lampe, Ellison, & Steinfield, 2006). Likewise, Pew research found that 91% of U.S. teens who use social network sites do so to connect with friends (Lenhart & Madden, 2007). They help people to navigate the networked social world insofar as an extended network may serve to validate identity information presented in profiles.

Thus, social network features have introduced a new organizational framing for online and mobile communities with implications for our daily life. However, the smooth technical integration of online communities into daily life is still challenging. It is quite evident in this context that mobile communications has the most important value. For many people, particularly younger users, cell phones, smart phones, and other handhelds primarily have a social function (Eagle & Pentland,

2005). One of the first definitions of social-mobile application was given by Lugano (TeliaSonera Finland) as mobile-social software, defined as a class of mobile applications whose scope is to support interaction among interconnected individuals (Lugano, 2007). Over the past years, Intel Research Seattle has designed, studied, and built several social applications like Houston (Consolvo, Everitt, Smith, & Landay, 2006; University of Washington and Intel Research Seattle, 2008; Schmidt, 2005), an application designed to investigate the utility of mobile interaction-support networks. Houston is oriented towards physical fitness and weight management, but the general principles apply to many other areas where friends share experiences and generate mutual support. With Houston, group members share step counts from their pedometers automatically via mobile phones – for example, "Joe made it to 10,000 steps today!"

We are already sharing our daily experiences with the community, as with twitter, where prominent events like "There's a plane in the Hudson. I'm on the ferry going to pick up the people. Crazy." are posted (Krums, 2009). In (Erfurth, Kern, Rossak, Braun, & Leßmann, 2008; Kern, Braun, Rossak, 2006) Erfurth and Kern present social mobile assistants as one way to bridge online and offline socially networked worlds. Porkahr et al. endorse this path by proposing "Agents: Technology for the Mainstream?" (Pokahr, Braubach & Lamersdorf, 2005). Using agents for the mainstream would open a new perspective of world. It soon becomes apparent that most problems require or involve multiple agents to represent the multiple perspectives or the competing interests (Bond, Gasser 1988). Moreover, the agents will need to interact with one another, either to achieve their individual objectives or to manage the dependencies that ensue from being situated in a common environment (Castefranchi, 1998; Jennings, 1993). These interactions can vary from simple information interchanges, to requests for particular actions to be performed, and on to cooperation, coordination and negotiation in order to arrange interdependent activities. It is imperative to take into account that agents make decisions about the nature and scope of interactions at run time. Thus, organizational relationships need to be represented explicitly. In many cases, these relationships are subject to ongoing change: social interaction means existing relationships evolve and new relations are created. To cope with this variety, dynamic and (self) understanding, the research area splits into different fields for protocols that enable organizational groupings, for mechanisms to ensure groupings act together, and structures to characterize the overall behavior of collectives (Jennings & Wooldridge, 1998; Wooldridge & Jennings, 1995; Ferber, Gutknecht & Michel, 2003; Pokahr, Braubach, & Lamersdorf, 2005). Moreover, a common agent vocabulary of concepts is missing. Wooldridge and Jennings cut a long story short by saying, "The problem is, that although the term is widely used, by many people working closely related areas, it defies attempts to produce a universally accepted definition." (Wooldridge & Jennings 1995). In "Is it an Agent or just a Program?" (Franklin & Graesser, 1996) Franklin and Graesser frame an answer by making a survey of accepted and partly contradictory definitions. They put this contradictory definition dilemma down to the key research activities "We suspect, that each of them grew directly out of the set of examples of agents that the definer has in mind." Based on Franklin and Graesser's survey we only give a brief insight into this definition process by picking out the AIMA and Hayes-Roth definition. Russel and Norvig present their AIMA definition as "An agent is anything that can be viewed as perceiving its environment through sensors and acting upon that environment through effectors." So the given definition is reliant on a grasp of the environment. For a good distinction between agent and program, concepts of environment, perception and effectors must be located. In contrast Hayes-Roth argue that agents make a decision as a result of mental activities "Intelligent agents continuously perform three functions: perception of dynamic conditions in the environment; action to affect conditions in the environment; and reasoning to interpret perceptions, solve problems, draw inferences and determine actions."

Consequently, the definitional challenge related to the term "agent" is still ongoing but there is a little consensus (Jennings, 1999). An increasing number of researchers find the following characterization useful (Wooldridge, 1997):

An agent is an encapsulated computer system that is situated in some environment and that is capable of flexible, autonomous action in that environment in order to meets its design objectives.

Following the characterization, Wooldridge and Jennings offer a weak and a strong notion according to quality characteristics. A weak notion describes essential properties as autonomy, social ability, reactivity and pro-activeness. A strong notion proposes that an agent has mental properties, such as knowledge, belief, intention, obligation, and adds mobility, veracity, benevolence and rationality.

Analyzing these multi-purposed definitions we can state that, in a nutshell, autonomous action is the essential capability for agents. For more information about agents we refer readers to "Mobile Agents" (Braun & Rossak, 2005) and "Developing Intelligent Agent Systems" (Padgham & Winikoff, 2004) as standard introductory books.

PERSONAL ASSISTANT/AGENT BASED INTERACTION

Software agents provide a new and fascinating design paradigm for the architecture and programming of today's distributed information systems. A software agent is a small software entity that is able to act autonomously and proactively on behalf of its principal in the virtual Internet world. For roaming into this world a software agent has the capability to migrate from one host to many other hosts in a network of heterogeneous computer systems driven by tasks specified by its owner. Such agents are referred to as mobile agents. To fulfill their tasks software agents need some kind of execution environment in which they live. This execution environment is called an agency or agent server and is comparable to application servers, for example those for Enterprise Java Beans or Java Servlets. The agent server provides a number of basic services to resident agents and controls an agent's local life-cycle.

Figure 2 shows two agent servers hosting a set of agents connected via a network. The agent server provides communication facilities for agents to communicate and collaborate locally. Remote communication may also be possible, although typically an agent migrates to the remote system to communicate with agents there. This ensures a loose coupling between agent servers. As the figure shows, *Agent M* is transferred over the network during a migration. Agent-based applications utilize the mobile agent system (MAS) middleware to realize flexible access to services within the network

Mobile agent technology helps the design of innovative software approaches by adding code mobility and local intelligence as built-in features of the development environment. Ferber describes his vision in (Ferber, 1999) as a virtual world in which agents directly represent human beings. Agents are also capable of communicating with each other in their own language while fulfilling complicated tasks on behalf of their principals (human counterparts). Obviously, this vision opens up many new challenges in various domains of research. In computer science, we speak mostly about work in the fields of artificial intelligence and software engineering.

Figure 2. Schematic overview of a mobile agent system

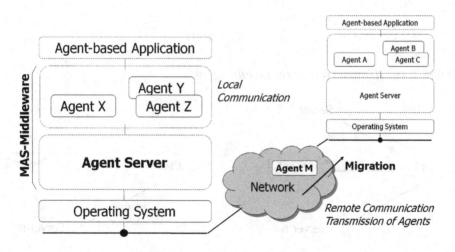

However, agent technology is common in other areas too. A good overview of theories, architectures, languages, and platforms is presented by (Pokahr, Braubach & Lamersdorf, 2005).

Typically a principal tells the agent what she or he wants to have done, and after a while the agent comes back with a (hopefully acceptable) solution. The main difference between traditional systems and mobile agents is the way of retrieving information. While traditional systems like client-server have a central focus and star-shaped data access paths, mobile agents follow a local approach and collect information in a round trip (see Figure 3). A mobile agent migrates proactively from host to host to fulfill a task. Thereby the state of the agent and its data are transferred between agent servers as well as its (byte-)code if necessary. After arriving at a server the agent continues its application algorithm based on already collected information.

Looking at details of the abstract process of task delegation, some issues come to the fore which lead to various research questions addressing:

- Task handover
  - ○ Formulation of agent's task
  - ○ Understanding principal's task
  - ○ Planning of subtasks and workflow
- Task execution
  - ○ Flexible service allocation and usage
  - ○ Communication/cooperation with (unknown) other agents
  - ○ Understanding of service features and results
- Result feedback
  - ○ Preparation of results
  - ○ Quality feedback of principal
  - ○ Way of contacting/reaching principal

Figure 3. (a) client-server vs. (b) mobile agent

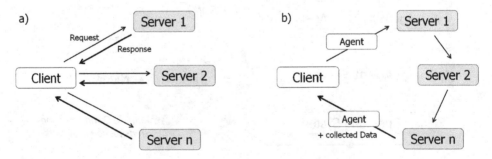

Mainly technological challenges have been addressed in the MobiSoft project – a joint initiative of industry and research. In the project we aimed at different application scenarios of personal assistants (on mobile devices) that range from information retrieval and control of legacy systems in industry to the support of human interactions in all places where people meet (Erfurth, Kern, Rossak, Braun & Leßmann, 2008). With the help of scenarios we were able to improve our agent system, for example enabling the execution of mobile agents on smart phones. Especially those scenarios focused on the support of human interactions and communities attracted further research interest. For this chapter we would like to pick out of MobiSoft the Campus.Net scenario – a scenario of utilizing resources flexibly in university surroundings. As Figure 4 indicates, different information sources and sinks are available at a university's campus. Most of the systems providing services run in different administrative regions typically without integration, and have often different ways of interaction. So a student has to access diverse systems to look for interesting courses, search for related books at the library, ask for enrolment, and meet some friends at the student's cafeteria and so on. Looking at the interaction between humans and technical systems, agents can help to simplify and to support. Let us consider an example to underpin this issue.

The mentioned student receives on her mobile phone a message from her personalised assistant – a mobile agent – like this (underlined words imply more detailed information):

"Next semester, there is an interesting course *on distributed systems. I've reserved for you one exemplar of the book at the library which is proposed by the course*

Figure 4. Campus.Net Available information resources in a university context

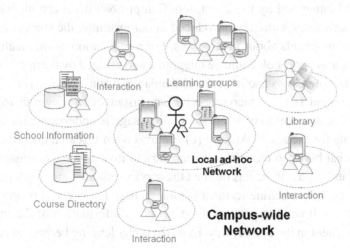

leader. Do you want to enrol for the course? And by the way, today your favourite meal is available at the student cafeteria! Would you like to meet your friends there?"

As this message indicates, a set of resources within the network is processed by a mobile agent autonomously. In advance the student has stated her preferences in a way her agent can analyze – a profile is used typically to personalize the agent, or more precisely the agent's algorithms. At regular intervals or at fixed time points the mobile agent checks for new information at available resources, for example at the schedule system for courses. On the basis of the information retrieved from the student's profile and the information found within the course repository, the mobile agent may visit other hosts – e.g., a library system or an enrolment system – to access further resources and to act proactively. Thereby the agent is roaming the network by traveling to different hosts which provide an execution environment, or accesses remote systems via standard interfaces e.g. using Web Services such as Amazon's Web Service to get details on a book. Due to the fact that the agent works asynchronously the student does not need to be online during this time. Additionally the agent is very fast and capable of visiting more services – some of them even unknown to the student. Finally it can provide a comprehensive overview of results, as indicated with the message above, including so far unknown alternatives, to support the final, typically user-driven decision.

Because agents operate on profiles, each student should set up her/his own profile. A profile means a structured form of student preferences according to her/his domain. It's like a "friend of a friend" data collection added with personal information about basic own information, friends, education and work. However this could only be a very small profile view. Moreover data stored at a profile depends on the centre of interest, and may differ from student to student and user to user.

The Campus.Net scenario has another interesting scope: Social networks can be accessed and integrated by the agent, too. Campus.Net itself can already be seen as a social network. As already introduced in our example, the student can choose to inform some friends about lunch plans. For a realization of this feature, social networks such as Facebook could be integrated and utilized by the agent. Generally the agent can connect to useful services available at run-time if (a) the service is known to the agent, (b) the concrete service is an instance of a known abstract service type, or (c) the description of a service and its usage is understandable or in some way learnable for the agent. At least (c) contains open research questions since in that case a chat between machines is necessary to investigate the semantics of the service and its results. W3C has defined the service-oriented architecture (SOA) to allow interoperable machine-to-machine interaction. However in practice in most cases humans still need to process the descriptive information of the interface to program the client in the correct way. Even (b) is challenging because services need to have a formal description, and a service ontology must also be established. It is essential to specify structural and semantic information on the service in a machine-processable format (e.g., using WSDL). Küster and König-Ries (2007) propose the DIANE service description (DSD), for instance. For mobile agent technology one research goal is a flexible and sometimes ad-hoc usage of suitable services available at run-time of the agent (and thus not fixed at compile time).

For sure the above outlined scenario is a future outlook of a possible usage of mobile agent technology. As part of the MobiSoft project, we investigated the preparedness of potential end users for such scenarios with a special focus on mobile devices. We received over 1000 submissions as a result of an online questionnaire (70% from students, 23% from university staff). The participants were asked to rank the importance of possibly available new services when using mobile agent technology, denoted here as software assistants. For 70% of the participants, services with mobile agents in the library sector were rated as important or very important. In contrast, 61% of participants stated that it would be less important or not important at all to have assistants for cafeteria menu information on mobile devices. Figure 5 presents the results of the question to rank the importance of a possible application of mobile agents in selected areas typically found at a university.

Despite the fact that the new technology of mobile agents is not yet well known, about 50% of the interviewed persons answered that they would perhaps use agents. Apparently the scenario "learning groups" has a strong community focus. About

Figure 5. Survey Results Importance of selected mobile applications

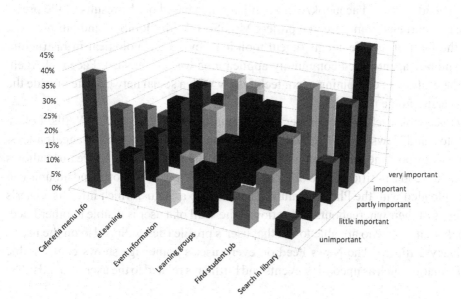

1/3 of interviewees answered that this scenario would be very important or at least important. Another third of the population sees this scenario as partly important. These results motivated our further research steps towards a combination of mobile agents and social networks. Campus.Net with its social network components was a first step in understanding social and technical characteristics of (social) software applications for smart phones to support human-to-machine communication or human-to-social network communication.

Solutions and Recommendations

With a combination of Facebook and mobile agents as an example, we target our research on the seamless integration of human life and social networks sites with a special focus on mobile users. Facebook, created in 2004, is one popular social network, used on a very regular basis especially by younger people: The typical user spends about 20 minutes a day on the site, and two-thirds of users log in at least once a day (Cassidy, 2006). With our social-mobile application FacebookAgent (Schau, Erfurth, Pasold, & Rossak, 2009) a community member is linked with Facebook via a personalized mobile software agent. This agent is a virtual substitute for the member and is able to update the member's personal data (e.g. current location) autonomously and inform the user of events arising at the Facebook site. FacebookAgent is also runnable on mobile devices to support mobile community members. It uses Facebook features and carries them to the user's device. Additional community features outside Facebook are possible too, such as for finding interesting people nearby.

The idea of the FacebookAgent application is based on the results of the previously mentioned joint research project MobiSoft. With MobiSoft and our research in the field of mobile agents (agent toolkit Tracy), a technological infrastructure for mobile agent-based community applications was established. FacebookAgent is the trial run in combining agent technology with a social network site outside the university home network.

Facebook itself has a number of community features, including Walls, Pokes, Photos, and News Feed. The Wall is a space on every user's profile page. It allows friends to post messages and attachments for the user. The Pokes feature allows users to send a notification to other users (a virtual "poke"). Photos and albums can be uploaded with the Photos feature. There is also a Status, which informs a user's friends of their whereabouts and actions. The Wall of a user is visible to other Facebook members who are able to see that user's profile (depending also on the user's privacy settings). The News Feed on every user's homepage shows configurable information such as upcoming events and birthdays related to the user's friends. The mentioned Facebook features are, or rather can be, utilized by the FacebookAgent application. The content is controlled or modified by agents on behalf of the user.

Figure 6 shows alternatives for the agent-based communication with Facebook (or other social networks). On the left-hand side of the tree subfigures a mobile device with one or more agents is shown. The device stands for the user who wants to access a social network from her/his device. The right-hand site is the social network site. Agents are presented as game pieces: 'A' stands for application agent, 'R' for runner agent, and 'I' for interface agent. Dotted agents are mobile and possibly away at the moment. Subfigure (a) presents the simplest approach: One mobile application agent is used for the entire communication between end user and social network. Due to the fact that the agent is mobile, this solution has the drawback that the application is not available to the end user during the roaming times of the agent. This leads to the idea of runner agents shown in subfigure (b). Runner agents take care of a stable communication channel between partners and local access. The application is accessible for the end user site as well as for events from social networks. The application agent is a substitute for the end user within a social network. The agent is even able to react directly to events coming from other community members, for example, without a communication to the end user. The end user may have more than one application agent to separate different features (a kind of component-oriented realization). This approach is more flexible than the latter. Subfigure (c) indicates the integration of several social networks. In this case the end user has an interface agent which integrates different social networks using a set of specialized application agents. This user-centered approach enables an end user to utilize only one application (the interface agent) to stay connected with different communities. Personal information (stored in a single profile) need not be entered several times. The interface agent takes care of up-to-date information within connected social networks using application agents (and runner agents as well). For the end user the communication is simplified and more convenient.

For the Facebook application we realized approach (b) above. We needed to establish an application agent acting as a substitute for the user in Facebook. For the communication with Facebook there is also an agent on the user's device which delivers updates to the Facebook site proactively and for the management of the user's profile. Both agents will gather additional information connected with the user, such as filters and preferences. Such information belongs to a user's profile too, but may not be accessible to other members. The user may want to be informed about an agent's results or regarding events within systems of interests (e.g., community systems). So the agent could now decide on the basis of the user's preferences on which device the principal should be informed, or simply try to reach the user on different devices. While trying to implement this we faced some technical difficulties and constraints in connecting to Facebook and exchanging data. For

Figure 6. Communication model for a human-centered approach to form communities

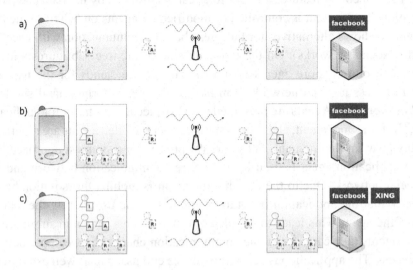

instance there is no possibility to store user data at Facebook; usage of the features by software (not humans) is not intended. But we figured out an architecture and an interaction model to realize the interesting combination. In the end we were not able to use all Facebook features. However, we could successfully combine these technologies on a low level. The resulting agent infrastructure is a basis for a future extension of the FacebookAgent as well as for the integration of further social networks using agents.

Figure 7 presents (a) traditional relations within a social network (e.g. friendships), and (b) our user-centered approach. Relations in a social network need to be established manually and can be bidirectional or just one way by accessing information of another member. In the user-centered approach multiple social networks can be integrated. The user is supported by the mentioned interface agent and a set of application agents which react to events according to the user's preferences defined in a profile; for example, a contact request can be declined by such an agent. The application agents can also act proactively to deploy new information about the user.

For "real" social network systems like Dogster or match2blue the direct communication between humans through their mobile devices is important. Looking at our Facebook extension the user's agent is able to connect to another agent without connecting to the Facebook site. This mobile ad-hoc scenario leads to challenges in human-to-machine interaction as well as machine-to-machine interaction. The interaction of a human with her or his mobile device is connected with issues of ergonomics (e.g., reduced display size) and usability (e.g., interaction modes). Between mobile devices the interaction is difficult on a technical level. Due to the

Figure 7. a) Relationships in social network vs. b) user-centered integration of social networks

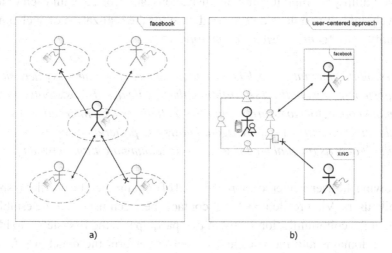

heterogeneity of the devices the communication is sometimes not reliable. However, this field of mobile communities is fascinating.

The feature of direct communications between humans is an interesting enhancement of social networks for the attraction of new members outside the community system. With the new possibilities provided by mobile phones and the experiences from the research project MobiSoft, community issues and mobility can be combined more easily. A user-centered approach of connecting people who share similar interests and exchanging information is the focus of our research. The mobile device is used for discovery of and interaction with people, for example using Bluetooth communication for people in the direct neighborhood. People with overlapping profiles (profiles that contain similar interests) will be connected and can enlarge, or start to form, communities with two or more members.

A similar approach for information sharing and collaboration without considering profiles can be found in (Heinemann, Kangasharju, Lyardet, & Mühlhäuser, 2003). There, information Clouds – iClouds – are introduced as the set of people sharing the same communication horizon and providing information on the basis of offer (have)- and search (wish)-lists.

Profiles, usually stored in central community systems, have to be carried on mobile devices as we did for the FacebookAgent. Each user profile within the social networks is just a full or partial copy of the unique user-centered profile of the user. If a user has enabled her/his device to join communities (scan mode) or search for people of interest the software works autonomously in the background and communicates with other devices (discovery). For the autonomous communication between these networked devices mobile agents will be used as a preferred solution. Their ability to migrate autonomously, compare profiles with each other and proactively inform people is a very good base for the realization of such a mobile community – an *Agent Assisted Community*.

Agent Assisted Communities are defined as user-centered communities where members are supported by personalized substitutes – the mobile agents/assistants – acting as autonomous connectors to form communities including social interactions especially in mobile environments. A mobile agent knows the preferences of its owner using its profile. It acts as an enabler for the real life communication between people.

Following the user-centered approach, a set of domain specific profiles is spanned by mobile users. Via profile matching, contacts between users can be established. Looking at the communication between two participants the first step is to identify the shared domains and the vocabulary used to perform the matching. As a first approach a common communication protocol for syntactic comparison is available.

Once we have found "compatible" domains represented by their sub-profiles in the first step, an in-depth look at the semantics is necessary to check whether used terms have the same meaning. In (Williams & Ren, 2001), the DOGGIE approach enables agents to locate similar semantic concepts. This promising approach can also help in identifying homonyms and synonyms. After passing these two steps, the matching process can be started in order to identify shared interests. Every established contact with other users as potential community members is important to form a community and to discover the (shared) interests of others, even if only one compatible domain was found by the contact and the other mentioned steps were not successful. Of course the contact is more interesting when shared interests can be identified.

As a result of this approach, communities are formed in an automatic and user-centered way. In contrast to a traditional client-server approach, the user is put into the middle. In addition, this user-centered approach integrates mobile and non-mobile users. Due to characteristics such as autonomy, personalization and adaptability, mobile agents are an adequate connector between users and their communities. Finally the interaction between humans is improved, enhanced and more efficient.

FUTURE RESEARCH DIRECTIONS

We think agent technology has strong potential in the improvement of interaction between humans. More proof-of-concept approaches are necessary to tackle different research questions and to allow trial runs to verify theoretical ideas. For such trial runs of agents an underlying infrastructure is essential to allow autonomous and proactive behavior. Services need to be available ready for a usage by agents. Furthermore agents need to be equipped with knowledge to reach decisions in their goal-oriented behavior. There is also a planning module needed to help the agent to pre-plan an execution workflow. As in many areas of research the semantics of the information has to be captured by the agent. For the identification of relevance of certain information an agent has to find out the meaning. There is no sufficient solution available at the moment. Typically, ontologies and keyword-based approaches are used.

Additionally on the technical side it is not very convenient to program agents, especially to map a plan from a high abstraction level. From the software engineering viewpoint there is a lack of notations to model agent-based applications efficiently. There is also a need for a holistic methodology to use the technology in practice. How to go on from a model to identify agent aspects, separate them and incrementally refine them? Additionally the agent could be equipped with reusable modules, or let's say tools, from a toolbox to gain necessary capabilities for the requested task, such as the capability to negotiate or to buy train tickets. This would help development of application-specific agents from a repository of modules on a high level. We would also like to be able to specify a task on the user's level, with the agent able to define the execution plan on its own, including the detection of necessary modules from the mentioned toolbox. What is the right workflow for the agent's execution? How can we plan the execution in advance without knowing the current situation within the network? Is the agent able to adjust a predefined plan? A lot of interesting challenges are faced here. We are sure that we can find some of the answers and incrementally improve acceptable solution approaches.

In recent years there have been a lot of discussions on topics such as economics, security and safety. Some of the challenges could be tackled, others need to be investigated. A discussion here would be out of focus. So we refer readers to Braun and Rossak (2005) for more details on these topics and open issues.

Especially interesting are also mobile scenarios where mobile devices are used to exchange information, e.g. to connect to a community system or to interact with other mobile users within an ad-hoc network. Recently started research projects will focus on such scenarios. In the security research program by Germany's Federal Ministry of Education and Research some projects look at the improvement of the interaction of rescue teams with the focus on inter-organizational information exchange. The resulting infrastructure is planned to be generic and should therefore be applicable in other ad-hoc scenarios as well.

CONCLUSION

In our networked society the interaction of humans is in many cases web based. This means information is exchanged using internet facilities such as simple mails or web based IT systems specialized for interaction within a community. Typically community members need to log in to platforms and need to scan for relevant information and events as well as to update their personal information. Within the chapter we have looked at possible improvements when using mobile software agents. Using the technology, communication and interaction between machines can be reformed in a flexible way adequate for the continuously changing environments faced in the web. Communication channels need not be fixed, since agents can look after message delivery autonomously.

The mobility of a user is also an interesting aspect for the application of agent technology in the area of social networks and community systems. An agent could be used as a virtual substitute of a community member. While traveling around, the agent can keep the member informed on relevant events within the community. Thereby the relevance of events can be user-defined on the basis of well differentiated profiles. The difficulty for the agent is to detect such events. With its knowledge regarding the potential meaning of monitored actions and information it has to decide how to handle an event that occurred within a community system. Agents can also be used to update a user's status information at community sites automatically. With the introduced interface agent the interaction between humans and machines is user-centered. This personalized agent covers different (social network) systems and communication channels so that the interaction with similar systems is integrated and centralized. For the user this means (s)he has everything in one place and can focus on the interaction with friends regardless of which social network they belong to.

Another interesting feature we are investigating is the attraction of new contacts outside the web. With an agent-based application on mobile phones, people with similar interests can be found using ad-hoc connection capabilities like Bluetooth. The phone application scans for people (phones) nearby to connect to and looks for the same interests by matching profiles. This could be used to extend online communities into the real world. Contacts established in the real world can be transferred into or also established in the virtual world of the web.

With the FacebookAgent we made a first simple proof-of-concept for a successful combination of mobile agents and a social network. This is an extensible trial run that we use to pinpoint difficulties and gaps. In another project we have developed a combination of Second Life and mobile agents. In such a virtual world, characters monitored or controlled by agents can react to inquiries or forward these to humans. Agents are even able to take over the execution of simple tasks within the virtual world or/and within connected social networks. The number of users is growing in such social networks, and the expectations on communication facilities is changing. This also has an influence on our daily life. Campbell and Park (2008) looked at social implications of mobile telephony. They stated that "mobile communication adds a unique new flavor to the social landscape" (Campbell and Park, 2008, p. 381). To overcome arising challenges such as information overload, new technical solutions are essential; software agents as personal assistants are a promising approach.

REFERENCES

Acquisti, A., & Gross, R. (2006). Imagined communities: Awareness, information sharing, and privacy on the Facebook. *6th Workshop on Privacy Enhancing Technologies*, (pp. 36–58). Cambridge.

Boyd, D. (2006). Friends, Friendsters, and Top 8: Writing community into being on social network sites. *First Monday, 11*(12).

Boyd, D. M., & Ellison, N. B. (2007). Social Network Sites: Definition, History, and Scholarship. *Journal of Computer-Mediated Communication, 13*(1), 210–230. doi:10.1111/j.1083-6101.2007.00393.x

Braun, P., & Rossak, W. (2005). *Mobile Agents - Basic concepts, mobility models & the Tracy toolkit.* dpunkt.verlag.

Campbell, S. W., & Park, Y. J. (2008). Social implications of mobile telephony: The rise of personal. *Social Compass, 2*(2), 371–387. doi:10.1111/j.1751-9020.2007.00080.x

Cassidy, J. (2006, 05 15). *The Online Life - Me Media.* Retrieved 08 21, 2009, from The New Yorker: http://www.newyorker.com/archive/2006/05/15/060515fa_fact_cassidy

Castefranchi, C. (1998). Modelling social action for AI agents. *Artificial Intelligence, 103*(1-2), 157–182. doi:10.1016/S0004-3702(98)00056-3

Consolvo, S., Everitt, K., Smith, I., & Landay, J. A. (2006). *Design requirements for technologies that encourage physical activity. SIGCHI conference on Human Factors in computing systems* (pp. 457–466). Montréal, Québec: ACM Press.

Eagle, N., & Pentland, A. (2005). Social serendipity: Mobilizing social software. *IEEE Pervasive Computing / IEEE Computer Society [and] IEEE Communications Society, 4*(2), 28–34. doi:10.1109/MPRV.2005.37

Erfurth, C., Kern, S., Rossak, W., Braun, P., & Leßmann, A. (2008). MobiSoft: Networked Personal Assistants for Mobile Users in Everyday Life. In M. Klusch, M. Pechoucek, & A. Polleres (Ed.), *Cooperative Information Agents, Volume 5180 of Lecture Notes in Computer Science* (pp. 147–161). New York: Springer.

Ferber, J. (1999). *Multi-Agent Systems: An Introduction to Distributed Artificial Intelligence*. Reading, MA: Addison-Wesley.

Ferber, J., Gutknecht, O., & Michael, F. (2003). In Giorgini, P., Mueller, J. P., & Odell, J. (Eds.), *AOSE 2003, LNCS 2935* (pp. 214–230). Heidelberg, Germany: Springer.

Franklin, S., & Graesser, A. (1997). Is it agent, or just a program? In Mueller, J. P., Wooldridge, M. J., & Jennings, N. R. (Eds.), *Intelligent Agents III* (pp. 21–36). Berlin: Springer.

Goble, G. (2009, 01 12). *The History of Social Networking*. Retrieved 08 21, 2009, from Sympatico/MSN: http://digitaltrends.technology.sympatico.msn.ca/feature/99/The+History+of+Social+Networking.html

Heinemann, A., Kangasharju, J., Lyardet, F., & Mühlhäuser, M. (2003). iClouds - Peer-to-Peer Information Sharing in Mobile Environments. In H. Koch, L. Börszörményi, & H. Hellwagner (Ed.), *Euro-Par 2003. Int. Conf. on Parallel and Distributed Computing. LNCS Series*, pp. 1038-1045. Klagenfurt: Springer.

Jennings, N. R. (1993). Commitments and conventions: The foundation of coordination in multi-agent systems. *The Knowledge Engineering Review*, 8(3), 223–250. doi:10.1017/S0269888900000205

Jennings, N. R. (1999). On agent-based software engineering. *Artificial Intelligent 117 (2000)*, pp. 277-296

Jennings, N. R., & Wooldrige, M. (1998). *Agent Technology: Foundations, Applications and Markets* (Jennings, N. R., & Wooldridge, M., Eds.). Berlin: Springer.

Kern, S., Braun, P., & Rossak, W. (2006). Mobisoft: An Agent-Based Middleware for Social-Mobile Applications. In R. Meersman, Z. Tari, & P. Herrero (Ed.), *On the Move to Meaningful Internet Systems Workshops. Volume 4277 of Lecture Notes in Computer Science*. pp. 984–993. Montpellier: Springer.

Koh, W., & Mui, L. (2001). *An Information Theoretic Approach to Ontology-based In-terest Matching*. Seattle: Artificial Intelligence, Ontology Learning Workshop.

Krums, J. (2009, 01 15). *There's a plane in the Hudson*. Retrieved 08 21, 2009, from Twitpic: http://twitpic.com/135xa

Küster, U., & König-Ries, B. (2007). Semantic Service Discovery with DIANE Service Descriptions. In *Proceedings of the International Workshop on Service Composition & SWS Challenge at the 2007 IEEE/WIC/ACM International Conference on Web Intelligence (WI 2007)*. pp. 152-156. Silicon Valley, CA: IEEE Computer Society.

Lampe, C., Ellison, N., & Steinfield, C. (2006). *A Face(book) in the crowd: Social searching vs. social browsing. Computer supported cooperative work* (pp. 167–170). Banff, Alberta: ACM Press.

Lampe, C., Ellison, N., & Steinfield, C. (2007). *A familiar Face(book): Profile elements as signals in an online social network. Human Factors in Computing Systems* (pp. 435–444). San Jose: ACM Press.

Lenhart, A., & Madden, M. (2007, 04 18). *Teens, Privacy and Online Social Networks*. Retrieved 08 21, 2009, from Pew Internet and American Life Project: http://www.pewinternet.org/Reports/2007/Teens-Privacy-and-Online-Social-Networks.aspx

Lugano, G. (2007). Mobile Social Software: Definition, Scope and Applications. *eChallenges 2007 conference* (pp. 1434-1442). The Netherlands: The Hague.

Pokahr, A., Braubach, L., & Lamersdorf, W. (2005, 11). Agenten: Technologie für den Mainstream? *it - Information Technology*, pp. 300–307.

Schmidt, I. (2005). Social-Mobile Applications. *IEEE Computer, 38*(4), 84–85.

Shirky, C. (12. 05 2003). *People on page: YASNS...*. Retrieved 08 21, 2009 von Corante's Many-to-Many: http://many.corante.com/archives/2003/05/12/people_on_page_yasns.php

The Nielsen Company. (2009). *Global Faces and Networked Places*. Nielsen Online.

University of Washington and Intel Research Seattle. (2008). *UbiFit*. Retrieved 08 21, 2009, from http://dub.washington.edu/projects/ubifit/

Williams, A. B., & Ren, Z. (2001). *Agents teaching agents to share meaning. Autonomous Agents* (pp. 465–472). Montreal: ACM Press.

Wooldridge, M. (1997). Agent-based software engineering. *IEEE Proceedings Software Engineering, 144*(1), 26–37. doi:10.1049/ip-sen:19971026

Wooldridge, M., & Jennings, N. R. (1995). Intelligent agents: Theory and practice. *The Knowledge Engineering Review, 10*(2), 115–152. doi:10.1017/S0269888900008122

Wooldridge, M., & Jennings, N. R. (1995). *Agent Theories, Architectures and Languages: A Survey*. Berlin: Springer Verlag.

ADDITIONAL READING

Braun, P., Erfurth, C., & Rossak, W. (2000). *An Introduction to the Tracy Mobile Agent System. Jenaer Schriften zur Mathematik und Informatik.* Friedrich Schiller University Jena.

Braun, P., Müller, I., Geisenhainer, S., Schau, V., & Rossak, W. (2004). *A Service-oriented Software Architecture for Mobile Agent Toolkits. Engineering of Computer Based Systems* (pp. 550–556). Brno: IEEE Computer Society.

Braun, P., Müller, I., Geisenhainer, S., Schau, V., & Rossak, W. (2004). Agent Migration as an Optional Service in an Extendable Agent Toolkit Architecture. In A. Karmouch, L. Korba, & E. R. Madeira (Ed.), *MATA, volume 3284 of Lecture Notes in Computer Science* (pp. 127-136). Springer.

Eichler, G., Erfurth, C., & Schau, V. (2007). *Enhancing Communities by Social Interactions in Mobile Environments.*

Lewis, M. (1998). Designing for Human-Agent Interaction. *AI Magazine, 19*(2), 67–78.

Padgham, L., & Winikoff, M. (2004). *Developing Intelligent Agent Systems: A practical guide.* Wiley. doi:10.1002/0470861223

Toledo Munoz, Maria B. (2006). *Agentenbasierte Modellierung und Analyse von Verbindungen im Produktentstehungsprozess.* Herzogenrath: Shaker Verlag.

Weiss, G. (1999). *Multiagent Systems: A Modern Approach to Distributed Artificial Intelligence.* Cambridge, MA: MIT Press.

Chapter 9
Your Personal, Virtual Librarian

Alexander Krumpholz
CSIRO ICT Centre & Australian National University, Australia

David Hawking
Funnelback, Australia

Tom Gedeon
Australian National University, Australia

ABSTRACT

Searching scientific literature is a common and critical activity for research scientists, students, and professionals such as medical clinicians. These search tasks can be time consuming and repetitive, but literature search and management tools are already making the job much easier. This chapter analyses the literature retrieval process, reviews some currently available tools and elaborates on potential future support for the knowledge worker by an intelligent automated assistant. A special focus of this chapter is the automatic retrieval of medical literature and the exploration of the answer space.

INTRODUCTION

Before the Internet revolution, researchers physically went to the library to find the publications they needed for their studies. They spent hours trying to fish the right index cards out of little drawers in numerous rows of cabinets to identify books and papers that might guide their work. Librarians then fetched the needed materials and passed them out to the reader. The turnaround time could be hours, days, or

DOI: 10.4018/978-1-61520-851-7.ch009

even weeks if the publication had to be ordered from overseas. Later, librarians got access to computers and translated readers' needs into queries to retrieve the meta-information about the requested literature. Beyond their retrieval tasks, experienced librarians also helped students to identify popular books or drew their scientists' attention to new publications in their field.

Today, almost every researcher has a computer on their desk and is able to send queries to search engines all over the world—including literature retrieval engines—and retrieve references, even full papers, within minutes. However, do the new systems provide you with all the benefits you got from your librarian? Are they the perfect solution for your literature retrieval needs, or is there much room for improvement?

We will describe existing systems currently available commercially or free, and present current research efforts to improve literature retrieval. The need for literature retrieval depends on the role and the field of the researcher as well as the task they wish to achieve. This chapter focuses on literature retrieval for computer scientists, and on medical literature retrieval for clinicians or medical researchers.

Information Needs

In what circumstances do scientists search the literature?

We will discuss six typical scenarios:

- Finding a specific publication
- Finding related publications
- Staying up to date in the field
- Entering a new field
- Special domain: Medical research.

Finding a Specific Publication

Almost all scientific publications provide a list of references to related material, similar to the way that URLs are used to refer to Web pages on the Internet. While the hyperlink mechanism embedded in the World Wide Web allows us to follow a URL by clicking on the anchor text, bibliographic references once had to be resolved by visiting the library, accessing the referenced journal issue and finding the cited article within. A scientist may need to access cited references to fully understand the paper they are reading or to learn about related work. References to specific publications may also be made by reviewers when the scientist submits his own work for publication. Furthermore, specific references are often made in casual conversations: "I really liked your presentation, but have you come across the paper by Smith and Jones from the University of...?".

Nowadays, various Internet portals can be used to locate abstracts quickly, and even to download the full text or printable version of the publication. Tools to manage retrieved bibliographical records for automatic use by text processing systems are essential and used by students or scientists.

Finding Related Publications

Traditionally, related publications have been found by searching for publications in the same classification as the primary article, or by following journals or conference proceedings in relevant areas. Through its own reference list, each new article might lead to other specific publications and, possibly, other venues to be monitored. Once research groups or individuals working on similar topics have been identified, their progress can be followed and collaboration becomes a possibility. Today, more automated means of identifying related publications have been developed and are available on some Web portals.

Staying up to Date in the Field

Once, staying on top of the field involved skimming through key journals and conference proceedings as they were published. Through conferences, discussions and exchanges with other researchers, scientists could be alerted to new projects, fertilising new ideas and collaborations. In addition to these traditional ways, modern Web-based technologies have provided notification services to provide keyword-based alerts to the publication of relevant new literature. Such services have been implemented economically and are often offered free of charge.

Entering a New Field

Entering a new field involves getting introduced to new terminology, new concepts and relationships between them. Scientific papers are usually too narrow and detailed to quickly obtain a bird's-eye view of a subject, although review articles are available for many topics. Some work has been done to automatically generate such reviews. An alternative approach is to use books and course material to provide good introductions, but there can be significant delays between the journal publication of cutting-edge research and its appearance in longer texts.

Special Domain Medical Research

Retrieval of medical literature is an activity that stands to have a profound effect on our health and wellbeing. Awareness of current medical knowledge can help medical practitioners to make better decisions and so lead to better health outcomes, or avoid adverse events. It is no surprise that vast resources have been invested in organising medical knowledge through ontologies such as Snomed (Stearns et al., 2001) and thesauri like MeSH ("Medical Subject Headings", n.d.). Since medical publications tend to be rich in jargon, advanced knowledge extraction techniques achieve good results. This has enabled the development of specialized visualization prototypes (Plake et al., 2006) and even expert systems.

With the development of *evidence-based medicine*—a term formally defined by the Evidence-Based Medicine Working Group in the 1990s (Evidence-Based Medicine Working Group et al., 1992)(Claridge & Fabian, 2005)—the need to find scientific literature in the medical field and to judge its value has become even more important. Observations reported in case studies trigger randomized controlled trials. Systematic reviews take all medical literature relevant to a given research question, summarize them, weigh the level of evidence they represent and provide a critical discussion. Clinical Practice Guidelines are step-by-step descriptions on how to diagnose and treat a patient with certain symptoms and co-morbidities (co-occurrences of additional diseases) and are generally based on systematic reviews. Due to the needs of evidence-based medicine and the specialization in the medical field, clinical literature retrieval is well developed and rich in features.

The prevalence of computer support in clinical settings has led to electronic health records increasingly being used to store clinical data such as symptoms, diagnoses, test results and treatments for each patient. While privacy issues still cause many concerns about how to share and exploit information, local solutions are implemented to help clinicians to make better-grounded decisions faster. Controlled sharing of electronic patient records between hospitals, clinics and practitioners has the potential to improve the quality of patient treatment and to reduce costs in the health care sector.

Interestingly, Rockliff et al. (2005) show that the services of real librarians remain of high value. They describe 'Chasing the Sun', a project between the South Australian Health Services Libraries' Consortium (SAHSLC) in Australia and the South West Information for Clinical Effectiveness (SWICE) network in the United Kingdom. This out-of-hours emergency virtual reference service allows night shift clinicians in either country to get help related to patient care using a skilled librarian as an intermediary.

Retrieval Process

Ad hoc Web search is a process well known to Internet users. Starting with a favourite search engine, a user enters a query containing some search terms and gets a list of matching documents—mostly Web pages—as a result. Most users only skim the first few results and may alter the query and search again without even leaving the first result page. These steps are repeated until the searcher is satisfied or gives up. The main types of change to the query include modifying the query terms (e.g., when better expressions have been seen in the first results), and adding/removing terms to reduce/increase the number of results. While interaction with literature retrieval systems is quite similar to Web retrieval, specific metadata is often exploited to allow additional means of interaction such as links to other publications by the same author.

Common steps in a search session are:

* Identification of the information need
* Selection of a corpus to query
* Selection of a search tool
* Formulation of a query
* Retrieving the search result
* Identification of the relevant items in the result set
* Identification of the relevant section of each result

Each of those steps has to be conducted manually by the searcher.

Identification of the Information Need

Initially, the user has to become aware of the need to find publications. Depending on the user's current task, it can be one of the needs described above. Often the user needs to find related publications or is trying to gain understanding of a certain topic.

Selection of a Corpus to Query

Then the user has to select the corpus to use. The corpus in this context is the document collection to be indexed by a retrieval system. Corpora differ in their comprehensiveness, currency and correctness. Some collections have full text versions of the documents available; others only store the bibliographic metadata or abstracts. The user's choice of corpus may depend upon the age of the publications they are seeking.

Selection of a Search Tool

When a collection is indexed by different parties, the user must also decide which search system to use. Freely available corpora are used by researchers to explore new ways of pre-processing the data in order to provide additional support to the searcher. Some prototypes are available free of charge for everyone on the Internet to explore, evaluate and send feedback. Such prototypes however are often unknown to researchers who are focusing on their work rather than tracking such developments.

Formulation of a Query

Finding the ideal search terms is often not a trivial task. Information retrieval systems have to match the query to the indexed corpus to find the documents best matching the users query. This matching makes it necessary for the user to know the jargon and writing style used in the corpus. The information retrieval community has developed mechanisms like *stop word lists* to remove words not relevant for the matching process, *stemming* to include documents containing identical words with different inflections, and *query expansion* to add synonyms of query terms to the query. Searchers must try to find a query that achieves a good balance between *precision* and *recall*, i.e., a query that retrieves everything of importance yet nothing of irrelevance. Recall expresses the proportion of relevant documents in the corpus that have been retrieved. Precision indicates the proportion of the retrieved documents that are relevant. Usually a query that achieves high precision will suffer from poor recall and vice versa. It's important to recognize that the user's need might not be well expressed in the user's query.

But why should we aim for the ideal search terms in times when users can make use of modern interfaces that allow them to iteratively reformulate queries interactively and submit hundreds of queries in a single session? On one hand because it is a frustrating task to miss out on the bulk of results just because the correct term has not been used. A PubMed search for *"high blood pressure"* for example currently returns 8,163 results if it is directly used as a query. PubMed however automatically expands queries before executing them to include the appropriate Medical Subject Headings (MeSH). Once the query is expanded to *"hypertension" [MeSH Terms] OR "hypertension" [All Fields] OR ("high" [All Fields] AND "blood" [All Fields] AND "pressure" [All Fields]) OR "high blood pressure" [All Fields]*, PubMed is able to allocate 376,007 matches. On the other hand, this chapter introduces an intelligent assistant that should at least support the user in the query formulation process by automatically generating an initial query, which can be modified by the user.

Retrieving the Search Result

The result of a Web search is often a ranked list of matching web pages or documents. In literature retrieval, the result set is usually a list of publications, represented by bibliographical records containing metadata such as the article title, the journal title, authors, publisher and the publication date.

Identifying the Relevant Items in the Result Set

Results returned by the system generally match the user's query in some way, but it is very unusual for all of them to be actually useful. The user must skim the results to find the ones most likely to help them with their task. Polysemies—words with multiple meanings—are a source of results matching the query but not the information need. The query term *apple* may return documents related to fruits as well as those related to computing equipment. Established methods to help the process of disambiguation include clustering and relevance feedback. Web search engines have been developed that build clusters according to the content of the result documents and present them in a way that allows the searcher to narrow the results to a particular cluster. Relevance feedback systems trace the user's interaction with the result set to identify results that are of interest to the user and from them to derive and submit a more complex query more closely related to the user's actual information need.

Identification of the Relevant Section of Each Result

Finally, the searcher has to find the part of each result document matching the query to find the section of interest to decide if the whole document has to be read and potentially cited. The size of publications available electronically for indexing is increasing and the work on information retrieval systems that deliver only parts of documents has commenced long ago (Salton et al., 1993) (Wilkinson, 1994). There are also tools for highlighting relevant sections, or individual query term occurrences, within long documents.

Techniques for Matching and Ranking Documents

Web search engines typically identify a set of candidate documents using a very narrow matching criterion such as "contains all of the query words in either singular or plural forms". They then rank the candidate set by combining degree-of-query-match with a number of query-independent factors such as popularity (estimated from user click frequencies), authoritativeness (estimated from patterns of hyper-linking) and inverse spam score.

The literature retrieval process is analogous but differs in many important ways. Popularity and authoritativeness may be estimated from analogous indicators such as number of downloads and time-weighted citation frequency. Note that for certain research tasks all documents satisfying the inclusion criteria must be considered, regardless of popularity or authority. (Spam is hopefully never an issue!) The In-exBib system (Krumpholz & Hawking, 2006) shows that the anchor text exploited by Web search engines also has an analogue in literature retrieval and can be used to extend recall.

Choosing a candidate set in literature search is much more of a challenge, because of the diversity of language typically used to discuss a single scientific concept or issue. This might sound naïve given that each field has well defined terminology, but overlapping fields do not necessarily use the same terms for the same concept and sometimes the correct terminology is just not being used. At the time of writing this chapter, the PubMed search *"high blood pressure" [All Fields] NOT hypertension[All Fields]* returns 2125 results, and slight variations like *"higher blood pressure" [All Fields] NOT hypertension[All Fields]* or *"increased blood pressure" [All Fields] NOT hypertension[All Fields]* yield result sets of hundreds of documents.

On the Web, when a layperson submits a simple query like "bird flu" they can confidently expect to find a set of pages giving good advice and information on that subject. However, a great deal of scientific literature relevant to that topic will not match those terms. The query must be expanded to include obvious terms such as influenza, H5N1 and many highly specialized terms relating to viruses, proteins, and the human immune system. Which query is ideal is highly context-dependent: What is the searcher's field of interest? Why are they searching on this particular occasion? What do they already know?

By convention, scientific articles are structured into sections such as Abstract, Related Work, Method, Results and Conclusions. They typically include other structural elements such as figures, tables and equations. There has been some recent research interest in whether document structure can be exploited in order to improve the retrieval performance, the matching process and the units of retrieval. Query matches in certain elements of a document (such as its title or conclusions) may be weighted more heavily than those in the general text of the document.

The rest of this section focuses on how to exploit structure and search context.

Structured Document Retrieval

The Initiative for the Evaluation of XML retrieval (INEX) has been active since 2002 as a platform for XML retrieval experiments (Fuhr et al., 2002). Its participants normally build an information retrieval collection and use the relevance values attached to each result for each given query to compare their search engines and improve performance (and derive better evaluation metrics). In an annual process, the participants download the corpus and suggest meaningful topics, which are collected by the organisers. After the elimination of redundant and meaningless queries, the remaining ones are distributed to the participants, who use their search engine to produce a list of potential hits for each topic. Those hits are collected and judged by the community. Once the relevance of each result for each query has been assessed, the collection can be used to calculate a set of quality measures characterizing a specific result set for a given query. Those metrics are used to compare different search engines or different tuning parameters on a given search engine. Results are not full documents as in traditional document retrieval, but parts of documents specified with XPath (Berglund et al., 2002) expressions, allowing specification of individual XML elements or regions within XML documents.

Scientific publications are written once, but may be read hundreds or thousands of times. The structure of scientific publications is defined to support the reader's need to access relevant literature. The title is used to get a first glimpse of relevance, the abstract is read for a better understanding and the conclusions are often consumed next, while figures or images can quickly give an idea of what the paper is reporting. Based on the information gathered, the reader assesses the likely value of reading the whole paper thoroughly. The importance of images in communicating the essence of a scientific paper has also been identified by (Xu et al., 2008), who show their PubMed results as thumbnail images of the containing graphs. This allows searchers to quickly identify publications relevant to their research in some cases and to identify previously seen papers in others.

Scientific articles in the medical field have a much higher degree of structure than publications in other research areas like computer science. The abstract is usually already partitioned, clearly describing the type of study undertaken, the demographics of the subjects, the results and so on. The Instructions for Authors by the Journal of the American Medical Association for example specify the requirements for different paper types in fine-grained detail. (http://jama.ama-assn.org/misc/ifora.dtl):

Abstracts for Reports of Original Data: Reports of original data should include an abstract of no more than 300 words using the following headings: Context, Objective, Design, Setting, Patients (or Participants), Interventions (include only if there are any), Main Outcome Measure(s), Results, and Conclusions. For brevity, parts of the abstract may be written as phrases rather than complete sentences.

This paragraph is followed by a description for each of the defined sections.

But is this enough? An intelligent system should be able to rely on concepts and their relations described in a publication without the need of interpretation and the inherent risk of misinterpretation by natural language processing (NLP) systems, as they try to map natural language into knowledge representation data structures. Since a researcher creates only a few publications per year, but is supposed to consume the essence of thousands of them at the same time, it only makes sense to shift the effort away from the reader to the writer.

One step in this direction is the creation of metadata by numerous indexers at the National Library of Medicine in the USA. Every publication in PubMed is tagged with a set of relevant medical subject heading (MeSH) terms, allowing a searcher to compose their query from a controlled vocabulary.

Context

It seems obvious that a literature retrieval system should be able to perform better if it can exploit the contextual information in addition to the explicitly specified query. Indeed there are a number of studies supporting this expectation. For example (Teevan et al., 2005) show that Web search results can be improved if an initial raw result set is reranked locally using information derived from the user's previous interactions and the documents they have on their own computer. (Kelly & Teevan, 2003) survey the use of human behaviours in deriving implicit measures for use in ranking or re-ranking.

Contextualized methods have the potential to assist with disambiguating ambiguous terms and with generating more effective queries, however there are many open questions about whether automatically derived profiles are best applied at the user's computer, where full context is available without privacy concerns, or at a remote retrieval system, where there is unlimited potential to affect matching and ranking.

EXISTING LITERATURE RETRIEVAL TOOLS

This section introduces some illustrative literature retrieval tools and maps them to the previously described researchers' needs.

Finding a Specific Publication

Databases

With the availability of computers and the Internet, publishers and scientific associations started to offer online access to their full text articles for their members through online portals.

The Association for Computing Machinery (ACM) (http://www.acm.org/), as an example, built the ACM Digital Library and offers access through the ACM Portal (http://portal.acm.org/), while the Institute of Electrical and Electronics Engineers (IEEE) (http://www.ieee.org/) created the IEEE Xplore digital library providing a search interface called IEEE Xplore (http://ieeexplore.ieee.org/).

Nowadays, most publishers of scientific material allow searching their articles, eBooks and so on through their portals like Springer's (http://www.springer.com/) SpringerLink (http://www.springerlink.com/) and Elsevier's (http://www.elsevier.com/) ScienceDirect (http://www.sciencedirect.com/)

However, those portals are usually limited to their own publications and allow only members to get access to the full text or PDF version of the publications or sell each article individually. The advantage of publishers' portals is in the high quality of the meta-data attached.

Manually Compiled Collections

The DBLP Computer Science Bibliography (Ley, 1997) (Ley, 2002) (http://www.informatik.uni-trier.de/~ley/db/) based at Universität Trier is a database of bibliographic references. Development on DBLP commenced in 1993 as a collection of computer science related publications. The high quality of manually maintained bibliographical references (Ley & Reuther, 2006) allowed the development of tools implementing bibliometrics developed long ago by (Garfield, 1963) and (Small, 1973). Despite the development of far larger indices, DBLP is still used frequently.

Other researchers improved the DBLP database by adding an enhanced search component called CompleteSearch DBLP (http://dblp.mpi-inf.mpg.de/dblp-mirror/index.php) (Bast & Weber, 2007) as well as faceted search capabilities (Tunkelang, 2009) via an interface named FacetedDBLP (Diederich et al., 2007) (http://dblp.l3s.de/dblp++.php).

Automatic Indices

Citeseer (http://citeseer.ist.psu.edu/) was developed by NEC in 1997 (Lawrence et al., 1999) and moved to Pennsylvania State University in 2003. It started as an attempt to bring the bibliographic information previously published distributed on websites of publishers, research organizations and individual authors into one searchable index and to automate indexing citations and citation linking. Citeseer also acts as a research platform and the improved system, CiteseerX (http://citeseerx.ist.psu.edu/), incorporates additional features like citation statistics, related document identification and query-sensitive summaries. CiteseerX now indexes over 1.4 million documents and over 27 million citations.

ScientificCommons (http://www.scientificcommons.org/) is an index built by the Institute for Media and Communications Management at the University of St.Gallen in Switzerland. (Kirchhoff et al., 2008). According to their website they indexed 13 million publications by January 2007.

Google Scholar (http://scholar.google.com) is Google's take on literature retrieval. Compared to other systems, Google started relatively late to offer a specialized portal for scientific publications, but has grown to probably the largest index. While numbers are not openly published on the Google Scholar website, simple searches claim hundreds of millions results. Google approaches publishers to streamline access to all their publication material. Google also analyses citations to build citation graphs and allow searching for publications that link to the current one.

Since the metadata is extracted automatically, the metadata provided by such systems tends to contain more errors.

Finding Related Publications

Finding related publications is based on a given context. This context can be based on other publications, the current work of the author, the author's long-term research interests and many other features.

Some bibliographic search systems like CiteseerX shows publications related to a given one. Such relatedness can for example be identified by similarity of the terms contained in both texts, by the number of shared references cited in both papers or the number of publications citing both texts.

The Mac OS X application Papers helps the researcher to build a library of documents, by supporting queries to most repositories and the easy incorporation of search results including the meta data into the user's local collection. In cases where a URL to a PDF-version of a publication is provided, the user can double-click the entry and the file will be automatically downloaded and stored with the metadata. The paper can then be printed or read and annotated on screen within the same application.

In terms of finding related publications, the application creates an editable list containing the authors of the publications of the collection, and the author view as shown in Figure 1 can be configured to automatically check for recent publications when an author is selected. This helps to find follow-up publications and become aware of the author's recent work. In an analogous way, recent articles for known journals are retrieved on the selection of a journal.

Staying up to Date in the Field

Traditionally, researchers tend to stay on top of their field via subscriptions to newsletters and journals, by visiting symposiums and conferences, and by exchanging references with colleagues. The latter seems to be used in increasing rates since

Web 2.0 based tools to share bookmarks and bibliographical metadata collections are more commonly available. An additional feature of modern bibliographic search sites is the availability of email or RSS notification.

Notification Services

The search interface of PubMed as shown in Figure 2 allows the user to specify RSS feed as a result output option. This allows researchers to specify their information need in a very precise form. The RSS feeds can be added to so-called feed aggregators that collect the incoming RSS items and present them for example in a list similar to an email inbox. (http://www.nlm.nih.gov/pubs/techbull/mj05/mj05_rss.html)

Sente (http://www.thirdstreetsoftware.com/) is a Mac OS X application that allows the user to manage references and their PDF files. Additionally, the user can define hierarchical collections by defining queries. The queries associated with those collections will be executed in the background and new publications will be indicated similar to incoming mail.

BioMed Central (BMC) Bioinformatics allows researchers to specify their research interests and send email notifications once new publications match the searcher's profile as illustrated in Figure 3. The service covers the broader interest, but is not as selective as PubMed's RSS implementation. (http://www.biomedcentral.com/)

Figure 1. Screenshot showing Paper app's author view (©2010 mekentosj.com Used with permission)

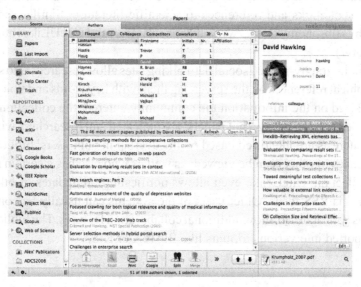

Figure 2. Screenshot showing PubMed's RSS Feed creation (Image courtesy of the U.S. National Library of Medicine)

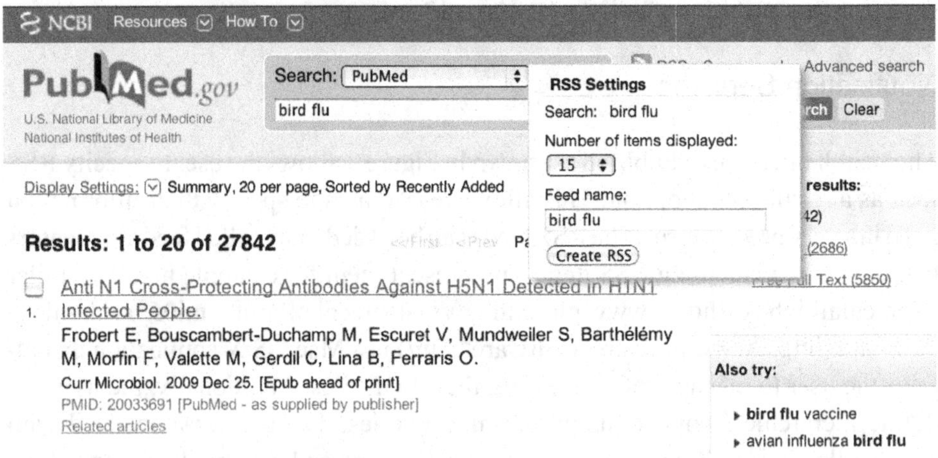

Social Networks

The rise of the Web 2.0 technologies enabled the development of Web applications that were as feature rich as binary applications for desktop computers. Their server-based nature also allowed those applications to share data between users and user groups. One class of such social networks is based on the idea of sharing bibliographic references and web links.

The publisher Elsevier (http://www.elsevier.com/) offers the free service called 2collab (http://www.2collab.com) that allows researchers and students to manage and share bookmarks and references to scientific literature. Similar services are provided by Bibsonomy (http://www.bibsonomy.org/) and CiteULike (http://www.citeulike.org/).

Such bibliography-related social networking sites allow researchers to store their bibliographical references on the server, tag them with key words and upload a PDF version. Based on the information the community entered, the collection of references can be browsed by tag, 'hot papers' are indicated and researchers with similar research interests are identified based on the overlap in both users' bibliographies. The references of others can be viewed, as well as who else has a certain reference in their collection. CiteULike even allows notification on updates of other user's collections via RSS feeds. Other users of the systems can usually be contacted or linked in as colleagues to allow additional collaboration features. The bibliographies can be exported into various formats like BibTeX or RIS.

Figure 3. Screenshot showing BioMed Central's email notification service setup (© BioMed Central, 2010. Used with permission)

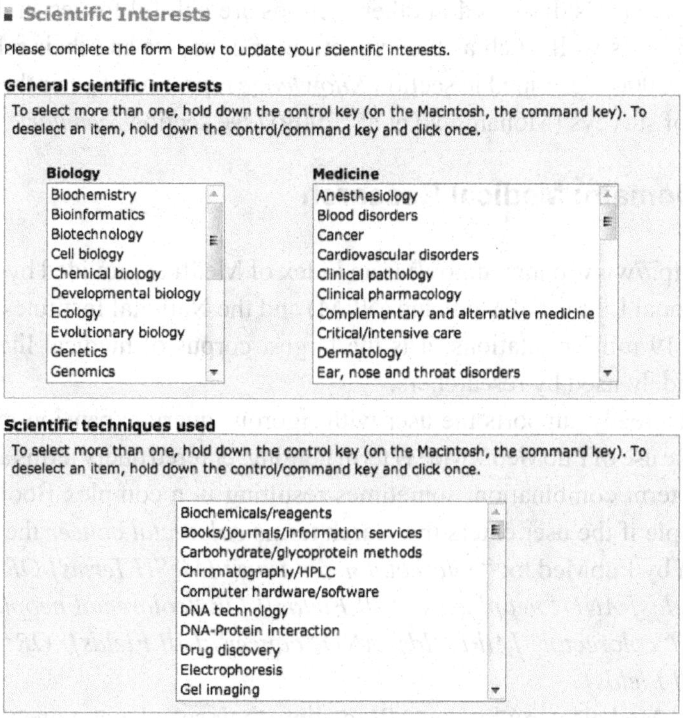

Entering a New Field

Someone who wants to enter a new science area needs to understand the field's terminology, concepts and their relationships and which questions have been solved or are still open problems. Lecturers at universities often spend vast amounts of time preparing course material or even books that are specifically designed to introduce students to new areas.

Researchers who have to do a thorough literature review sometimes summarize the current state of literature in surveys. Such surveys cover the publications of selected topics or concepts well and are a valuable source of information for students and other researchers. Journals like the ACM computing surveys publishing nothing but such surveys.

Due to the relatively high quality of community-authored websites like Wikipedia (http://www.wikipedia.org/) and knol (http://knol.google.com/) they are also becoming a viable entry point for getting an overview of a field or concept. While they cannot be taken as source of scientific knowledge like reviews, they are often well written and provide a quick overview including links to more specific or generic concepts and scientific publications.

Many of the tools discussed in other sections are helpful for researchers entering a new field as well, such as the extraction of concepts and their relationships (Plake et al., 2006) described in section *Knowledge representation* or the automatic generation of surveys (Mohammad et al., 2009) (see section *Summaries*).

Special Domain: Medical Research

PubMed (http://www.pubmed.gov/) is an index of Medline provided by the United States' National Library of Medicine (NLM) and the National Institutes of Health. With about 19 million citations, it is the largest corpus of medical literature and therefore widely used by researchers.

PubMed already supports the user with rigorous query expansion facilities. In order to make use of PubMed's MeSH term tagging, entered query terms are mapped into MeSH term combination, sometimes resulting in a complex Boolean query. As an example if the user enters the search terms *colorectal cancer* the query will be rewritten by PubMed to: *"colorectal neoplasms" [MeSH Terms] OR ("colorectal" [All Fields] AND "neoplasms" [All Fields]) OR "colorectal neoplasms" [All Fields] OR ("colorectal" [All Fields] AND "cancer" [All Fields]) OR "colorectal cancer" [All Fields]*

Since PubMed also provides an API to allow their search component to be used in complex scenarios, a number of research prototypes incorporate PubMed's search features to create new retrieval tools. This section describes tools that are based on PubMed such as AliBaba, a knowledge extraction and visualization tool, and GoPubMed, a service providing a comprehensive interface to semantically navigate through the PubMed results to a given query.

Knowledge Representation

Ali Baba is a research prototype built by the Knowledge Management in Bioinformatics research group at the Humboldt University in Berlin (Plake et al., 2006). It performs a PubMed query, analyses the results and visually presents an interactive graph showing the semantic relationship between biological concepts, which they call entities, contained in the result set. One of the problems with PubMed and similar resources is the plethora of documents they contain and the vast amount of matches they produce to common query terms. AliBaba helps the user to visualize the concepts described as well as relationships between them in an interactive graph. Extracting concepts mentioned together within one sentence, for example, identifies relationships between such concepts. Selected GUI components link back to the publications from which that knowledge was gained. This helps the searcher to obtain an overview quickly.

AliBaba performs entity as well as relationship extraction by learning language patterns and deriving consensus patterns representing clusters of identified initial patterns for performance reasons. The entities extracted belong to classes like cells, diseases, drugs, proteins, species and tissues. The techniques used in AliBaba have been described in various papers including (Plake et al., 2006) and (Palaga et al., 2009).

The screenshot in Figure 4 is an example from the AliBaba Website (Knowledge Management in Bioinformatics Group, Department of Computer Science, Humbold-Universität zu Berlin). It is described there as follows:

A Patient with cough becomes unresponsive after normal dosage of codeine— what is going on? The query entered in Ali Baba was "codeine intoxication".

Ali Baba shows the relationship between codeine (marked in the graph with blue frame), cough, morphine, and poisioning. Poisioning is also connected to morphine and CYP2D6. The solution thus is that codeine is bioactivated by CYP2D6 into morphine, certain patients show an ultrarapid form of this metabolism, which leads to a life-threatening intoxication (see (Gasche et al., 2004)). The connection codeine->CYP2D6->morphine is directly visible in Ali Baba. ("AliBaba Screenshots", n.d.).

Figure 4. Screenshot showing AliBaba's user interface (© 2006-2010 Ulf Leser. Used with permission)

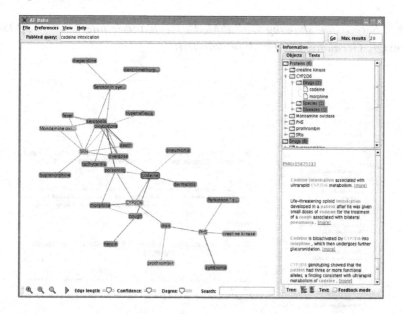

Faceted Interfaces

The German company Transinsight provides another interface to PubMed: Go-PubMed (Delfs et al., 2004) as illustrated in Figure 5. It shows matching sentences of the abstract, with search terms highlighted, and provides ontology-based ways to navigate through the search results, concepts discovered within and metadata, such as authors, publishers and year of publications. It shows statistics for the metadata as well as timelines indicating when publications including the search terms have been published. These features of GoPubMed help searchers to explore and understand new fields.

Additional features such as ontology building tools are provided by the commercial extension, called GoPubMed Pro. (http://www.gopubmed.org/)

Novo|seek's interface (http://www.novoseek.org/) is visually similar to Go-PubMed, allows users to filter by medical concepts and bibliographic properties, including authors and journals (see (Allende, 2009)). In addition to the PubMed corpus, it also indexes full text articles and around 500,000 research grants from Canada and the US provided by SciSight (http://www.scisight.com/).

The point of faceted interfaces is to use hierarchies of facets based on properties of the collection's structure or artificially created ones to provide the user means to navigate through the collection. Often the interface is enhanced with the estimated number of results to give the user advance information about the potential result set of each facet.

Figure 5. Screenshot showing GoPubMed's faceted user interface (© 2005-2010 Transinsigh, Germany. Used with permission)

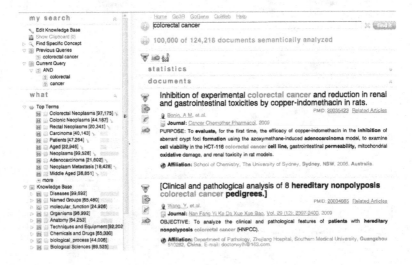

Result Visualisation

ManyEyes (http://manyeyes.alphaworks.ibm.com/manyeyes) is a site by IBM alphaWorks that allows Internet users to create, explore and discuss interactive visualisations of their datasets (Viegas et al., 2007). Users pick or upload a dataset, select a predefined visualisation type and configure it according to their visualisation ideas. Various PubMed related datasets are already available on the server and 20 visualisations about PubMed have been created and discussed by the community. Figure 6 shows an overview of the first ten visualisations matching the search term *pubmed*.

The delivery of the search results in a graphical alternative to a ranked list might take some burden off the user. Instead of parsing each result, understanding its key points and building a mental image of the answer space, the user sees a graphical representation of an aspect of the matching documents and their relations. This can potentially be of great help in getting an overview of the field.

Other work on the visualisation of PubMed results can be seen on the website of the graph visualisation software AiSee (http://www.aisee.com/graph_of_the_month/pubmed.htm) by the German company AbsInt Angewandte Informatik GmbH. It shows visualisations based on data processed using tools like botXminer (http://www.aisee.com/graph_of_the_month/botxm.htm), which has been described in (Mudunuri et al., 2006) or the publication network graph utility PubNet (http://www.aisee.com/graph_of_the_month/pubmed.htm) by Douglas et al. (2005).

Figure 6. Many Eyes shows a variety of example graphs representing PubMed search results (© 2010, IBM Corporation. Used with permission)

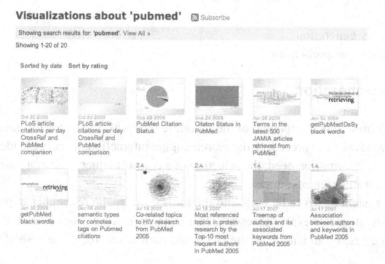

Tailored Delivery

Tailoring the delivery is the process of adapting a search engine's output specifically for the current user or user group. In order to allow for a system to deliver user-specific output, it has to represent preferences of the user. Such information is stored in a user model and can be predefined to match the needs of known classes of user like clinical practitioners versus nurses, or learned for specific users.

MiSearch (http://misearch.ncibi.org/) offers adaptive PubMed search (States et al., 2009). Using relevance feedback techniques, the system identifies preferred MeSH terms, substance names and author names, and uses this information to rank result sets of future queries according to the searcher's interests. Relevance feedback has been explored in the information retrieval field since the early 1970s (Rocchio, 1971).

AN INTELLIGENT LITERATURE RETRIEVAL SYSTEM

The section *Retrieval process* described common steps in a search session. Using an intelligent system of the sort we envisage, the user experience will not feel like *searching*. Rather, all the steps in the retrieval process, such as query formulation, retrieval, and result delivery, will integrate seamlessly in a behind-the-scenes workflow whose behaviour can be modified by the user either implicitly through monitoring interactions or explicitly. In order to achieve this, an intelligent literature retrieval assistant should have a user model, task model and knowledge structure model in order to effectively support the searcher.

Some aspects of an intelligent assistant for literature retrieval will be described here. The user should be supported in

- Query generation
- Result comprehension

Query Generation

The first important component of the literature retrieval assistant is the automation of the retrieval steps preceding the search engine interaction, namely the identification of the information need, the selection of a corpus to query and of a search tool, and the formulation of a query.

The system needs to be built into the tools used by the researcher in the phase where literature retrieval is necessary. This can be a program, such as a word processor in the case of an author, or the electronic patient record, in the case of clinical decision support. As part of the user model, the assistant should know about the user's education, for example if the information is needed by an undergraduate student, a post-doc or a professor with years of experience in the field.

In the medical field, the user's current role or job position could be used to decide which type of publication is likely to be most useful: for example, whether a randomized clinical trial, a clinical guideline, or even a consumer information sheet would be more helpful.

Utilizing the user's previous publications as part of the search context, the intelligent search assistant can help to disambiguate query terms in favour of the user's research interests.

Three main points according to (Budzik et al., 2001) are

- Relevance of active goals
- Word-sense ambiguity
- Audience appropriateness.

One way to derive the user's context is to attach the literature retrieval assistant to applications used by the searcher. Some effort has been made to explore the context of the user and offer matching search results, including working prototypes.

(Budzik et al., 2001) designed information management assistants and implemented a system called Watson that ran on a user's computer, observing the user's current context and task. This information was used to automatically retrieve documents for immediate display to the user. Alternatively graphical user interface components to trigger a search were offered to the user.

The information management assistant extracted the information need, based on the user's action and task models, as well as the content representation, based on the currently manipulated document and content models. Using information source descriptors, queries were sent to external information sources and the results were collected and presented to the user.

Watson incorporated adapters to access documents from applications like Microsoft Word and Web browsers and could be configured to retrieve similar or related documents. Based on text analysis, information entities such as addresses could be extracted and augmented by a link to a map service showing the location of the address. When the user created an empty image and a caption, the system used the caption text as query terms and displayed matching images from the Web. Since the rest of the document formed the context of that query, the results generally matched well and did not need to be clustered for disambiguation.

Watson was available as a free desktop tool for the Windows platform, but has been developed into a server-based platform for Web publishers and is now commercialized as Perfect Market. (http://www.perfectmarket.com/) by Idea Labs (http://www.idealab.com/).

A less generic type of application onto which to attach a literature retrieval assistant would be authoring software. Just as text editors evolved into word processors, special purpose authoring software is being developed for screenplay writers, novel writers and scientific writers.

One such development is the digital scholar's workbench (Barnes, 2007). It helps students and scientists to focus on writing their publications, while taking care of the publication workflow. The workbench supports the conversion of produced word processor documents into DocBook XML (ref) for storage in a revision control system as well as long-term preservation. It automatically generates XHTML versions of the student's website and PDF for printing.

Other systems, such as Scrivener (http://www.literatureandlatte.com/scrivener. html) for Mac OS X, support the research phase by providing a storage space for background material including web pages, images, word processing documents, notes, and so on. It then aids the author in writing long documents by allowing the creation of text snippets of arbitrary size that can easily be arranged and rearranged within the structure of the document.

In systems like the ones described above, the currently written publication could be taken to automatically allocate publications that are close to the currently written one and should be cited similar to what Watson (Budzik et al., 2001) is capable of doing. However in addition to only taking the current document into account, the context should also make use of the current location in the document for a more tactical view, or the authors' previously published articles, and their bibliographies to identify long-term interests.

This could even go down to a finer grain, for example by highlighting paragraphs as coming from another publication, reminding the author to quote text correctly in order to avoid unintentional plagiarism.

In the clinical context, (Price et al., 2002) describe their prototype called Smart-Query, which was integrated into an electronic health record system. They used relevant terms out of the patient record, converted them into MeSH terms and used them to query PubMed and other data sources. They also built a model of pathological test results and the interpretations of those results. This allows, for example, the mapping of the lab report entry "Meas ICA, Wh B" to the search term "Calcium", "Hypercalcemia" or "Hypocalcemia".

(Cimino & Del Fiol, 2007) describes *infobuttons*, a more recent prototype exploring ways to link from clinical systems to online information resources.

Result Delivery

Once the search results are retrieved, the user needs to understand the content of the retrieved information and the relations between publications. The concept of showing a list of ranked result documents as offered by traditional web search tools is often not the most intuitive way to present results. The user needs to find an answer to a question quickly and should not have to wade through long lists of results. A lot of effort is therefore going into the research on better user interfaces, with results being displayed for example as interactive graphs or even geographic maps, trying to generate direct benefit for the user.

Another key question is how to alert the user of the availability of search results. The user should not feel interrupted by a paperclip-like annoyance (Swartz, 2003). Instead the results should be shown on demand or probably via a non-interruptive notification in the graphical user interface. As example of a less interruptive interface, the Watson prototype (Budzik et al., 2001) was able to search for images to embed in a document based on the caption text. Since the user already indicated the need for a new image, the results are likely not to be seen as in interruption.

It should be noted that various research areas address the result delivery task; the examples given here are very selective.

Result Visualisation

Visualizations showing citation graph data or relationships in medical subjects have been increasingly explored recently. Some of those visualizations are interactive and allow the searcher to browse the answer space. (Whitelaw, 2009) explains his work on the Visible Archive project (http://visiblearchive.blogspot.com/) that aims to make the vast amount of documents in the Australian National Archive more accessible. Visualizations like the one in Figure 7 show the number of publications along timelines, indicate the size and the series, and the amount available digitally as well as related material.

A literature retrieval assistant in the future should have the ability to explore relations beyond those explicitly available, such as citations. If and when technologies to extract semantics from general text become sufficiently advanced, systems linking concepts like those available in the medical field today will become generally available.

Figure 7. One of the interactive interfaces created by the VisualArchive project. It shows series from the Australian National Archive as squares. The size of each square indicates the physical size of the collection in storage, the inner square indicates the percentage of the series available digitally. Selecting a series shows a summary and links to all series that are related. (© 2009 Mitchell Whitelaw. Used with permission)

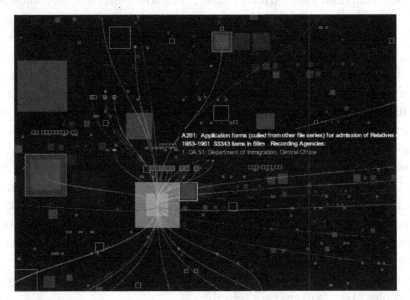

Summaries

Once automatically generated summaries are of sufficient quality, they will help to describe a field to get a quick overview and might also be useful for creating an update for a researcher returning from an absence.

(Mohammad et al., 2009) compare ways of automatically generating technical surveys. They use multi-document summarizing techniques based on the citation texts.

With the increasing rate of research papers and articles being published, researchers have an increased need to quickly estimate the relevance of a text for their research interests. Apart from the title, the abstract is used to get a first impression about the content of a publication. The abstract, however, is written by the author. A more objective description of a publication might be gained by looking how authors citing that publication describe it.

A recent development in information retrieval is an increased focus on the delivery aspect of the search result. The traditional way of returning a ranked list has transformed into ways of aggregating different result types like images, movies and geo-referenced documents. This research area is now referred to as aggregated search. The workshop on aggregated search at the SIGIR 2008 conference focused on this topic. One of the more advanced approaches is the automated generation of documents based on the needs of the searcher. (Wan et al., 2008) describe a system that plans the structure of a result document, triggers searches in heterogeneous information sources, analyses the results, and summarises them to compile the result document.

Responsiveness to the User

Fellow human beings respond to a number of signals we present unconsciously about our responses to information. There is increasing work on computer understanding of such signals. It is accepted that one of the most significant signals is the direction of eye gaze. The pattern of eye gaze has been used for determining user task (Iqbal & Bailey, 2004) and for tuning enterprise search (Hawking et al., 2009). There are two constructive models of eye gaze motion for reading based on the properties of the oculomotor system, and effects of word recognition and can explain many of the experimental phenomena faced in reading (the E-Z Reader model—(Pollatsek et al., 2006) and SWIFT—(Engbert et al., 2005)). When fused with a predictive eye gaze model (e.g. (Gedeon et al., 2008)), they could be used to make some predictions as to the degree of comprehension or even appropriateness of the information presented. The latter is possible because the eye gaze path is under cognitive but not conscious control (e.g., for faces see (Palermo & Rhodes, 2007)), and so the content of view affects the way the eyes move.

The next step would be to use this information in the query formulation phase or at least to use the predicted user response to pre-fetch further information and so on.

Future Research Directions

Why do big organizations not have a pool of secretaries helping all managers, but rather one personal secretary for each manager, usually called a 'personal assistant'? It is because secretaries can play a much more valuable role if they go beyond just typing letters or mechanically completing administrative tasks, and instead grow to be the extended arm of their manager. A good secretary knows all the preferences of their manager, their preferred travel arrangements, their goals and how they like to achieve them, how to handle their incoming calls and email, how they organize their daily routines and even how they like their coffee. It usually takes a while for a new secretary to become a manager's most important companion.

Similarly, an automated literature retrieval assistant can be much more effective if it is contextualized—i.e., if it knows about its user, their tasks and information needs. It has to gather this information and learn about the user's preferences in order to build a user model, a task model and a knowledge structure model.

The literature retrieval assistant could make assumptions about a researcher's interests by taking into account their recent publications and drafts, the bibliography file they used, the references they accessed on online bibliographical sites like the ones discussed above, and the research areas of colleagues connected to them via work-related social networks such as LinkedIn (http://www.linkedin.com/) or Xing (http://www.xing.com/). Analysing the publications read by the user, as well as their type and publisher, the system can create a model of the searcher's information need. In the medical context, does the user prefer to read clinical guidelines, systematic reviews, randomized clinical trials or case studies?

But a literature retrieval assistant can be particularly helpful when a researcher's context is changing. It could analyse the publications in a field to help researchers entering a new research area at the start of a new project or when changing jobs. How did the field develop? What have been the major terms and streams, did they merge with other areas or divert into separate directions? What are the key publications in the area? Who are the key players, researchers, organisations, companies? The area could be even be presented in a way that would help newcomers to quickly gain an understanding of where ideas originated and what are the open issues. Interactive timelines and influence graphs coupled with automatically generated summaries could potentially be highly effective in this regard.

Research in the bio-informatics area has progressed well in recent years and currently available tools can take a lot of the burden off the medical researchers by extracting and pre-processing knowledge from scientific literature and aggregating it into comprehensible graphs. Modern tools allow the researcher to interactively explore the answer space by filtering the publications using medical terms from thesauri or even focus on genomes, tissues, and other medical entities and their relations. Future breakthroughs in technologies related to the automated processing of documents written in natural language may one day significantly improve bio-medical retrieval by allowing searches of relationships between biological entities such as genes and proteins.

A future intelligent literature assistant may assist medical practitioners and specialists in their daily routines. Systems that make use of task or working context, for example using data of the current patient's electronic health record to provide decision support about diagnosis or care, have been explored but are not generally available to practitioners.

EVALUATING PERFORMANCE

It is all very well to use one's intuition to design an intelligent literature search assistant and to propose all sorts of exciting features, but eventually we need to ask: Is the assistant useful as a whole? How useful? Is it more useful than other assistants? What about its specific features – do they make the system more useful, or do they make it worse?

Search for scientific literature is a sub-area of the well established field of *Information Retrieval*, which has usually based its measures on *precision:* the proportion of a retrieved set of documents which are judged useful; and *recall*: the proportion of the total number of useful (or relevant) documents which have been retrieved. In fact, information retrieval has been described as a signal detection problem (Swets, 1963) where useful documents are seen as signal and irrelevant ones as noise. Swets proposed that a retrieval system, like a missile-detecting radar, could be characterised with an ROC (Receiver Operating Characteristic) curve. In the retrieval case recall is plotted against *fallout:* the proportion of irrelevant documents in the collection, which have been retrieved. Definitions of precision, recall and fallout assume a binary definition of usefulness, but this is over-simplistic -- humans are often capable of distinguishing multiple levels of utility.

Obviously, judgments of the usefulness of a document retrieved are subjective and highly dependent upon the information need that prompted the search. Returning to the information need scenarios in beginning of the chapter, it would be natural to expect that the different scenarios would lead to very different judgments. For example, an expert searching for new material in their field would judge as useless many documents that would be very useful to a novice entering the field.

Long-Ago Evaluations from Which we can Learn

We would now like to discuss two literature search evaluations conducted many decades ago, which illustrate important principles that will be of use to us in evaluating modern systems.

The first is the study conducted by Cleverdon and others at the Cranfield Aeronautical Laboratories (Cleverdon, 1967). These studies are acclaimed by many as providing the foundation for most modern evaluations of information retrieval systems, but interestingly, utility judgments in the Cranfield collection were explicitly related to a specific task. Researchers at Cranfield who deposited a technical report in the library were asked to judge all the other technical reports (over a thousand of them) on a multi-point scale of usefulness. Essentially: (1) does the paper completely obviate the need for the new report? or (2) was the new author able to avoid experiments or derivations by citing the older report? or (3) does the older report provide background information worth citing in the newer one, or is the older report irrelevant or otherwise not useful?

In some literature search scenarios, such as carrying out systematic reviews in medicine, achieving very high recall is important. Unfortunately, in such a scenario, recall should ideally be computed relative to "all published documents". In other words, useful/relevant documents should not be ignored even if they are not included within the scope of the search system being used. In these cases, the *coverage* of the collection is a vital factor. Fascinatingly, a study of the effectiveness of MEDLARS (pre-cursor of PubMed) published by Lancaster (1969) took this into account.

The MEDLARS evaluation sampled real searches conducted over a period and sampled the documents retrieved by the corresponding query. Sampled documents were printed and sent to the submitter along with the original query for judgment on a four-point scale. Uniform sampling is critical to ensuring that conclusions drawn from the experiments may be extrapolated to real-world usage. To estimate coverage, and therefore true recall, subject experts at the U.S National Library of Medicine identified candidate documents not included in MEDLARS that they believed could be relevant. These additional documents were also printed and included in the set of documents sent to the participants for evaluation.

Between them, these long-ago studies illustrate principles that should be applied to the evaluation of a virtual librarian:

- The evaluation of a retrieval system should occur in the context of a real task.
- Evaluations should uniformly sample the population of real searches applicable to the scenario to be evaluated, so that conclusions drawn may be meaningfully generalised.
- It is appropriate to take account of degrees of usefulness. More recent work by Järvelin and Kekäläinen (2000) has proposed a measure called Normalised Discounted Cumulative Gain (NDCG) which takes into account multiple levels of utility and which may be a good choice for a single number score on which to compare alternative systems.

Other Types of Evaluation Methodology

Where the scenario being evaluated is oriented to precision rather than recall, different types of evaluation can be considered. First, we can develop an effectiveness score based on the user's interactions with the system. How many documents did they open, print or email? How much time did they spend looking at a document? Second, we can present two alternative sets of retrieved documents side-by-side to randomly selected users on a large screen and ask them to compare the sets as a whole and make a preference judgment (Krumpholz & Hawking, 2006) (Thomas &

Hawking, 2006). This second method would be a very appropriate choice for comparing two alternative virtual librarians, or for comparing a base system against the same system with a particular enhancement. Evaluating result sets in their entirety by this method has many advantages, as outlined by Thomas and Hawking, but the method is not always applicable.

Other Evaluation Factors

Since, as we have seen, there are many different functions that a Virtual Librarian might perform, evaluation and comparison of systems obviously cannot be restricted to comparing the sets of documents retrieved. Some added-value enhancements such as automatic query generation and enhancement, automatic deduction of a user's task context, and sophisticated linguistic analysis of the content of documents, may indeed be measurable by their effect on the quality of results retrieved. However others, such as tools for exploring, summarising, visualising and navigating within the results set must be measured in other ways: perhaps the side-by-side preference approach is applicable here, or perhaps we must resort to the pattern of more traditional psychological experiments with Latin Square designs, controls for individual differences, rating scales and pre and post questionnaires.

A fully-fledged Virtual Librarian is a complex system with many components, hopefully performing tasks of which previously only humans were capable. It is clear that the methodology for any attempt to evaluate or compare such systems must be very carefully thought out and tailored not only to the features of the systems being evaluated, but to the scenarios being modelled.

CONCLUSION

The modern scientist can gain access to most current, and many past, journal articles and research papers without even leaving their desk. For many of us, still remembering dusty index cards in libraries, this is a major achievement of the library science and information retrieval community and of invaluable help for researches in all fields. It must be close to what Vannevar Bush envisaged, in his highly prescient description of the hypothetical *Memex* system (Bush, 1945)

However, an intelligent literature retrieval assistant of the future could take even more pressure off the researcher by automatically retrieving literature in the absence of a specific search and by adding value to retrieved literature through pointers to related work, automatic summaries of single and even multiple documents, highlighting of relationships between concepts and alerts to new and emerging ideas.

The field is still in very active development and we can expect to see a change of paradigm away from explicit search (pull paradigm) toward automated monitoring, delivery and knowledge extraction (push paradigm). Finding appropriate methodologies for evaluating and comparing the sophisticated intelligent assistants of future will be an additional challenge for researchers.

REFERENCES[1]

Barnes, I. (2007). The digital scholar's workbench. In Chan, L. & Martens, B., editors, ELPUB2007. *Openness in Digital Publishing: Awareness, Discovery and Access - Proceedings of the 11th International Conference on Electronic Publishing*, (pp. 285–296), Vienna, Austria.

Bast, H., & Weber, I. (2007). The completesearch engine: Interactive, efficient, and towards ir&db integration. In *CIDR, 7*, pp. 88–95. Citeseer.

Berglund, A., Boag, S., Chamberlin, D., Fernandez, M., Kay, M., Robie, J., & Simeon, J. (2002). *Xml path language (xpath) 2.0. W3C working draft.*

Berner, E., & Ball, M. (1998). *Clinical Decision Support Systems: Theory and Practice.* New York: Springer Verlag.

Budzik, J., Hammond, K., & Birnbaum, L. (2001). Information access in context. *Knowledge-Based Systems, 14*(1-2), 37–53. doi:10.1016/S0950-7051(00)00105-2

Bush, V. (1945). As we may think. *Atlantic Monthly, 176*, 101–108.

Cimino, J. J., & Del Fiol, G. (2007). *Clinical Decision Support: The Road Ahead, chapter Infobuttons and point of care access to knowledge.* New York: Academic Press.

Claridge, J. A., & Fabian, T. C. (2005). History and development of evidence- based medicine. *World Journal of Surgery, 29*(5), 547–553. doi:10.1007/s00268-005-7910-1

Cleverdon, C. (1967). The Cranfield tests on index language devices. *Aslib Proceedings*, 19,173–192. (republished In Sparck Jones, Karen and Peter Willett, eds, Readings in Information Retrieval.San Francisco: Morgan Kauffman. Collen, M. F. (1987). Health care information systems: a personal historic review. In Bluhm, (Ed.) *Proceedings of ACM conference on History of medical informatics*, pages 123–136, New York:ACM.

Delfs, R., Doms, A., Kozlenkov, A., & Schroeder, M. (2004). Gopubmed: ontology-based literature search applied to gene ontology and pubmed. In German Conference on Bioinformatics, pages 169–178. Citeseer.

Diederich, J., Balke, W., & Thaden, U. (2007). Demonstrating the semantic growbag: automatically creating topic facets for FacetedDBLP. In *Proceedings of the 7th ACM/IEEE-CS joint conference on Digital libraries*, page 505. ACM.

Douglas, S., Montelione, G., & Gerstein, M. (2005). Pubnet: a flexible system for visualizing literature derived networks. *Genome Biology, 6*(9). doi:10.1186/gb-2005-6-9-r80

Engbert, R., Nuthmann, A., Richter, E., & Kliegl, R. (2005). Swift: A dynamical model of saccade generation during reading. *Psychological Review, 112*, 777–813. doi:10.1037/0033-295X.112.4.777

Evidence-Based Medicine Working Group. Guyatt, G., Cairns, J., Churchill, D., Cook, D., Haynes, B., Hirsh, J., Irvine, J., Levine, M., Levine, M., Nishikawa, J., Sackett, D., Brill-Edwards, P., Gerstein, H., Gibson, J., Jaeschke, R., Kerigan, A., Neville, A., Panju, A., Detsky, A., Enkin, M., Frid, P., Gerrity, M., Laupacis, A., Lawrence, V., Menard, J., Moyer, V., Mulrow, C., Links, P., Oxman, A., Sinclair, J., and Tugwell, P. (1992). Evidence-based medicine: A new approach to teaching the practice of medicine. *Journal of the American Medical Association, 268*(17), 2420–2425. doi:10.1001/jama.268.17.2420

Fuhr, N., Gövert, N., Kazai, G., & Lalmas, M. (2002). INEX: INitiative for the Evaluation of XML retrieval. In *Proceedings of the SIGIR 2002 Workshop on XML and Information Retrieval*.

Garfield, E. (1963). Citation indexes in sociological and historical research. *American documentation, 14*(4),289–291.

Gasche, Y., Daali, Y., Fathi, M., Chiappe, A., Cottini, S., Dayer, P., & Desmeules, J. (2004). Codeine intoxication associated with ultrarapid CYP2D6 metabolism. *The New England Journal of Medicine, 351*(27), 2827–2831. doi:10.1056/NEJMoa041888

Gedeon, T., Zhu, D., & Mendis, B. S. U. (2008). Eye gaze assistance for a game-like interactive task. *International Journal of Computer Games Technology*, 2008.

Hawking, D., Thomas, P., Gedeon, T., Jones, T., & Rowlands, T. (2009). New methods for creating testfiles: Tuning enterprise search with c-test. In *SIGIR 2009 Workshop on the Future of IR Evaluation*, page 5.

Iqbal, S., & Bailey, B. (2004). Using eye gaze patterns to identify user tasks. In *The Grace Hopper Celebration of Women in Computing.* Citeseer.

Järvelin, K., & Kekäläinen, J. (2000). IR methods for retrieving highly relevant documents. In [Athens, Greece.]. *Proceedings of SIGIR, 00,* 41–48.

Kelly, D., & Teevan, J. (2003). Implicit feedback for inferring user preference: a bibliography. In *ACM SIGIR Forum, 37,* 18–28. New York: ACM

Kirchhoff, L., Stanoevska-Slabeva, K., Nicolai, T.& Fleck, M. (2008). *Using social network analysis to enhance information retrieval systems.*

Krumpholz, A. & Hawking, D. (2006). *InexBib - retrieving XML elements based on external evidence.*

Lancaster, F. (1969). Medlars: Report on the evaluation of its operating efficiency. [republished In Sparck Jones, Karen and Peter Willett, eds, Readings in Information Retrieval, Morgan Kauffman, San Francisco, 1997]. *American Documentation, 20,* 119–142. doi:10.1002/asi.4630200204

Lawrence, S., Bollacker, K., & Giles, C. L. (1999). Indexing and retrieval of scientific literature. In *Proceedings of the Eighth International Conference on Information and Knowledge Management,* pp. 139–146. New York: ACM.Ley, M. (1997). Die trierer informatik-bibliographie dblp. *GI Jahrestagung,* pages 257–266.

Ley, M. (2002). The dblp computer science bibliography: Evolution, research issues, perspectives. *Lecture Notes in Computer Science,* 1–10. doi:10.1007/3-540-45735-6_1

Ley, M., & Reuther, P. (2006). Maintaining an online bibliographical database: The problem of data quality. Actes des Sixi`emes Journ´ees Extraction et Gestion des Connaissances, Lille, France, pages 5–10.

Medical Subject Headings. (n.d.). Retrieved December 23, 2009 from National Library of Medicine Web site: http://www.nlm.nih.gov/mesh/

Mohammad, S., Dorr, B., Egan, M., Hassan, A., Muthukrishan, P., Qazvinian, V., et al. (2009). Using citations to generate surveys of scientific paradigms. In *Proceedings of Human Language Technologies: The Annual Conference of the North American Chapter of the Association for Computational Linguistics (NAACL-HLT 2007),* pages 584–592. Association for Computational Linguistics.

Mudunuri, U., Stephens, R., Bruining, D., Liu, D., & Lebeda, F. (2006). botxminer: mining biomedical literature with a new web-based application. *Nucleic Acids Research, 34*(Web Server issue):W748–W752.

Palaga, P., Nguyen, L., Leser, U., & Hakenberg, J. (2009). High-performance information extraction with AliBaba. In *Proceedings of the 12th International Conference on Extending Database Technology: Advances in Database Technology*, pp.1140–1143. New York: ACM.

Palermo, R., & Rhodes, G. (2007). Are you always on my mind? a review of how face perception and attention interact. *Neuropsychologia, 45*(1), 75–92. doi:10.1016/j. neuropsychologia.2006.04.025

Plake, C., Schiemann, T., Pankalla, M., Hakenberg, J., & Leser, U. (2006). Alibaba: Pubmed as a graph. *Bioinformatics (Oxford, England), 22*(19), 2444. doi:10.1093/ bioinformatics/btl408

Pollatsek, A., Reichle, E., & Rayner, K. (2006). Tests of the ez reader model: Exploring the interface between cognition and eye-movement control. *Cognitive Psychology, 52*(1), 1–56. doi:10.1016/j.cogpsych.2005.06.001

Price, S., Hersh, W., Olson, D., & Embi, P. (2002). Smartquery: context-sensitive links to medical knowledge sources from the electronic patient record. In *Proceedings of the AMIA Symposium*, page 627. American Medical Informatics Association.

Rocchio, J. J. (1971). Relevance feedback in information retrieval. In G. Salton,(Ed.) *The SMART Retrieval System—Experiments in Automatic Document Processing (pp.* 313–323).Upper Saddle River, NJ: Prentice Hall Inc.

Rockliff, S., Peterson, M., Martin, K., & Curtis, D. (2005). Chasing the sun: a virtual reference service between sahslc (sa) and swice (uk). *Health Information and Libraries Journal, 22*(2), 117–123. doi:10.1111/j.1471-1842.2005.00569.x

Salton, G., Allan, J., & Buckley, C. (1993). Approaches to passage retrieval in full text information systems. In *Proceedings of the 16th Annual International ACM SIGIR Conference on Research and Development in Information Retrieval*, page 58. New York: ACM.

Small, H. (1973). Co-citation in the scientific literature: A new measure of the relationship between two documents. *Journal of the American Society for Information Science American Society for Information Science, 24*(4), 265–269. doi:10.1002/ asi.4630240406

States, D. J., Ade, A. S., Wright, Z. C., Bookvich, A. V., & Athey, B. D. (2009). MiSearch adaptive PubMed search tool. *Bioinformatics (Oxford, England), 25*(7), 974–976. doi:10.1093/bioinformatics/btn033

Stearns, M., Price, C., Spackman, K., & Wang, A. (2001). SNOMED clinical terms: overview of the development process and project status. In *Proceedings of the AMIA Symposium,* (p.662). American Medical Informatics Association.

Swartz, L. (2003). *Why people hate the paperclip: Labels, appearance, behavior and social responces to user interface agents.* bachelor thesis.

Swets, J. A. (1963). Information retrieval systems. *Science, 141*(3577), 245–250. doi:10.1126/science.141.3577.245

Teevan, J., Dumais, S., & Horvitz, E. (2005). Personalizing search via automated analysis of interests and activities. In *Proceedings of the 28th Annual International ACM SIGIR Conference on Research and Development in Information Retrieval,* (p. 456). New York: ACM.

The Journal of the American Medical Association (2009). *JAMA Instructions for Authors.*

Thomas, P., & Hawking, D. (2006). Evaluation by comparing result sets in context. In [New York: ACM.]. *Proceedings of CIKM, 2006,* 94–101.

Tunkelang, D. (2009). *Faceted Search (Synthesis Lectures on Information Concepts, Retrieval, and Services).* Morgan and Claypool Publishers.

Viegas, F., Wattenberg, M., Van Ham, F., Kriss, J., & McKeon, M. (2007). Many Eyes: A site for visualization at internet scale. *IEEE Transactions on Visualization and Computer Graphics, 13*(6), 1121. doi:10.1109/TVCG.2007.70577

Wan, S., Paris, C., & Krumpholz, A. (2008). From aggravated to aggregated search: Improving utility through coherent organisations of an answer space. In Lalmas, M. & Murdock, V.,(Eds.) *Proceedings of the SIGIR 2008 Workshop on Aggregated Search,* Singapore.

Whitelaw, M. (2009). Exploring archival collections with interactive visualisation. In To appear in: *Proceedings of eResearch Australasia2009*: No boundaries.

Wilkinson, R. (1994). Effective retrieval of structured documents. In *Proceedings of the 17th annual international ACM SIGIR conference on Research and development in information retrieval,* (pp.311–317). New York: Springer-Verlag

Xu, S., McCusker, J., & Krauthammer, M. (2008). Yale image finder (yif): a new search engine for retrieving biomedical images. *Bioinformatics (Oxford, England), 24*(17), 1968. doi:10.1093/bioinformatics/btn340

ADDITIONAL READING[2]

Baeza-Yates, R., & Ribeiro-Neto, B. (1999). *Modern Information Retrieval*. Addison Wesley.

Blum, B. I. (1987). *Proceedings of ACM conference on History of Medical Informatics*, New York: ACM.

Greenes, R. A. (2006). *Clinical Decision Support: The Road Ahead*. New York: Academic Press.

Ingwersen, P., & Jarvelin, K. (2005). *The turn*. New York: Springer.

Kopliku, A. (2009). *Aggregated search: potential, issues and evaluation. Technical report*. France: Institut de Recherche en Informatique de Toulouse.

Lehmann, H. P., Abbott, P. A., Roderer, N. K., Rothschild, A., Mandell, S., Ferrer, J. A., Miller, R. E., & Ball, M. J. (2006). Aspects of Electronic Health Record Systems. *Health Informatics Series*. Springer Science+Business Media, Inc.

Manning, C. D., Raghavan, P., & Schütze, H. (2008). *Introduction to Information Retrieval*. Cambridge, UK: Cambridge University Press.

Murdock, V., & Lalmas, M. (2008). Workshop on aggregated search. *SIGIR Forum, 42*(2),80–83.

Shortliffe, E. H., & Cimino, J. J. (2006). *Biomedical Informatics: Computer Applications in Health Care and Biomedicine. Springer Science+Business Media* (3rd ed.). LLC.

Tunkelang, D. (2009). *Faceted Search (Synthesis Lectures on Information Concepts, Retrieval, and Services)*. San Rafael, CA: Morgan and Claypool Publishers.

ENDNOTES

[1]   Please notice that the Bibliography provided is very selective. Numerous publications exist in this field, some dating back half a century. Allende, R. A. (2009). Accelerating searches of research grants and scientific literature with novo|seek. *Nature Methods*, 6.

[2]   Introductions on Information retrieval are *Introduction to Information Retrieval* (Manning et al., 2008) and *Modern Information Retrieval* (Baeza-Yates & Ribeiro-Neto, 1999). *The turn – Integration of Information Seeking and Retrieval in Context* (Ingwersen & Jarvelin, 2005) is a book focusing on the

context aspect of information retrieval. The recently published book *Faceted Search* (Tunkelang, 2009) is a brief introduction to the topic. Aggregated search is addressed in *Workshop on Aggregated Search* (Murdock & Lalmas, 2008) and thoroughly discussed in the technical report *Aggregated search: potential, issues and evaluation* (Kopliku, 2009).

Readers interested in aspects of clinical literature retrieval and clinical decision-making might find *Clinical Decision Support – The Road Ahead* (Greenes, 2006) very helpful. Furthermore, books like *Biomedical Informatics: Computer Applications in Health Care and Biomedicine* (Shortliffe & Cimino, 2006) and *Aspects of Electronic Health Record Systems* (Lehmann et al., 2006) are helpful to get a better understanding of the clinical aspects of information science. The papers collected in the proceedings of the *ACM conference on History of medical informatics* provide an interesting insight into early experiences in the area (Blum, 1987).

Compilation of References

ACL. Agent Communications Language. (2006). Retrieved from http://www.fipa.org/repository/aclspec.html.

Acquisti, A., & Gross, R. (2006). Imagined communities: Awareness, information sharing, and privacy on the Facebook. *6th Workshop on Privacy Enhancing Technologies*, (pp. 36–58). Cambridge.

Adam, N. R., Dogramaci, O., Gangopadhyay, A., & Yesha, Y. (1999). *Electronic Commerce*. Upper Saddle River, NJ: Prentice Hall.

Adelsberger, H. H., Bick, M., & Hanke, Th. (2002). Einführung und Etablierung einer Kultur des Wissensteilens in Organisationen. In M. Engelien & J. Homann (Eds.), *Virtuelle Organisationen und Neue Medien* (pp. 529-552). Köln: Eul.

Aguilera, M. K., Strom, R. E., Sturman, D. C., Astley, M., & Chandra, T. D. (1999). Matching events in a content-based subscription system. *Proc. ACM Intl. Symp. On Principles of Distributed Computing (PODC)*, (pp. 53–61).

Aksac, A. (Alkatun). *Knowledge engineering and semantics for the quality based next generation knowledge web*. Master's thesis, Christian-Albrechts University Kiel, Dept. of Computer Science, May 2009.

Alavi, M., & Leidner, D. E. (1999). Knowledge management systems: issues, challenges, and benefits. *Journal of Communications of the AIS, 1(2es)*.

Alves, L. L., & Davis, C. A., Jr. (2006) *Interoperability through Web services: evaluating OGC standards in client development for spatial data infrastructures*. VIII Brazilian Symposium on GeoInformatics, 2006, INPE, 193–208. ArcGIS. Retrieved from http://www.esri.com/products.html

Anderson, D. L., & Lee, H. (1999). The New Frontier. In Achieving Supply Chain Excellence Through Technology. Montgomery Research (pp. 12–21). Synchronized Supply Chains.

Anisimov, V. V., & Fedorov, V. V. (2007). Modeling, Prediction and Adaptive Adjustment of Recruitment in Multicentre Trials. *Statistics in Medicine, 26(27), 4958–4975*. doi:10.1002/sim.2956

Arjmand, M., & Roach, S. (1999). Creating Greater Customer Value by Synchronizing the Supply Chain. *In Achieving Supply Chain Excellence Through Technology*, Montgomery Research, 154-159, also in http://arjmand.ascet.com.

B. Thalheim.(2007). The conceptual framework to user-oriented content management.

Baker, A.D., Van Dyke Parunak, H., & Kutluhan, E. (1999). Agents and the Internet: Infrastructure for Mass Customization. *IEEE Internet Computing*, Sept.-Oct., 62-69.

Bannert, M. (1996). *Gestaltung und Evaluation von EDV-Schulungsmaßnahmen. Eine empirische Studie zur Effektivität und Akzeptanz. Landau*. Empirische Pädagogik.

Barnes, I. (2007). The digital scholar's workbench. In Chan, L. & Martens, B., editors, EL-PUB2007. *Openness in Digital Publishing: Awareness, Discovery and Access - Proceedings of the 11th International Conference on Electronic Publishing*, (pp. 285–296), Vienna, Austria.

Bast, H., & Weber, I. (2007). The completesearch engine: Interactive, efficient, and towards ir&db integration. *In CIDR, 7, pp. 88–95*. Citeseer.

Bellifemine, F., Caire, G., Poggi, A., & Rimassa, G. (2003). JADE: A White Paper. *Exp 3(3), 6-19*.

Bergenti, F. & Poggi. A. (2001). LEAP: A FIPA Platform for Handheld and Mobile Devices. *In Proc. Eighth International Workshop on Agent Theories, Architectures, and Languages (ATAL-2001)*, Seattle, WA, 303-313.

Berglund, A., Boag, S., Chamberlin, D., Fernandez, M., Kay, M., Robie, J., & Simeon, J. (2002). *Xml path language (xpath) 2.0. W3C working draft*.

Berner, E., & Ball, M. (1998). *Clinical Decision Support Systems: Theory and Practice*. New York: Springer Verlag.

Bigus, J. P., Schlosnagle, D. A., Pilgrim, J. R., Mills, W. N. III, & Diago, Y. (2002). ABLE: A Toolkit for Building Multi-agent Autonomic Systems – Agent Building and Learning Environment. *IBM Systems Journal, (September): 1–19*.

Binemann-Zdanowicz, A., Thalheim, B., & Tschiedel, B. (2003). *Logistics for learning objects. In eTrain'2003*. Kluwer.

Bower, G. H., & Hilgard, E. (1984). *Theorien des Lernens*. Stuttgart: Klett-Cotta.

Boyd, D. (2006). Friends, Friendsters, and Top 8: Writing community into being on social network sites. *First Monday, 11(12)*.

Boyd, D. M., & Ellison, N. B. (2007). Social Network Sites: Definition, History, and Scholarship. *Journal of Computer-Mediated Communication, 13(1), 210–230.* doi:10.1111/j.1083-6101.2007.00393.x

Braun, P., & Rossak, W. (2005). *Mobile Agents - Basic concepts, mobility models & the Tracy toolkit.* dpunkt.verlag.

Brin, S., & Page, L. (1998). The Anatomy of a Large-Scale Hypertextual Web Search Engine, *International Journal of Computer Networks and ISDN Systems, 30, (1-7) 107-117.*

Bryant, R. E. (1986). Graph-based algorithms for Boolean function manipulation. *IEEE Transactions on Computers, C-35(8), 677–691.* doi:10.1109/TC.1986.1676819

Budzik, J., Hammond, K., & Birnbaum, L. (2001). Information access in context. *Knowledge-Based Systems, 14(1-2), 37–53.* doi:10.1016/S0950-7051(00)00105-2

Bullinger, H.-J., Wörner, K., & Prieto, J. (1997). *Wissensmanagement heute.* Stuttgart: Fraunhofer-Institut für Arbeitswirtschaft und Organisation.

Bush, V. (1945). As we may think. *Atlantic Monthly, 176, 101–108.*

Campbell, S. W., & Park, Y. J. (2008). Social implications of mobile telephony: The rise of personal. *Social Compass, 2(2), 371–387.* doi:10.1111/j.1751-9020.2007.00080.x

Capgemini. (2004). A Collection of Agent Technology Pilots and Projects. Retrieved from http://www.capgemini.com/resources/thought_leadership/putting_agents_towork/

Carroll, J. M. (1990). *The Nurnberg funnel: designing minimalist instruction for practical computer skill.* Cambridge, Mass: MIT press.

Cassidy, J. (2006, 05 15). *The Online Life - Me Media.* Retrieved 08 21, 2009, from The New Yorker: http://www.newyorker.com/archive/2006/05/15/060515fa_fact_cassidy

Castefranchi, C. (1998). Modelling social action for AI agents. *Artificial Intelligence, 103(1-2), 157–182.* doi:10.1016/S0004-3702(98)00056-3

Chi, E. H.-H., Konstan, J., Barry, P., & Riedl, J. (1997). A spreadsheet approach to information visualization. *In Proceedings of the 10th annual ACM symposium on User interface software and technology, (pp. 79-80).* New York: ACM Press.

Chi, E. H.-H., Riedl, J., Barry, P., & Konstan, J. (1998). Principles for information visualization spreadsheets. *IEEE Computer Graphics and Applications, 18(4), 30–38.* doi:10.1109/38.689659

Cimino, J. J., & Del Fiol, G. (2007). *Clinical Decision Support: The Road Ahead, chapter Infobuttons and point of care access to knowledge.* New York: Academic Press.

Claridge, J. A., & Fabian, T. C. (2005). History and development of evidence- based medicine. *World Journal of Surgery, 29(5), 547–553.* doi:10.1007/s00268-005-7910-1

Clark, J., & DeRose, S. J. (1999). *XML Path Language (XPath) Version 1.0. W3C Recommendation.* Retrieved December 21, 2009, from http://www.w3.org/TR/xpath

Cleverdon, C. (1967). The Cranfield tests on index language devices. *Aslib Proceedings, 19,173–192.* (republished In Sparck Jones, Karen and Peter Willett, eds, Readings in Information Retrieval.San Francisco: Morgan Kauffman. Collen, M. F. (1987). Health care information systems: a personal historic review. In Bluhm, (Ed.) *Proceedings of ACM conference on History of medical informatics, pages 123–136,* New York:ACM.

Consolvo, S., Everitt, K., Smith, I., & Landay, J. A. (2006). *Design requirements for technologies that encourage physical activity. SIGCHI conference on Human Factors in computing systems* (pp. 457–466). Montréal, Québec: ACM Press.

Cox, D. (1955). Some Statistical Methods Connected with Series of Events (with Discussion). *Journal of the Royal Statistical Society. Series B. Methodological, 17, 129–164.*

Cube, F. v. (1968). *Kybernetische Grundlagen des Lernens und Lehrens.* Stuttgart: Klett.

Daugs, R. (1979). *Programmierte Instruktion und Lerntechnologie im Sportunterricht.* München: Minerva.

Davis, J., & Bradski, G. (1999, September). Real-time Motion Template Gradients using Intel CVLib. *Paper presented at IEEE ICCV Workshop on Framerate Vision,* Kerkyra, Greece

Delfs, R., Doms, A., Kozlenkov, A., & Schroeder, M. (2004). Gopubmed: ontology- based literature search applied to gene ontology and pubmed. In German Conference on Bioinformatics, pages 169–178. Citeseer.

Demers, A. J., Gehrke, J., Hong, M., Riedewald, M., & White, W. M. (2006). Towards expressive publish/subscribe systems. *In Intl Conf. on Extending Database Technology (EDBT), pp. 627–644.*

Dieberger, A., Dourish, P., Höök, K., Resnick, P., & Wexelblat, A. (2000). Social navigation: Techniques for building more usable systems. [New York: ACM.]. *Interaction, 7(6), 36–45.* doi:10.1145/352580.352587

Diederich, J., Balke, W., & Thaden, U. (2007). Demonstrating the semantic grow- bag: automatically creating topic facets for FacetedDBLP. In *Proceedings of the 7th ACM/IEEE-CS joint conference on Digital libraries,* page 505. ACM.

Dix, A., Finlay, J., Abowd, G., & Beale, R. (1995). *Mensch Maschine Methodik.* München: Prentice Hall.

Dorer, K., & Calisti, M. (2005). An Adaptive Solution to Dynamic Transport Optimization. *In Proc. Of the Fourth International Joint Conference on Autonomous Agents & Multi-agent Systems, AAMAS '05, Utrecht, The Netherlands. Also* at:http://www.whitestein.com/pages/downloads/publications.

Douglas, S., Montelione, G., & Gerstein, M. (2005). Pubnet: a flexible system for visualizing literature derived networks. *Genome Biology, 6(9)*. doi:10.1186/gb-2005-6-9-r80

Dumas, J. S., & Redish, J. C. (1999). *A practical guide to usability testing.* Norwood, NJ: Ablex.

Düsterhöft, A., & Thalheim, B. (2001). Conceptual modeling of internet sites. *In Proc. ER'01, (LNCS 2224*, pp. 179-192). New York: Springer, 2001.

Eagle, N., & Pentland, A. (2005). Social serendipity: Mobilizing social software. *IEEE Pervasive Computing / IEEE Computer Society [and] IEEE Communications Society, 4(2), 28–34.* doi:10.1109/MPRV.2005.37

Ekin, A., Tekalp, A. M., & Mehrotra, R. (2003). Automatic soccer video analysis and summarization. *IEEE Transactions on Image Processing, 12(7), 796–807.* doi:10.1109/TIP.2003.812758

Engbert, R., Nuthmann, A., Richter, E., & Kliegl, R. (2005). Swift: A dynamical model of saccade generation during reading. *Psychological Review, 112, 777–813.* doi:10.1037/0033-295X.112.4.777

Ennals, R., & Gay, D. (2007). User-friendly functional programming for web mashups. *SIGPLAN Notices, 42(9), 223–234.* doi:10.1145/1291220.1291187

Erfurth, C., Kern, S., Rossak, W., Braun, P., & Leßmann, A. (2008). MobiSoft: Networked Personal Assistants for Mobile Users in Everyday Life. In M. Klusch, M. Pechoucek, & A. Polleres (Ed.), *Cooperative Information Agents, Volume 5180 of Lecture Notes in Computer Science (pp. 147–161).* New York: Springer.

Evidence-Based Medicine Working Group. Guyatt, G., Cairns, J., Churchill, D., Cook, D., Haynes, B., Hirsh, J., Irvine, J., Levine, M., Levine, M., Nishikawa, J., Sackett, D., Brill-Edwards, P., Gerstein, H., Gibson, J., Jaeschke, R., Kerigan, A., Neville, A., Panju, A., Detsky, A., Enkin, M., Frid, P., Gerrity, M., Laupacis, A., Lawrence, V., Menard, J., Moyer, V., Mulrow, C., Links, P., Oxman, A., Sinclair, J., and Tugwell, P. (1992). Evidence-based medicine: A new approach to teaching the practice of medicine. *Journal of the American Medical Association, 268(17), 2420–2425.* doi:10.1001/jama.268.17.2420

Ferber, J. (1999). *Multi-Agent Systems: An Introduction to Distributed Artificial Intelligence.* Reading, MA: Addison-Wesley.

Ferber, J., Gutknecht, O., & Michael, F. (2003). In Giorgini, P., Mueller, J. P., & Odell, J. (Eds.), *AOSE 2003, LNCS 2935* (pp. 214–230). Heidelberg, Germany: Springer.

Fiedler, G., & Thalheim, B. (2009). Towards semantic wikis: Modeling intensions, topics and origin in content management systems. *Information Modelling and Knowledge Bases, XX, 1–21.*

Fischer, G., Lemke, A. C., & Schwab, T. (1985). Knowledge-Based Help Systems. In L. Borman, & B. Curtis (Eds.), *Proceedings of CHI'85 Conference on Human Factors in Computing Systems* (pp. 161-167). New York:ACM.

Franklin, S., & Graesser, A. (1997). Is it agent, or just a program? In Mueller, J. P., Wooldridge, M. J., & Jennings, N. R. (Eds.), *Intelligent Agents III* (pp. 21–36). Berlin: Springer.

Frej, H. B., Rigaux, P., & Spyratos, N. (2006). User notification in taxonomy based digital libraries (invited paper). *Proc. of ACM SIG-DOC Conference on the Design of Communication,*(pp. 18-20).

Fuhr, N., Gövert, N., Kazai, G., & Lalmas, M. (2002). INEX: INitiative for the Evaluation of XML retrieval. *In Proceedings of the SIGIR 2002 Workshop on XML and Information Retrieval.*

Fujima, J., & Tanaka, Y. (2007). Web-application composition through direct editing of Web documents and multiplexing of information access scenarios. *Journal of Systems and Computers in Japan, 38(12)*, 1–13. doi:10.1002/scj.20861

Fujima, J., Lunzer, A., Hornbæk, K., & Tanaka, Y. (2004). Clip, connect, clone: combining application elements to build custom interfaces for information access. *In Proceedings of the 17th Annual ACM Symposium on User Interface Software and Technology*, (pp. 175-184). New York: ACM Press.

Fujima, J., Yoshihara, S., & Tanaka, Y. (2007). Web application orchestration using Excel. *In Proceedings of the 2007 IEEE/WIC/ACM International Conference on Web Intelligence* (pp. 743-749). Washington, DC: IEEE Computer Society.

Gagné, R. M. (1969). *Die Bedingungen des menschlichen Lernens*. Hannover: Schroedel.

Garfield, E. (1963). Citation indexes in sociological and historical research. *American documentation, 14(4),289–291.*

Gasche, Y., Daali, Y., Fathi, M., Chiappe, A., Cottini, S., Dayer, P., & Desmeules, J. (2004). Codeine intoxication associated with ultrarapid CYP2D6 metabolism. *The New England Journal of Medicine, 351(27), 2827–2831*. doi:10.1056/NEJMoa041888

Gedeon, T., Zhu, D., & Mendis, B. S. U. (2008). Eye gaze assistance for a game-like interactive task. *International Journal of Computer Games Technology, 2008.*

Ghiassi, M. (2001). An E-Commerce Production Model for Mass Customized Market. *Issues in Information Systems, 2, 106–112.*

Ghiassi, M., & Spera, C. (2003). a). Defining the Internet-based Supply Chain System for Mass Customized Markets. *Computers & Industrial Engineering Journal, 45(1), 17–41*. doi:10.1016/S0360-8352(03)00017-2

Ghiassi, M., & Spera, C. (2003b). A Collaborative and Adaptive Supply Chain Management System. *Proceedings of the 31st International Conference on Computers and Industrial Engineering.*, San Francisco, Ca., 473-479.

Gilmore, J. H., & Pine, B. J., II. (2000). Markets of One: Creating Customer-Unique Value Through Mass Customization. *A Harvard Business Review Book.* GPRS: General Packet Radio System. Retrieved from http://www.gsmworld.com/technology/gprs/index.html

Goble, G. (2009, 01 12). *The History of Social Networking.* Retrieved 08 21, 2009, from Sympatico / MSN: http://digitaltrends.technology.sympatico.msn.ca/feature/99/The+History+of+Social+Networking.html

Gough, J., & Smith, G. (1995). Efficient recognition of events in a distributed system. *Proc. Australasian Computer Science Conference.*

GRASS (Geographic Resources Analysis Support System). Retrieved from http://grass.itc.it/

H. Ma & B. Thalheim.(September 2008). *Web information systems co-design and web 2.0.* WISE 2008 Tutorial, Auckland.

Hawking, D., Thomas, P., Gedeon, T., Jones, T., & Rowlands, T. (2009). New methods for creating testfiles: Tuning enterprise search with c-test. In *SIGIR 2009 Workshop on the Future of IR Evaluation,* page 5.

Heine, C. & Durrer, F. (2001). Computer und neue Medien in der Schule. Erfahrungen mit EDV-gestützten Lernprogrammen und Erwerb von Computerkenntnissen während der Schulzeit. Befunde aus der Befragung der studienberechtigten Schulabgänger 1999. *HIS-Kurzinformation A5/2001.*

Heinemann, A., Kangasharju, J., Lyardet, F., & Mühlhäuser, M. (2003). iClouds - Peer-to-Peer Information Sharing in Mobile Environments. In H. Koch, L. Börszörményi, & H. Hellwagner (Ed.), Euro-Par 2003. *Int. Conf. on Parallel and Distributed Computing. LNCS Series,* pp. 1038-1045. Klagenfurt: Springer.

Igel, C., & Daugs, R. (2002). Mehrwertpotentiale internetbasierter Lehre. In Jantke, K. P., Wittig, W. S., & Herrmann, J. (Eds.), *Von E-Learning bis E-Payment* (pp. 8–19). Berlin: Akademische Verlagsgesellschaft.

Information Modeling and Knowledge Bases, XVII,30-49.

Iqbal, S., & Bailey, B. (2004). Using eye gaze patterns to identify user tasks. *In The Grace Hopper Celebration of Women in Computing.* Citeseer.

Itoh, M., Fujima, J., Ohigashi, M., & Tanaka, Y. (2007). Spreadsheet-based framework for interactive 3D visualization of Web resources. *In Proceedings of the 11th International Conference on Information Visualisation,* (pp. 65-73). Washington, DC: IEEE Computer Society.

Jaakkola, H., Thalheim, B., Kidawara, Y., Zettsu, K., Chen, Y., & Heimburger, A. (2008). Information modeling and global risk management systems. In Jaakkola, H., & Kiyoki, Y. (Eds.), EJC'2008, *Information Modeling and Knowledge Bases* XVI. Amsterdam: IOS Press.

Jaboyedoff, M. & Labiouse. V. CONEFALL: a program for the quick preliminary estimation of the rock-fall potential of propagation zones,. *Computer & Geosciences.*

JADE. http://jade.cselt.it & http://jade.tilab.com

Jain, A. K., Aparicio, M. IV, & Singh, M. P. (1999). Agents for Process Coherence in Virtual Enterprises. *Communications of the ACM, 42(3), 62–69.* doi:10.1145/295685.295702

Järvelin, K., & Kekäläinen, J. (2000). IR methods for retrieving highly relevant documents. In [Athens, Greece.]. *Proceedings of SIGIR, 00,* 41–48.

JCMA.(1988). *Protection Against Snow Handbook.*

Jennings, N. R. (1993). Commitments and conventions: The foundation of coordination in multi-agent systems. *The Knowledge Engineering Review, 8(3), 223–250.* doi:10.1017/S0269888900000205

Jennings, N. R. (1999). On agent-based software engineering. *Artificial Intelligent 117 (2000),* pp. 277-296

Jennings, N. R., & Wooldrige, M. (1998). *Agent Technology: Foundations, Applications and Markets* (Jennings, N. R., & Wooldridge, M., Eds.). Berlin: Springer.

Jones, S. P., Blackwell, A., & Burnett, M. (2003). A user-centered approach to functions in Excel. *In Proceedings of the Eighth ACM SIGPLAN International Conference on Functional Programming,* (pp. 165-176). New York: ACM Press.

Kalakota, R., Stallaert, J., & Whinston, A. B. (1998). Implementing Real-Time Supply Chain Optimization Systems. Global Supply Chain and Technology Management, *POMS, 60-75.*

Kandogan, E., Haber, E., Barrett, R., Cypher, A., Maglio, P., & Zhao, H. (2005). A1: enduser programming for web-based system administration. *In Proceedings of the 18th Annual ACM Symposium on User Interface Software and Technology,* (pp. 211-220). New York: ACM Press.

Keil-Slawik, R., Beuschel, W., Gaiser, B., Klemme, M., Pieper, C., & Selke, H. (1997). Multimedia in der universitären Lehre. Eine Bestandsaufnahme an deutschen Hochschulen. In I. Hamm & D. Müller-Böling (Eds.), *Hochschulentwicklung durch neue Medien* (pp. 73-122). Gütersloh: Verlag Bertelsmann-Stiftung.

Kelly, D., & Teevan, J. (2003). Implicit feedback for inferring user preference: a bibliography. *In ACM SIGIR Forum,* 37, 18–28. New York: ACM

Kern, S., Braun, P., & Rossak, W. (2006). Mobisoft: An Agent-Based Middleware for Social-Mobile Applications. In R. Meersman, Z. Tari, & P. Herrero (Ed.), *On the Move to Meaningful Internet Systems Workshops.* Volume 4277 of Lecture Notes in Computer Science. pp. 984–993. Montpellier: Springer.

Kerres, M. (2001). *Multimediale und telemediale Lernumgebungen. Konzeption und Entwicklung.* München, Wien: Oldenbourg.

Kirchhoff, L., Stanoevska-Slabeva, K., Nicolai, T.& Fleck, M. (2008). *Using social network analysis to enhance information retrieval systems.*

Kleimann, B., Weber, S., & Willige, J. (2005). *E-Learning aus Sicht der Studierenden. 10. Kurzbericht der HIS – Hochschul-Informations-System GmbH.* Retrieved February 22, 2007, from http://www.his.de/pdf/24/HISBUS_E-Learning10.02.2005.pdf

Klix, F. (1971). Information und Verhalten. Kybernetische Aspekte der organismischen Informationsverarbeitung. Einführung in naturwissenschaftliche Grundlagen der Allgemeinen Psychologie. (1. Aufl.). Berlin: Verlag der Wissenschaften.

Knuth, D. E. (2009). *The Art of Computer Programming: Bitwise Tricks & Techniques; Binary Decision Diagrams, volume 4,* fascicle 1. Reading, MA: Addison-Wesley.

Kobsa, A. (2005). User modeling and user-adapted interaction. *User Modeling and User-Adapted Interaction, 15(1-2), 185–190.* doi:10.1007/s11257-005-6468-9

Koh, W., & Mui, L. (2001). *An Information Theoretic Approach to Ontology-based In-terest Matching.* Seattle: Artificial Intelligence, Ontology Learning Workshop.

Kowski, S. (July 2009). *Verwaltung von Generatoren auf der Basis des Concept-Driven Engineerings.* Master's thesis, Christian-Albrechts University Kiel, Dept. of Computer Science.

Krumpholz, A. & Hawking, D. (2006). *InexBib - retrieving XML elements based on external evidence.*

Krums, J. (2009, 01 15). *There's a plane in the Hudson.* Retrieved 08 21, 2009, from Twitpic: http://twitpic.com/135xa

Küster, U., & König-Ries, B. (2007). Semantic Service Discovery with DIANE Service Descriptions. *In Proceedings of the International Workshop on Service Composition & SWS Challenge at the 2007 IEEE/WIC/ACM International Conference on Web Intelligence (WI 2007).* pp. 152-156. Silicon Valley, CA: IEEE Computer Society.

Laender, A. H. F., Ribeiro-Neto, B. A., da Silva, A. S., & Teixeira, J. S. (2002). A brief survey of web data extraction tools. *SIGMOD Record, 31(2), 84–93.* doi:10.1145/565117.565137

Lampe, C., Ellison, N., & Steinfield, C. (2006). *A Face(book) in the crowd: Social searching vs. social browsing. Computer supported cooperative work* (pp. 167–170). Banff, Alberta: ACM Press.

Lampe, C., Ellison, N., & Steinfield, C. (2007). *A familiar Face(book): Profile elements as signals in an online social network. Human Factors in Computing Systems* (pp. 435–444). San Jose: ACM Press.

Lancaster, F. (1969). Medlars: Report on the evaluation of its operating efficiency. [republished In Sparck Jones, Karen and Peter Willett, eds, Readings in Information Retrieval, Morgan Kauffman, San Francisco, 1997]. *American Documentation, 20, 119–142.* doi:10.1002/asi.4630200204

Lange, D. B., & Oshima, M. (1998). *Programming and Developing Java Mobile Agents with Aglets.* Reading, MA: Addison-Wesley.

Lawrence, S., Bollacker, K., & Giles, C. L. (1999). Indexing and retrieval of scientific literature. In *Proceedings of the Eighth International Conference on Information and Knowledge Management,* pp. 139–146. New York: ACM.Ley, M. (1997). Die trierer informatik-bibliographie dblp. GI Jahrestagung, pages 257–266.

Lenhart, A., & Madden, M. (2007, 04 18). *Teens, Privacy and Online Social Networks.* Retrieved 08 21, 2009, from Pew Internet and American Life Project: http://www.pewinternet.org/Reports/2007/Teens-Privacy-and-Online-Social-Networks.aspx

Lewin, K., Heublein, U., Kindt, M. & Föge, A. (1996). *Bestandaufnahme zur Organisation mediengestützter Lehre an Hochschulen. HIS Kurzinformationen 7/96.*

Ley, M. (2002). The dblp computer science bibliography: Evolution, research issues, perspectives. Lecture Notes in *Computer Science,* 1–10. doi:10.1007/3-540-45735-6_1

Ley, M., & Reuther, P. (2006). Maintaining an online bibliographical database: The problem of data quality. Actes des Sixi`emes Journ´ees Extraction et Gestion des Connaissances, Lille, France, pages 5–10.

Lin, J., Wong, J., Nichols, J., Cypher, A., & Lau, T. A. (2009). End-user programming of mashups with vegemite. In *Proceedings of the 13th international conference on Intelligent user interfaces* (pp. 97-106). New York: ACM Press.

Loyd, B. H., & Gressard, C. P. (1984). The effects of sex, age, and computer experience on computer attitudes. *Association for Educational Data Systems Journal, 18(4), 67–76.*

Lugano, G. (2007). Mobile Social Software: Definition, Scope and Applications. *eChallenges 2007 conference* (pp. 1434-1442). The Netherlands: The Hague.

Ma, M. (1999). Agents in E-Commerce. *Communications of the ACM, 42(3), 79–80.* doi:10.1145/295685.295708

Maeno, K. & Fukuda, M. (2000). *Avalanche and Snowstorm.*

Maes, P., Guttman, R. H., & Moukas, A. G. (1999). Agents that Buy and Sell. *Communications of the ACM, 42(3), 81–91.* doi:10.1145/295685.295716

Medical Subject Headings. (n.d.). Retrieved December 23, 2009 from National Library of Medicine Web site: http://www.nlm.nih.gov/mesh/

MIDP. Mobile Information Device Profile. Retrieved from http://java.sun.com/products/midp/index.jsp

Minato, S. (1992). BEM-II: An arithmetic Boolean expression manipulator using BDDs. *IEICE Transactions on Fundamentals. E (Norwalk, Conn.), 76-A(10)*, 1721–1729.

Minato, S. (1996). *Binary Decision Diagrams and Applications for VLSI CAD*. Amsterdam: Kluwer Academic Publishers.

Mohammad, S., Dorr, B., Egan, M., Hassan, A., Muthukrishan, P., Qazvinian, V., et al. (2009). Using citations to generate surveys of scientific paradigms. In *Proceedings of Human Language Technologies: The Annual Conference of the North American Chapter of the Association for Computational Linguistics (NAACL-HLT 2007)*, pages 584–592. Association for Computational Linguistics.

Moreno, A., Valls, A., & Viejo, A. (2005). Using JADE-LEAP to Implement Agents in Mobile Devices (Research Report 03-008, DEIM, URV).Retrieved fromhttp://www.etse.urv.es/recerca/banzai/toni/MAS/papers.html Pancerella, A., & Berry, N. (1999). Adding Intelligent Agents to Existing EI Frameworks. *IEEE Internet Computing, Sept.-Oct., 60-61*.

Moritz, T., Noack, R., Schewe, K.-D., & Thalheim, B. (2007). Intention-driven screenography. In *Proceedings ISTA 2007*,(Vol. LNI 107, pp. 128-139).

Moritz, T., Schewe, K.-D., & Thalheim, B. (2005). Strategic modeling of web information systems and its impact on visual design patterns. In Frasincar, F., Houben, G.-J., & Vdovjak, R. (Eds.), *WISM'05* (pp. 5–13). Sydney.

Mudunuri, U., Stephens, R., Bruining, D., Liu, D., & Lebeda, F. (2006). botxminer: mining biomedical literature with a new web-based application. *Nucleic Acids Research, 34*(Web Server issue):W748–W752.

Murphy, G. L. (2001). *The big book of concepts*. Cambridge, MA: MIT Press.

Nakamura, Y., & Kanade, T. (1997). Semantic analysis for video contents extraction—spotting by association in news video. *Proceedings of the fifth ACM international conference on Multimedia* (pp.393-401). New York: ACM Press.

Nebel, I.-T., & Paschke, R. (2004). Integration domänenspezifischer Informationen in Benutzerprofile für adaptive e-Learning-Systeme. In K.P. Fähnrich, K.P. Jantke & W.S. Wittig (eds.), *Conference Proceedings of the Leipziger Informatiktage '04 - LIT'04* (pp. 264-272).

Ohigashi, M., & Tanaka, Y. (2005). *Shadows on 3D: Hosting 2D legacy applications into a 3D meme media environment*. In Leipziger Informatik-Tage 2005(LNI 72, pp. 401–410).

Ohigashi, M., Guo, Z. S., & Tanaka, Y. (2006). Integration of a 2D legacy GIS, legacy simulations, and legacy databases into a 3D geographic simulation, SIGDOC '06: *Proceedings of the 24th Annual Conference on Design of Communication*, pp.149–156.

Okada, Y., & Tanaka, Y. (1995). IntelligentBox: A constructive visual software development system for interactive 3D graphic applications. *Proc. of Computer Animation, 95, 114–125.*

Open, C. V. retrieved December 22, 2009, from http://opencv.willowgarage.com/

OpenGIS Standards and Specifications. Retrieved from http://www.opengeospatial.org/standards

Oracle: Oracle BPEL Process Manager Quick Start Guide (2006). Retrieved December 21, 2009, from http://download.oracle.com/docs/cd/B31017_01/integrate.1013/b28983.pdf

Ortner, J. (2002). Barrieren des Wissensmanagements. In M. Bornemann & M. Sammer (Eds.), Anwendungsorientiertes Wissensmanagement: Ansätze und Fallstudien aus der betrieblichen und universitären Praxis (pp. 73–114). Wiesbaden: Gabler.

Paech, B. (2000). *Aufgabenorientierte Softwareentwicklung*. Berlin: Springer.

Palaga, P., Nguyen, L., Leser, U., & Hakenberg, J. (2009). High-performance information extraction with AliBaba. In *Proceedings of the 12th International Conference on Extending Database Technology: Advances in Database Technology*, pp.1140–1143. New York: ACM.

Palermo, R., & Rhodes, G. (2007). Are you always on my mind? a review of how face perception and attention interact. *Neuropsychologia, 45(1), 75–92.* doi:10.1016/j.neuropsychologia.2006.04.025

Patel, N. R., & Tourtellotte, E. (2009). Drug Supply for Adaptive Trials. http://www.cytel.com/Knowledge/stimulating_adaptive_1_08.pdf

Peltz, C. (2003). Web services orchestration and choreography. *IEEE Computer, 36(10), 46–52.*

Piersol, K. W. (1986). Object-oriented spreadsheets: The analytic spreadsheet package. In *Proceedings on Object-Oriented Programming Systems, Languages and Applications* (pp. 385–390). New York: ACM Press.

Plake, C., Schiemann, T., Pankalla, M., Hakenberg, J., & Leser, U. (2006). Alibaba: Pubmed as a graph. *Bioinformatics (Oxford, England), 22(19), 2444.* doi:10.1093/bioinformatics/btl408

Pokahr, A., Braubach, L., & Lamersdorf, W. (2005, 11). Agenten: Technologie für den Mainstream? *it - Information Technology*, pp. 300–307.

Polanyi, M. (1983). *Tacit Dimension*. Gloucester, MA: Peter Smith Pub Inc.

Pollatsek, A., Reichle, E., & Rayner, K. (2006). Tests of the ez reader model: Exploring the interface between cognition and eye-movement control. *Cognitive Psychology, 52(1), 1–56.* doi:10.1016/j.cogpsych.2005.06.001

Price, S., Hersh, W., Olson, D., & Embi, P. (2002). Smartquery: context-sensitive links to medical knowledge sources from the electronic patient record. In *Proceedings of the AMIA Symposium*, page 627. American Medical Informatics Association.

R. Kaschek, K.-D. Schewe, B. Thalheim, & Lei Zhang.(2003). Integrating context in conceptual modelling for web information systems, web services, e-business, and the semantic web. In *WES 2003*, (LNCS 3095, pp. 77-88). New York: Springer.

Rocchio, J. J. (1971). Relevance feedback in information retrieval. In G. Salton,(Ed.) *The SMART Retrieval System—Experiments in Automatic Document Processing* (pp. 313–323).Upper Saddle River, NJ: Prentice Hall Inc.

Rockliff, S., Peterson, M., Martin, K., & Curtis, D. (2005). Chasing the sun: a virtual reference service between sahslc (sa) and swice (uk). *Health Information and Libraries Journal, 22(2)*, *117–123*. doi:10.1111/j.1471-1842.2005.00569.x

RosettaNet. (1998). http://www.rosettanet.org

Safra, J. E., & Yeshua, I. (2003). *Encyclopedia Britannica*. Merriam-Webster.

Sakagami, H., & Kamba, T. (1997). Learning Personal Preferences on Online Newspaper Articles from User Behaviors., *International Journal of Computer Networks and ISDN Systems, 29,(8-13) 1447-1456.*

Salton, G., Allan, J., & Buckley, C. (1993). Approaches to passage retrieval in full text information systems. In *Proceedings of the 16th Annual International ACM SIGIR Conference on Research and Development in Information Retrieval*, page 58. New York: ACM.

Sandholm, T. (1999). Automated Negotiation. *Communications of the ACM, 42(3), 84–85.* doi:10.1145/295685.295866

Schewe, K.-D., & Thalheim, B. (2004). Reasoning about web information systems using story algebra. *In ADBIS'2004*, (LNCS 3255, pages 54-66,)

Schewe, K.-D., & Thalheim, B. (2006). *Usage-based storyboarding for web information systems.* Technical Report 2006-13. Christian Albrechts University Kiel, Institute of Computer Science and Applied Mathematics, Kiel.

Schewe, K.-D., & Thalheim, B. (2007). Development of collaboration frameworks for web information systems. *In 20th Int. Joint Conf. on Artiꟷcal Intelligence, Section EMC07 (Evolutionary models of collaboration)*, (pp. 27-32), Hyderabad.

Schewe, K.-D., & Thalheim, B. (2007). Personalisation of web information systems. *Data & Knowledge Engineering, 62(1), 101–117.* doi:10.1016/j.datak.2006.07.007

Schewe, K.-D., & Thalheim, B. (2008). Context analysis: Towards pragmatics of information system design. In A. Hinze & M. Kirchberg,(eds.) *Fifth Asia-Pacific Conference on Conceptual Modelling (APCCM2008)*, (volume 79 of CRPIT, pp.69-78) Hobart, Australia.

Schewe, K.-D., & Thalheim, B. (2008). Life cases: A kernel element for web information systems engineering. *In Web Information Systems and Technologies, Volume 8*. (Lecture Notes in Business Information Processing,).Berlin: Springer.

Schmidt, I. (2005). Social-Mobile Applications. *IEEE Computer, 38(4), 84–85*.

Schründer-Lenzen, A. (1995). *Weibliches Selbstkonzept und Computerkultur*. Weinheim: Deutscher Studienverlag.

Schüppel, J. (1996). *Wissensmanagement: Organisatorisches Lernen im Spannungsfeld von Wissens- und Lernbarrieren*. Wiesbaden: Gabler.

Senn, S. (1998). Some Controversies in Planning and Analysing Multi-centre Trials. *Statistics in Medicine, 17(15-16), 1753–1756*. doi:10.1002/(SICI)1097-0258(19980815/30)17:15/16<1753::AID-SIM977>3.0.CO;2-X

Seo, Y., & Zhang, B. (2000). Learning user's preferences by analyzing web-browsing behaviors. *Proceedings of International Conference on Autonomous Agents* (pp.381-387). New York: ACM.

Shah, J. B. (2002). ST, HP VMI Program Hitting Its Stride. *Electronics Business News (EBN)*, 42,http://www.ebnonline.com.

Shirky, C. (12. 05 2003). *People on page: YASNS*.... Retrieved 08 21, 2009 von Corante's Many-to-Many: http://many.corante.com/archives/2003/05/12/people_on_page_yasns.php

Siepmann, B. (1993). *Effektives EDV-Training*. Doctoral dissertation, University Bochum.

Singh, R., Salam, A. F., & Iyer, L. (2005). Agents in E-Supply Chains. *Communications of the ACM, 48(6), 109–115*. doi:10.1145/1064830.1064835

Small, H. (1973). Co-citation in the scientific literature: A new measure of the relationship between two documents. *Journal of the American Society for Information Science American Society for Information Science, 24(4), 265–269*. doi:10.1002/asi.4630240406

Søby, M. (2003). *Digital Competence: from ICT skills to digital "bildung"*. Oslo ITU, University of Oslo.

States, D. J., Ade, A. S., Wright, Z. C., Bookvich, A. V., & Athey, B. D. (2009). MiSearch adaptive PubMed search tool. *Bioinformatics (Oxford, England), 25(7), 974–976*. doi:10.1093/bioinformatics/btn033

Stearns, M., Price, C., Spackman, K., & Wang, A. (2001). SNOMED clinical terms: overview of the development process and project status. In *Proceedings of the AMIA Symposium*, (p.662). American Medical Informatics Association.

Sturm, R. (2008). *Internetbasiertes Wissensmanagement in Sportwissenschaft und Sport: eine empirische Studie zur Nutzung des Knowledge-Management-Systems „Bewegung und Training*. Retrieved December 1, 2009, from http://scidok.sulb.uni-saarland.de/volltexte/2008/1510/

Sturm, R., & Igel, C. (2005). Überlegungen zur empirischen Analyse des Nutzungsverhaltens des Knowledge Management Systems, Bewegung und Training". In U. Lucke, K. Nölting & D. Tavangarian (Eds.), Workshop *Proceedings DeLFI 2005 and GMW05*(pp. 103-112). Rostock, 13-16 September 2005. Berlin: Logos Verlag

Sugibuchi, & T., Tanaka, Y. (2004). Integrated Framework for the Visualization of Relational Databases and RelatedWeb Content. *Proceedings of Fourth IEEE Pacific-Rim Conference On Multimedia (CD-ROM)*. Tokyo, Japan.

Sundermeyer, K. (2001). Collaborative Supply Net Management. In Baader, F., Brewka, G., & Eiter, T. (Eds.), KI:2001, *Advances in Artificial Intelligence (pp. 467–470)*. doi:10.1007/3-540-45422-5_35

Swartz, L. (2003). *Why people hate the paperclip: Labels, appearance, behavior and social responces to user interface agents.* bachelor thesis.

Swets, J. A. (1963). Information retrieval systems. *Science, 141(3577), 245–250.* doi:10.1126/science.141.3577.245

Syeda-Mahmood, T., & Ponceleon, D. (2001). Learning video browsing behavior and its application in the generation of video previews. *Proceedings of the ninth ACM international conference on Multimedia* (pp.119-128). New York: ACM Press.

Takashima, A., Yamamoto, Y., & Nakakoji, K. (2004). A Model and a Tool for Active Watching: Knowledge Construction through Interacting with Video. *Proceedings of INTERACTION: Systems, Practice and Theory* (pp.331-358). Sydney, Australia: Creativity and Cognition Studios Press.

Takatsuka, M., & Gahegan, M. (2002). GeoVISTA Studio: a codeless visual programming environment for geoscientific data analysis and visualization. *Computers & Geosciences, 28(10), 1131–1144.* doi:10.1016/S0098-3004(02)00031-6

Tanaka, Y. (2003). *Meme media and meme market architectures: Knowledge media for editing, distributing, and managing intellectual resources.* New York: IEEE Press & Wiley-Interscience. doi:10.1002/047172307X

Tanaka, Y. (2003). *Meme Media and Meme Market Architectures: Knowledge Media for Editing, Distributing, and Managing Intellectual Resources.* IEEE Press, John Wiley & Sons. doi:10.1002/047172307X

Tanaka, Y. (2003). *Meme Media and Meme Market Architectures: Knowledge Media for Editing, Distributing, and Managing Intellectual Resources.* Hoboken, NJ: Wiley-IEEE Press. WEKA. retrieved December 22, 2009, from http://www.cs.waikato.ac.nz/ml/weka/

Tanaka, Y., & Imataki, T. (1989). IntelligentPad: A hypermedia system allowing functional compositions of active media objects through direct manipulations. In *Proceedings of the IFIP 11th World Computer Congress* (pp. 541-546). North-Holland/IFIP.

Tanaka, Y., Ito, K., & Fujima, J. (2006). Meme media for clipping and combining web resources. *World Wide Web (Bussum), 9(2),* 117–142. doi:10.1007/s11280-005-3043-6

Tani, S., Hamaguchi, K., & Yajima, S. (1996). The Complexity of the Optimal Variable Ordering Problems of a Shared Binary Decision Diagram, *IEICE transactions on information and systems. E (Norwalk, Conn.), 79-D(4),* 271–281.

Teevan, J., Dumais, S., & Horvitz, E. (2005). Personalizing search via automated analysis of interests and activities. In *Proceedings of the 28th Annual International ACM SIGIR Conference on Research and Development in Information Retrieval,* (p. 456). New York: ACM.

The ACM computing classification system. (1999). Retrieved August 4, 2009, from http://www.acm.org/class

The Journal of the American Medical Association (2009). *JAMA Instructions for Authors.*

The Nielsen Company. (2009). *Global Faces and Networked Places.* Nielsen Online.

Thomas, P., & Hawking, D. (2006). Evaluation by comparing result sets in context. In [New York: ACM.]. *Proceedings of CIKM, 2006,* 94–101.

Tröger, B. (2004). *Nutzungsanalysen im Blick auf fachliche und interdisziplinäre Webportale – Ergebnisse und Konsequenzen.* B.I.T.online brochure 1/2004. Retrieved October 30, 2006, from http://www.b-i-t-online.de/hefte/2004-01/troeger.htm

Tunkelang, D. (2009). *Faceted Search (Synthesis Lectures on Information Concepts, Retrieval, and Services).* Morgan and Claypool Publishers.

University of Washington and Intel Research Seattle. (2008). *UbiFit.* Retrieved 08 21, 2009, from http://dub.washington.edu/projects/ubifit/

Upson, C., & Faulhaber, J. Thomas, Kamins, D., Laidlaw, D.H., Schlegel, D., Vroom, J., Gurwitz, R. & van Dam, A. (1989). The application visualization system: A computational environment for scientific visualization. *IEEE Computer Graphics and Applications, 9(4),* 30–42. doi:10.1109/38.31462

Viegas, F., Wattenberg, M., Van Ham, F., Kriss, J., & McKeon, M. (2007). Many Eyes: A site for visualization at internet scale. *IEEE Transactions on Visualization and Computer Graphics, 13(6),* 1121. doi:10.1109/TVCG.2007.70577

Wan, S., Paris, C., & Krumpholz, A. (2008). From aggravated to aggregated search: Improving utility through coherent organisations of an answer space. In Lalmas, M. & Murdock, V.,(Eds.) *Proceedings of the SIGIR 2008 Workshop on Aggregated Search,* Singapore.

Wang, G., Yang, S., & Han, Y. (2009). Mashroom: end-user mashup programming using nested tables. In *Proceedings of the 18th international conference on World Wide Web.* (pp. 861-870). New York: ACM Press.

Whitelaw, M. (2009). Exploring archival collections with interactive visualisation. In To appear in: *Proceedings of eResearch Australasia2009: No boundaries*.

Wilke, J. (2002). Using Agent-Based Simulation to Analyze Supply Chain Value and Performance. *Supply Chain World Conference and Exhibition, New Orleans, La*.

Wilkinson, R. (1994). Effective retrieval of structured documents. In *Proceedings of the 17th annual international ACM SIGIR conference on Research and development in information retrieval*, (pp.311–317). New York: Springer-Verlag

Williams, A. B., & Ren, Z. (2001). *Agents teaching agents to share meaning. Autonomous Agents* (pp. 465–472). Montreal: ACM Press.

Witkowski, A., Bellamkonda, S., Bozkaya, T., Naimat, A., Sheng, L., Subramanian, S., & Waingold, A. (2005). Query by Excel. In *Proceedings of the 31st International Conference on Very Large Data Bases*, (pp. 1204-1215). VLDB Endowment.

Wooldridge, M. (1997). Agent-based software engineering. IEEE *Proceedings Software Engineering, 144(1)*, 26–37. doi:10.1049/ip-sen:19971026

Wooldridge, M., & Jennings, N. R. (1995). *Agent Theories, Architectures and Languages: A Survey*. Berlin: Springer Verlag.

Wooldridge, M., & Jennings, N. R. (1995). Intelligent agents: Theory and practice. *The Knowledge Engineering Review, 10(2)*, 115–152. doi:10.1017/S0269888900008122

Xu, S., McCusker, J., & Krauthammer, M. (2008). Yale image finder (yif): a new search engine for retrieving biomedical images. *Bioinformatics (Oxford, England), 24(17), 1968*. doi:10.1093/bioinformatics/btn340

Y. Kiyoki & B. Thalheim.(2008). Knowledge technology for next generation web. *PPP Application to DAAD: Partnership Program with Japan*. September

Yamamoto, Y., Nakakoji, K., & Takashima, A. (2005). The Landscape of Time-based Visual Presentation Primitives for Richer Video Experience. In Costabile, M. F., & Paterno, F. (Eds.), *Human-Computer Interaction: INTERACT 2005* (pp. 795–808). Heidelberg, Germany: Springer Berlin. doi:10.1007/11555261_63

Yan, T. W., & Garcia-Molina, H. (1999). The SIFT information dissemination system. [TODS]. *ACM Transactions on Database Systems, 24(4), 529–565*. doi:10.1145/331983.331992

Yu, B., Ma, W. Y., Nahrstedt, K., & Zhang, H. J. (2003). Video Summarization Based on User Log Enhanced Link Analysis. *Proceedings of the eleventh ACM international conference on Multimedia 03* (pp. 382-391). New York, NY: ACM.

About the Contributors

Gunther Kreuzberger works at the Ilmenau Technical University. Having received a masters degree in computer science in 1996 for the implementation of a neuro-fuzzy system, his research then focussed on multi-agent systems for therapy planning. In 1998 he joined the Institute of Media and Communication Science and became a senior lecturer and executive assistant to the collegiate administrative committee. As a lecturer he is nowadays in charge of lectures and seminars in the fields of digital communication, electronic documents and interactive media such as digital games or iTV. His research interests cover higher education courses on interactive media/ digital games, collaborative IT-enhanced life-long learning, and media applications for children as well as elderly people.

Aran Lunzer is a British researcher in Human-Computer Interaction, currently employed at Hokkaido University as an Associate Professor with special responsibilities for overseas research liaison. After undergraduate studies in Engineering at Cambridge University, he worked from 1986 to 1991 on software technology for IBM UK Laboratories, then returned to full-time study to obtain his PhD in Computing Science from the University of Glasgow. From 2002 to 2004, between spells in Japan, he was an Assistant Research Professor at the University of Copenhagen.

Aran's research is focused on what he calls "subjunctive interfaces", which are interfaces that support users in examining and comparing alternative results during trial-and-error use of software applications. He believes this is a necessary but generally lacking form of support in domains such as simulation, design, and data retrieval. In 2008/9 he has been building and refining a subjunctive interface for a cancer treatment simulator, as part of a large EU Integrated Project.

Roland Kaschek studied mathematics at the university of Oldenburg (Germany). He received a joint Soviet-German PhD grant for study in Novosibirsk and Moscow in 1986-1987, and obtained his PhD in mathematics from the University of Oldenburg in 1990. After that he was an Assistant Professor at the University of Klagenfurt (Austria); at that time he worked on various aspects of information systems design, database design and business process design. From 1999 to 2002 he was an informatics consultant with UBS AG in Zurich (Switzerland), working on software architecture, software quality and data warehousing. Then until 2008 he was Associate Professor with Massey University in Palmerston North (New Zealand), where he continued to deal with information systems design issues and in particular became involved in Web information systems design and eLearning. He was then appointed Full Professor with the KIMEP in Almaty (Kazakhstan) until 2009, and was additionally a guest lecturer or professor with universities in Austria, Brazil, Germany, Thailand, and the Ukraine. Currently he is a mathematics and informatics teacher at Gymnasium Gerresheim in Düsseldorf (Germany).

* * *

Aylin Akaltun, nee Aksac, studied Computer Science and Engineering at Christian-Albrechts-University at Kiel in Germany (2002 - 2009) and was awarded a diploma in 2009. Her major interests are database theory and database management systems, knowledge management systems (representation and reasoning) and development of Service-oriented architecture. Currently, she works as software engineer at COR & FJA which is one of the leading software and consulting companies for insurers, banks and company pension schemes providers in Germany.

Christian Erfurth has been holding teaching and research positions in the Friedrich Schiller University (FSU) Jena, Germany, since 2000. He is PostDoc at the computer science department. His research interests include distributed systems, software architectures, model-driven development, and agile development processes. Christian Erfurth holds a Diploma in computer science. He finished his PhD on proactive navigation of mobile agents in the year 2004, which was awarded in 2005. He has organized national and international workshops. Christian Erfurth is the leader of the agent group at the department. At the moment he is also responsible for two national research projects of FSU Jena with a couple of industry and other research partners.

Jun Fujima is pursuing research related to software design based on meme media architecture and its application to various research domains such as interfaces for information management and access, Web-based system design, and human-computer interaction. He earned his bachelor's and master's degree at Hokkaido University, Japan in 1999 and 2001 respectively. Then he obtained his PhD in Electronics and Information Engineering at Meme Media Laboratory in Hokkaido University in 2006. From 2006 to 2009, he worked as a postdoctoral fellow at Hokkaido University. He is currently a research programmer in the Children's Media Department of Fraunhofer IDMT, Germany.

Tom Gedeon is Chair Professor of Computer Science at the Australian National University. He has worked previously at Murdoch University and the University of New South Wales. His BSc and PhD are from the University of Western Australia. He is a former president of the Asia-Pacific Neural Network Assembly, has been nominated for VC's awards for postgraduate supervision at three Universities, and has a number of journal board roles. Tom's research focuses on the development of automated systems for information extraction, and for the synthesis of the extracted information into humanly useful information resources (hierarchical knowledge), mostly using fuzzy systems and neural networks, as well as by cognitive modeling based on biologically plausible information flow constraints. Application areas of the research include mining, security and medical applications, particularly in the construction of intelligent interfaces which understand human eye gaze as well as facial expression and other human behavioural cues.

Manoochehr Ghiassi is a professor of Information Systems, a Breetwor fellow, and director of the MSIS program at Santa Clara University, Santa Clara, CA. He received a B.S. from Tehran University, and an M.S. in Economics from Southern Illinois University at Carbondale. He also holds an M.S. in Computer Science and a Ph.D. in Industrial Engineering both from the University of Illinois at Urbana-Champaign. His current research interests include artificial neural network, business intelligence, software engineering, software testing, supply chain management, and simulation modeling. He is a member of the IEEE, and the ACM.

Zhen-Sheng Guo is a doctor-course student at Knowledge Media Laboratory, Graduate School of Information Science and Technology, Hokkaido University, Japan. He is an international student from China. His research interests include 3D geographic information systems, new frameworks for integrating legacy system with geographic information systems, and the original approach of integrating Web Services with 3D geographic information systems.

David Hawking is an Information Retrieval researcher. Between 1998 and 2008 he was a research scientist at CSIRO. In July 2008 he took up a full-time position at the Funnelback enterprise search company in the role of Chief Scientist. His interests lie in the areas of enterprise and Web Search. He is particularly interested in search evaluation in realistic contexts, distributed search techniques, enterprise/ intranet search, improvement of search through exploitation of context, personal search and search efficiency. He is a member of the editorial board for the Information Retrieval journal (INRT). David holds an Adjunct professorship in the College of Engineering and Computer Science at the Australian National University and supervises PhD students at both ANU and the University of Sydney.

Christoph Igel, born 1968 in Saarbrücken (Germany). 1989-1996: Studies of political science, science of history, sport science and education science at Saarland University (Germany). 1997-2003: Scientific assistant with the Department of Human Movement and Training Science at the Institute of Sport Science of Saarland University (Germany). 2002-2008: Deputy Head of the Competence Center "Virtual Saar University" at Saarland University (Germany). In 2007: Habilitation (formal qualification as university lecturer) at the Faculty of Psychology and Sport Studies at Westfälische Wilhelms-Universität Münster (Germany). Since 2009: Scientific Director of the Competence Center "Virtual Saar University" at Saarland University (Germany). In 2009: Chief Learning Officer 2009 in Germany (awarded by the journal "Wirtschaft & Weiterbildung" (economy and continuing education). From 2010: Managing Director of the Centre for e-Learning Technology at Saarland University and German Research Center for Artificial Intelligence (Saarbrücken, Germany).

Klaus Peter Jantke, born in Berlin, Germany, studied Mathematics at Humboldt University Berlin. He graduated with an honours degree in Theoretical Computer Science and received both his doctorate and his habilitation at Humboldt. Jantke won the Weierstrass Award for his diploma thesis and the Humboldt Prize for his PhD. Klaus Jantke started his academic career as a full professor at Kuwait University and simultaneously at Leipzig University of Technology, aged 35. Since then he has been teaching at several German Universities such as Chemnitz, Cottbus, Darmstadt, Ilmenau, Leipzig, and Saarbrücken. He sees himself as a logician in the school of Heinrich Scholz and Karl Schröter. Jantke's scientific interest ranges from universal algebra and algorithmic learning through digital games to qualitative and quantitative research into the impact of media. Fraunhofer Society, Germany's largest research institution with currently 17,000 scientists and 60 institutes in operation, decided to establish its own children's media research center. In January 2008, Klaus Jantke was put in charge of developing this research center in Erfurt, Germany,

Alexander Krumpholz is Research Engineer at the CSIRO ICT Centre. He joined CSIRO in 2001 and contributed to several projects before joining the ICT Centre's Information Retrieval group led by David Hawking. Alexander is also a Ph.D. student at the Australian National University studying structural aspects of medical literature retrieval. Alexander investigates ways to exploit structure embedded in a document collection or metadata describing aspects of such a collection to improve the retrieval quality. In his current project he is developing a system that brings relevant medical publications to a medical practitioner's attention. The relevance is based on the user's current context, e.g. a patient's record.

Patrick Maisch studied law at Christian-Albrechts-University at Kiel, Germany. He is author of various commercial applications and web solutions. Since 2008 he is postgraduate at the Department of Computer Science, in the group of Prof. Bernhard Thalheim.

Shin-ichi Minato is an Associate Professor of Graduate School of Information Science and Technology, Hokkaido University. He also serves a Project Director of ERATO (Exploratory Research for Advanced Technology) MINATO Discrete Structure Manipulation System Project, executed by JST (Japan Science and Technology Agency). He received the B.E., M.E., and D.E. degrees from Kyoto University in 1988, 1990, and 1995 respectively. He had been working at NTT Laboratories since 1990 until March 2004. He was a Visiting Scholar at Computer Science Department of Stanford University in 1997 (for one year). He joined Hokkaido University in 2004. He started the ERATO Project from Oct. 2009. His research topics include efficient representations and manipulation algorithms for large-scale discrete structure data. He published "Binary Decision Diagrams and Applications for VLSI CAD" (Kluwer,1995). He is a member of IEEE, IEICE, IPSJ, and JSAI.

Cosimo Spera is the Chief Executive Officer of Zipidy Inc., a Fulbright Scholar and a NATO and MINE Fellow. He holds a Ph.D. in Operations Research from Yale University and the University of Siena, Italy and an MS in Applied Mathematics from the University of Siena. His current research interests include supply chain management, agent technology, adaptive and learning systems. He is a member of the INFORMS and MPS societies.

Nicolas Spyratos holds a Diploma in Electrical Engineering from the National Technical University of Athens (Greece), a M.Sc. from the University of Ottawa

(Canada), a Ph.D. from Carleton University (Canada), and Thèse d'Etat from the University of Paris South (France). Since 1983 he is full professor of Computer Science at the University of Paris South, Orsay Center, and the head of the database group at the Informatics Research Laboratory (LRI). Prior to his present position he has worked for IBM in Greece, for Bell-Northern Research and the Federal Department of Communications in Canada, and for INRIA, the University of Orleans and the National Research Council (CNRS) in France. He is the author of over 150 publications in international conferences and journals and his current research interests include conceptual modeling, information integration and digital libraries.

Roberta Sturm, born 1977 in Bucharest (Romania). 1996-2001: Studies of sport science focusing informatics at University of Technology Darmstadt (Germany). 2001-2009: Scientific assistant with the Competence Center "Virtual Saar University" at Saarland University (Germany). In 2008: Doctoral Thesis: Web based knowledge management in sport science and sport. In 2009: Senior Business Consultant with the imc AG Saarbrücken (Germany). From 2010: Principal Researcher with the Centre for e-Learning Technology at Saarland University and German Research Center for Artificial Intelligence (Saarbrücken, Germany). Major work fields: IT- and project manager of R&D projects regarding the use of new media, information- and knowledge management, new web technologies, communication and collaboration tools, assessment technologies, authoring- and IT-training systems.

Akio Takashima is an assistant professor at School of Computer Science, Tokyo University of Technology, Japan. He received a Ph.D degree in engineering from Nara Institute of Science and Technology, Japan. His research interests include human computer interaction, interaction design, video interface, overview and detail in time, visualization, knowledge media, computer supported cooperative work, project based learning, and profile based education. He is currently a member of Tangible Software Engineering Education Project that aims to satisfy students' needs in software engineering education.

Yuzuru Tanaka is a professor at the Department of Computer Science, Graduate School of Information Science and Technology, Hokkaido University, and the director of Meme Media Laboratory, Hokkaido University. He is also a visiting professor of National Institute of Informatics. His research areas covered multiprocessor architectures, database schema-design theory, hardware algorithms for searching and sorting, multiport memory architectures, database machine architectures, full text search of document image files, and automatic cut detection in movies and full video search. His current research areas cover meme media architectures, knowledge federation frameworks, and their application to e-Science based on meme media application frameworks such as database and Web visualization frameworks and virtual experiment environment frameworks. He worked as a board member of Japanese Society for Artificial Intelligence (1991-1994), a councilor of Japanese Society for Artificial Intelligence (1995-), a board member of Information Processing Society of Japan (1995-1996, 1999-2000, 2008-), an associate member of Japanese Academy of Science (2006-2008), and an advisory board member of NTT Research Laboratory (2004-).

Bernhard Thalheim holds an MSc in Mathematics from Dresden University of Technology, a PhD in Mathematics from Lomonosov University Moscow, and a DSc in Computer Science from Dresden University of Technology. His major research interests are database theory, logic in databases, discrete mathematics, knowledge systems, and systems development methodologies, in particular for web information systems. He has been programme committee chair and general chair for several international events such as ADBIS, ASM, EJC, ER, FoIKS, MFDBS, NLDB, and WISE. He is currently full professor at Christian-Albrechts-University at Kiel in Germany after working at Dresden University of Technology (1979-88) (since 1986 Associate Prof.), Kuwait University (1988-1990) (Visiting Prof.), Rostock University (1990-1993)(Full prof.), and Cottbus University of Technology (1993-2003)(Full prof.).

Shohei Yoshihara earned his masters degree in Graduate School of Information Science and Technology, Hokkaido University in 2007. His master's work focused on the research and development of a spreadsheet-based orchestration environment. He is currently employed by NEC Software in Japan.

Volkmar Schau is a research staff member of Computer Science at the Friedrich Schiller University Jena. In 2000 he was invited to join the mobile agent working group at the university to study about agent technologies and toolkits. As a group member he was the key developer for TRACY2 mobile agent platform. Mr. Schau and his partners were awarded with a grant from a federal entrepreneur program supporting a spin-off. In 2003 the company "the agent factory GmbH" was established. Working as Chief Executive Officer Mr. Schau developed his product vision of human centered mobile social networks, based on mobile intelligent agents located at mobile devices, e.g. cell phones. In 2006 Mr. Schau was offered the opportunity to follow his vision further by starting his PhD thesis at the university in Jena. The promising field for agent research induced Bell Labs Innovations to invite Mr. Schau in 2007 and 2008.

Index